The Labour Market Under New Labour

D0183838

Also by the editors:

The State of Working Britain, (eds) Paul Gregg and Jonathan Wadsworth

The State of Working Britain: Update 2001, (eds) Paul Gregg, Richard Dickens and Jonathan Wadsworth

The Labour Market Under New Labour

The State of Working Britain 2003

Edited by

Richard Dickens

Centre for Economic Performance, the London School of Economics and Queen Mary, University of London
UK

Paul Gregg

Centre for Economic Performance, the London School of Economics and University of Bristol
UK

and

Jonathan Wadsworth

Centre for Economic Performance, the London School of Economics and Royal Holloway College, University of London
UK

First published 2003 by
PALGRAVE MACMILLAN
Houndmills, Basingstoke, Hampshire RG21 6XS and
175 Fifth Avenue, New York, N.Y. 10010
Companies and representatives throughout the world

PALGRAVE MACMILLAN is the global academic imprint of the Palgrave
Macmillan division of St. Martin's Press, LLC and of Palgrave Macmillan Ltd.
Macmillan® is a registered trademark in the United States, United Kingdom
and other countries. Palgrave is a registered trademark in the European Union
and other countries.

ISBN 1–4039–1629–2 hardback
ISBN 1–4039–1630–6 paperback

This book is printed on paper suitable for recycling and
made from fully managed and sustained forest sources.

A catalogue record for this book is available
from the British Library.

Library of Congress Cataloging-in-Publication Data
The labour market under new Labour : the state of working Britain / edited by
  Richard Dickens, Paul Gregg, and Jonathan Wadsworth.
    p. cm.
  Includes bibliographical references and index.
    ISBN 1–4039-1629-2 (cloth) — ISBN 1–4039–1630–6 (pbk.)
    1. Labour market—Great Britain. 2. Labor policy—Great Britain.
  3. Manpower policy—Great Britain. 4. Unemployment—Great Britain.
  5. Labour Party (Great Britain)

  HD5765.A6.L24 2003
  331.12'0941—dc21

                                                          2003054759

10   9   8   7   6   5   4   3   2   1
12   11   10   09   08   07   06   05   04   03

Printed and bound in Great Britain by
Antony Rowe Ltd, Chippenham and Eastbourne

Contents

List of Figures

List of Tables

Acknowledgements

Contributors Richard Disney and Denise Hawkes would like to thank Carl Emmerson for providing the information from the Family Expenditure Survey. Helen Robinson is most grateful to Gerry Makepeace for providing useful comments. The Crown Copyright LFS, FES, GHS and BHPS data used in the chapters of this book have been made available by the Office for National Statistics through the ESRC Data Archive. Neither the ONS nor the Data Archive bear any responsibility for the analysis or interpretation of the data reported here. The editors would like to thank Julia Shvets for her careful transformation of the book's figures and Helen Durrant for her excellent administrative assistance. They would also like to thank Michele Pellizzari and Tanvi Desai for their initial help with preparation of the figures. The data that underlie the figures used in this book can be downloaded from the following website: http://cep.lse.ac.uk/state2

Abbreviations and Acronyms

ASLEF	Associated Society of Locomotive Engineers and Firemen
BCS	British Cohort Study
BHPS	British Household Panel Survey
BTEC	The Business and Technician Education Council
CHB	Child Benefit
CTC	Child Tax Credit
DB	Defined benefit
DC	Defined contribution
DfEE	Department for Education and Employment
DfES	Department for Education and Skills
DTI	Department of Trade and Industry
DWP	Department for Work and Pensions
EITC	Earned Income Tax Credit
EMA	Education Maintenance Allowance
FC	Family Credit
FES	Family Expenditure Survey
GHS	General Household Survey
GMB	Britain's General Union
GNVQ	General National Vocational Qualification
HB	Housing Benefit
HNC	Higher National Certificate
HND	Higher National Diploma
IALS	International Adult Literacy Survey
IS	Income Support
ISC	Independent Schools Council
ISTC	Institute of Scientific and Technical Communicators
IVB	Invalidity Benefit (now Incapacity Benefit)
JSA	Jobseeker's Allowance
JUVOS	Joint Unemployment and Vacancies Operating System
LFS	Labour Force Survey
LHPD	Limiting health problem or disability
LLSI	Limiting long-standing illness
LPC	Low Pay Commission
MFIP	Minnesota Family Investment Program
MSF-Amicus	Manufacturing Science Finance
NCDS	The National Child Development Study
NDDP	New Deal for Disabled Persons
NDLP	New Deal for Lone Parents

NDLTU	New Deal for Long-Term Unemployed
NDP	New Deal for Partners
NDYP	New Deal for Young People
ND25+	New Deal 25 Plus
ND50+	New Deal 50 Plus
NES	New Earnings Survey
NMW	National Minimum Wage
NVQ	National Vocational Qualification
ONS	Office for National Statistics
PRP	Performance related pay
RSA	Royal Society of Arts Examinations Board
SDA	Standard Service Agreement
SSP	(Canadian) Self-Sufficiency Project
TGWU	Transport and General Workers Union
WFI	Work Focused Interviews
WFTC	Working Families Tax Credit
WTC	Working Tax Credit
YCS	Youth Cohort Study

Notes on Contributors

Richard Blundell is Research Director of the Institute for Fiscal Studies and Director of the ESRC Centre for the Microeconomic Analysis of Public Policy. He is also Leverhulme Research Professor at University College London.

Richard Dickens is a Research Fellow at the Centre for Economic Performance, London School of Economics and a Lecturer in Economics at Queen Mary, University of London.

Richard Disney is Professor of Economics at the University of Nottingham and Research Fellow at the Institute for Fiscal Studies, London.

Peter Dolton is a Professor at the University of Newcastle Upon Tyne Business School. He is also an affiliate member of the Centre for the Economics of Education at the Centre for Economic Performance, London School of Economics.

David T. Ellwood is Lucius N. Littauer Professor of Political Economy at the John F. Kennedy School of Government, Harvard University.

Giulia Faggio is a Research Officer at the Centre for Economic Performance, London School of Economics.

Alissa Goodman is Programme Director of the Education, Employment and Evaluation Sector at the Institute for Fiscal Studies, London.

Maarten Goos is an occasional Research Assistant at the Centre for Economic Performance, London School of Economics.

Francis Green is Professor of Economics at the University of Kent. He is also an Associate Member of two ESRC research centres: the Centre for Economic Performance at the London School of Economics, and the Centre on Skills, Knowledge and Economic Performance (SKOPE) at the Universities of Oxford and Warwick.

Paul Gregg is a Senior Research Fellow at the Centre for Economic Performance, London School of Economics and a Reader in Economics at the University of Bristol. He is also a member of the Council of Economic Advisers at HM Treasury.

Susan Harkness is a Lecturer in Economics at the University of Bristol.

Denise Hawkes is a Research Officer at the Centre for Longitudinal Studies (CLS), which is part of the Bedford Group for Lifecourse and Statistical Studies, Institute of Education.

Stephen Machin is Professor of Economics at University College London and Group Leader of the Centre for the Economics of Education at the Centre for Economic Performance, London School of Economics.

Alan Manning is the Director of the Labour Markets Programme at the Centre for Economic Performance, and Professor of Economics, London School of Economics.

Leslie McGranahan is a Research Economist in the Education, Employment and Evaluation sector based at the Institute for Fiscal Studies, London.

Steven McIntosh is a Research Officer at the Centre for Economic Performance.

David Metcalf is Professor of Industrial Relations, London School of Economics and the Director of the Leverhulme Trust Programme on the Future of Trade Unions in Modern Britain at the Centre for Economic Performance, London School of Economics.

Stephen Nickell is a Professor of Economics at the London School of Economics and an External Member of the Bank of England Monetary Policy Committee.

Howard Reed is Director of the Work and Income Sector at the Institute for Fiscal Studies, London.

Helen Robinson is a Lecturer in Economics and Leverhulme Research Fellow at Cardiff Business School, Cardiff University.

Andrew Shephard is a Research Economist at the Institute for Fiscal Studies, London.

John Van Reenen is Director of the Innovation and Productivity Programme at the Centre for Economic Performance, London School of Economics.

Jonathan Wadsworth is a Researcher at the Centre for Economic Performance, London School of Economics and a Lecturer in Economics at Royal Holloway College, London.

Introduction

In the 20 years preceding the election of the Labour administration in May 1997, there had been many dramatic changes to the nature of labour market institutions and policy management in Britain. The long period of Conservative government had swept away many of the corporatist relations between the state, firms and unions. Incomes policies were abandoned. Trade union activities became highly regulated and restricted and union membership went into freefall. The tools of Keynesian demand management were thrown away and the basic tenets of US-style laissez faire capitalism embraced. The 30-year period after the war had produced growth and increased living standards in Britain, though to a lesser extent than in many other OECD countries. Significantly, most individuals appeared to benefit from this growth.

The Thatcherite experiment aimed to improve efficiency and gave little emphasis to equity concerns. By 1997, and despite two sharp recessions, the case for improved efficiency looked strong. The UK economy had seen GDP per capita rising relative to its other European counterparts. Inflation was low and employment levels were high and increasing. The resulting equity outcomes, however, were catastrophic. Wage inequality rose to its highest level since before the war. Unemployment had risen to 40-year record levels and more men than ever were dropping out of the labour force well before official retirement age. Hence, an unprecedented one in five working-age households contained no one in employment, leading to record numbers reliant on welfare payments. Despite significant increases in the numbers of working mothers, child poverty was inordinately high, with one in five children living in a family where no one worked, and one in three living in relative poverty. Britain had managed to achieve an unsightly combination of levels of wage inequality comparable to those in the US alongside levels of welfare dependency akin to several of the larger mainland European countries. Indeed, welfare dependency among families with children was substantially higher in Britain than in mainland Europe.

The incoming Labour government sought to try and marry the relative efficiency gains of the Conservative years with a greater emphasis on social justice and opportunity. Flushed with the innovative zeal of the newly elected,

1

the incoming government quickly enacted a series of major policy initiatives intended to deal with these labour market problems, notably the New Deal, the National Minimum Wage and the Working Families Tax Credit. Labour also signalled its intention to honour the European Social Charter which aimed to ensure safeguards for employees over working hours, protection from discrimination and to facilitate union representation. It was, in the words of the party's helmsman, 'time to do'.

This book considers whether things really did get better in the British labour market over the course of the Labour administration. The previous *State of Working Britain* volume set the scene, pointing out issues that, we believed, were in the most urgent need of attention. Using the insights of a range of labour market experts, this new volume attempts to assess not just whether things got better in general, but also whether the specific policy strategies that were put in place under Labour did make a difference. The book covers employment and unemployment, hours of work and job satisfaction, the status of trade unions, wages, education and training. A number of specific policies are assessed, the New Deals for the unemployed and lone parents, the Working Families Tax Credit, the National Minimum Wage and the Educational Maintenance Allowance. The book also offers comments on other issues that policy either left behind or has still not addressed adequately.

The broad consensus that flows from the assessments in this volume is that many labour market issues have stabilised after the dramatic changes witnessed over the preceding two decades. Inequality in the distributions of work and wages has largely stopped getting any worse (Machin, Chapter 12, Gregg and Wadsworth, Chapter 2, Disney and Hawkes, Chapter 4). The decline in trade union presence has also slowed (see Metcalf, Chapter 11). There has, however, been no substantial reversal of the big changes in these areas that occurred in the years of Conservative administration.

GDP per capita has risen strongly and, for the first time in a generation, all parts of society have enjoyed rapidly rising living standards. This is a happy alignment of efficiency and equity, but the increases in inequality that were so dramatic under the Conservatives have been left largely undiminished. Likewise, the specific policy developments initiated by Labour have proven to be essentially successful and without major adverse side effects, but they have been modest in their accomplishments. The National Minimum Wage (NMW), for example, has raised wages for the lowest paid million or so Britons with evidence of any job losses confined only to the most heavily affected sector. However, the numbers covered have proven to be far lower than originally suggested by the Low Pay Commission, as were any pay gains provided by the NMW (see Dickens and Manning, Chapter 13). The net policy impact has thus been positive but small.

Long-term unemployment has fallen sharply partly due to the New Deals (see Blundell, Reed, Van Reenen and Shephard, Chapter 1). The improvement in employment among lone parents has been dramatic. Around 120,000 more lone parents are working more than 16 hours a week directly as a result of policy reform (see Gregg and Harkness, Chapter 7). The living standards of the poorest families with children have risen rapidly and relative child poverty has fallen, reflecting increases both in welfare payments and in employment (see Dickens and Ellwood, Chapter 19).

In other areas there has been no improvement, even continued deterioration. Employment among the less skilled has fallen in large parts of the country even during the strong recovery (see Gregg and Wadsworth, Chapter 6). Male inactivity has continued to rise among this group and among the sick and disabled (see Faggio and Nickell, Chapter 3). For many ethnic minority groups the recovery has seen rising employment rates but the employment deficit relative to the white British born population remains (see Wadsworth, Chapter 8). The decline in social mobility evident in the 1980s has, at least as far as access to higher education is concerned, not been redressed (see Machin, Chapter 18). There is also evidence that the nature of jobs created during the recovery has polarised, with a simultaneous rise in high and low paying jobs (Goos and Manning, Chapter 5). McIntosh (Chapter 16) shows that returns to vocational qualifications are valued increasingly unequally. Public sector and gender pay differentials are explored by Dolton and McIntosh (Chapter 14) and Robinson (Chapter 15), and evidence suggests that the progress of women in the labour market has slowed and that public sector workers have seen declining relative pay, particularly among graduates and those living and working in the South.

The book also considers a number of other highly topical issues that affect the labour market, even if not directly the result of government policy. The nature of jobs that are being created, the composition of households, job satisfaction, hours of work, and worker effort (see the respective chapters by Goos and Manning, Gregg and Wadsworth, Green [Chapter 9] and Harkness [Chapter 10]) have all changed noticeably in recent years. The way we work now is different from that of 20 years ago and it is important that these trends are documented.

Setting the scene: efficiency

Table I.1 compares the performance of the UK economy since 1960 with several other OECD countries. Between 1960 and 1979 living standards in the UK rose rapidly, compared to other periods of history, but were rising less than in most other OECD countries. By 1979, GDP per head had fallen well below that of Canada, Germany, Sweden, France and even Italy and Japan had caught up with the UK. After 1979, the UK's relative performance improved, matching that of the US whilst other countries slipped back. As shown by Card and Freeman (2002), this was largely due to mainland Europe experiencing a sharp slowdown in productivity growth and reduced hours of work rather than growth rates increasing in the UK. UK growth was achieved

Table I.1 GDP per head for OECD countries (US$ 1999), 1960–2002

	UK	US	Germany West	Germany Unified	France	Italy	Spain	Sweden	Canada	Japan
1960	10,437	13,603	11,064	–	8,829	7,765	4,385	10,329	10,936	4,828
1979	15,894	22,562	19,944	–	17,522	16,711	11,976	17,502	19,765	15,938
1996	21,716	30,608	25,545	23,463	21,938	22,796	17,011	21,199	23,895	24,767
2002	24,771	34,076	–	25,549	24,808	25,026	20,475	24,880	28,138	25,128
Relative to US = 100										
1960	77	100	81	–	64	57	32	76	80	35
1979	70	100	88	–	78	74	53	78	88	71
1996	71	100	83	77	72	74	56	69	78	81
2002	73	100	–	75	73	73	60	73	83	73

Sources: University of Groningen and Conference Board GGDC Database: http//www.eco.rug.nl/ggdc

4

by higher employment levels and longer hours of work offsetting lower relative levels of capital investment. Since 1996, the UK has maintained its strong relative performance, along with Spain and Sweden. Indeed the larger European economies and even Japan have converged toward a narrow range of 73–75 per cent of US levels of GDP per head.

As Table I.2 shows, growth in the years of Labour administration has been somewhat faster than during the (longer) Conservative era. Under Labour, growth has been extremely jobs-rich which means that productivity as measured by output per worker has been weaker than under the Conservative years. Historically as living standards rose, individuals and institutions settled on shorter working hours, which allowed more time to enjoy increased wealth. Unusually this trend stopped during the Conservative era. Despite there being more part-time working, this was largely offset by longer hours among the professional and managerial classes. As documented by Green in Chapter 9, hours of work have fallen quite sharply since the mid-1990s. This is, in part, due to increased holiday entitlements resulting from the implementation of the European Working Time Directive, but also because of a sharp reduction in the numbers of managerial staff working very long hours. Hence, productivity adjusted for hours of work looks very similar between the periods 1979–96 and 1997–2002. Ongoing productivity growth has allowed average real earnings to continue growing at around 2 percentage points a year, much the same as under the Conservatives, though Labour's record on inflation is much better. On the basis of these trends it seems that Labour's macro record on growth and productivity has therefore been successful relative to other major European economies and has at least matched that achieved under the Conservatives.

Table I.2 Annual growth rates of GDP, population, employment, inflation, earnings, productivity and hours worked

	1979–1996	1997–2002
GDP (%)	2.17	2.57
Working age population (%)	0.45	0.63
Employment (%)	0.27	1.10
Unemployment rate (percentage points)	0.12	–0.52
Inactivity rate (percentage points)	0.03	–0.03
GDP per employee (%)	1.87	1.47
Average weekly hours worked (%)	–0.19	–0.46
GDP per hour worked	2.06	1.93
Inflation (percentage points)	6.5	2.4
Real average earnings (percentage points)	2.2	2.3

Source: Updated from Nickell (2002) using ONS data and hours data from *Labour Market Trends* (January 2003) Table A.1 and *Employment Gazette* (various issues 1983–97) Table 5.6.

Labour was fortunate that when it took office, the economy had been growing again for four years, but the benefits of growth had yet to permeate widely. Unemployment had begun to fall without any sign of emerging inflationary pressure. The government announced its intention of following international guidelines, something since lacking in other respects, by giving greater prominence to the International Labour Office (ILO) definition of unemployment rather than the claimant count based on the numbers eligible to receive benefit, which was and remains, susceptible to changes in eligibility rules.[1] As Figure I.1 and Table I.3 show, both counts were falling before 1997 but continued to fall thereafter. The ILO unemployment rate has now hovered around 5 per cent, some 1.5 million individuals, for the last two years, around half the level observed in 1993 and almost 30 per cent below the level inherited in 1997. This has led some commentators to conclude, perhaps rather rashly, that the labour market is now close to full employment. Still, there is currently little sign of substantial inflationary pressure stemming from the labour market. This has led some to revise down, again, their estimates of the NAIRU (the rate of unemployment below which inflationary pressures start to build). Any worries that the labour market could sustain a 5 per cent unemployment rate without generating substantial inflationary pressures caused by labour shortages have proved unfounded.[2]

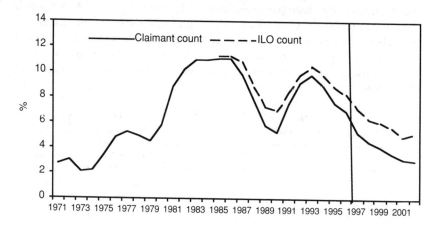

Figure I.1   Unemployment rates, 1971–2002

Source: National Statistics, http://www.statistics.gov.uk/statbase/tsdlistfiles.asp

Long-term unemployment, aside from the human cost, thought of as a significant indicator of wage pressure (the long-term unemployed find it harder to get jobs and so do not constitute part of the reserve army of labour which keeps wages down), has also continued to fall to quite low levels (Table I.4).

Table I.3 Unemployment, 1984–2002

Year	ILO unemployment (000s)	(%)	Claimant unemployment (000s)	(%)
Total				
1984	3,240	11.9	3,160	11.0
1990	1,990	6.9	1,660	5.5
1993	2,950	10.5	2,920	9.9
1997	2,040	7.2	1,600	5.4
2002	1,520	5.2	960	3.2
Men				
1984	1,930	12.0	2,200	12.9
1990	1,170	7.1	1,230	7.2
1993	1,970	12.5	2,240	13.5
1997	1,280	8.2	1,230	7.5
2002	910	5.8	720	4.4
Women				
1984	1,310	11.6	960	8.2
1990	830	6.6	430	3.3
1993	980	7.9	680	5.3
1997	760	5.9	380	2.8
2002	620	4.6	240	1.7

Notes: Data are for United Kingdom, not seasonally adjusted. Unemployment is for aged 16+ and not available on consistent basis before 1984.

Source: National Statistics. http://www.statistics.gov.uk/statbase/tsdlistfiles.asp

Table I.4 Long-term unemployment (over 12 months) in Great Britain

	All Level (000s)	Share (%)	Men Level (000s)	Share (%)	Women Level (000s)	Share (%)
1994	1,250	44.7	938	50.6	313	33.2
1997	785	37.6	560	44.0	240	26.4
1999	516	28.5	520	33.4	230	20.5
2000	452	26.8	450	32.5	210	18.1
2002	343	21.8	410	25.6	170	16.0

Source: *Labour Market Trends*.

However, labour market performance should not be assessed solely on the basis of the unemployment numbers. Unemployment can fall because individuals leave the labour force rather than find a job. As such, it is as important to monitor what is happening to employment and also to inactivity. EU member countries have recently agreed on the European Employment

Strategy. This is essentially a set of guidelines, rather than specific binding targets, aimed at promoting full employment and social cohesion in member countries. The targets were based on employment rather than unemployment with an aspiration that each country should have an aggregate employment rate of 70 per cent by 2010, a 60 per cent employment rate among women and a 50 per cent employment rate among the 55+ age group.

As Table I.5 shows, Britain had already reached these objectives in 1990. Since then, the aggregate employment rate has fallen and risen with the subsequent economic cycle but these targets are still being surpassed. There has been a net gain of over 2.5 million jobs since 1993 and 1.5 million since 1997. The number of individuals in employment is indeed higher than ever, but, because the population is growing, the employment *rate* (employment divided by the population of working age) is still below the rate experienced at the end of the 1980s recovery.

Table I.5   Britain's employment performance, 1975–2002

	Total		Men		Women		55+	
	(000s)	(%)	(000s)	(%)	(000s)	(%)	(000s)	(%)
1975	22,560	72.7	14,180	87.8	8,380	56.4	3,100	72.5
1979	23,400	73.3	14,410	86.8	8,990	58.6	3,200	69.2
1984	22,370	67.4	13,330	76.6	9,030	57.3	2,590	57.5
1990	25,560	75.0	14,690	82.4	10,870	66.8	2,470	58.8
1993	24,030	70.1	13,410	74.8	10,620	64.9	2,260	54.0
1997	25,140	72.5	14,060	77.4	11,080	67.0	2,340	55.6
2000	26,220	74.3	14,650	79.2	11,570	68.9	2,610	58.4
2002	26,760	74.4	14,900	79.0	11,860	69.4	2,940	60.6

Notes: Population of working age (men 16–64, Women 16–59). Figures weighted and rounded to nearest 10,000. 55+ columns are men and women together.

Source: LFS, authors' calculations.

This benign picture of falling unemployment and rising employment with little inflationary pressure has not been unique to Britain. As Table I.6 shows, Sweden, the Netherlands, Austria and Denmark have also managed ILO unemployment rates of 5 per cent or less in 2002. But the recent contrast of high and rising unemployment in France, Germany, Italy and even the US and Japan is stark.

In sum, the period of Labour government has seen strong GDP growth, reasonable productivity growth and a sustained period of low inflation and unemployment. On any assessment, then, this has been a period of success in terms of economic efficiency. Of course, it does not follow necessarily that policy reforms under Labour drove these benign outcomes and some other countries with different approaches to labour market policy have performed

Table 1.6 Comparative labour market performance, 1975–2002

	UK	EU	USA	Canada	France	Australia	Japan	Netherlands	Sweden	Austria	Italy	Denmark
Unemployed (%)												
1990	6.9	8.2	5.6	8.1	8.6	6.7	2.1	5.9	1.7	n/a	8.9	7.2
1997	6.9	10.4	4.9	9.1	11.8	8.3	3.4	4.9	9.9	4.4	11.6	5.3
2000	5.4	7.8	4.0	6.8	9.3	6.3	4.7	2.8	5.6	3.7	10.4	4.4
2002	5.1	7.6	5.8	7.7	8.7	6.3	5.4	2.7	4.9	4.1	9.0	4.5
Employed (%)												
1990	72.5	61.4	72.2	70.3	59.9	67.9	68.6	61.1	83.1	n/a	52.6	75.4
1997	70.8	60.9	73.5	68.0	58.9	66.3	70.0	67.5	70.7	67.2	51.6	75.4
2000	72.4	63.8	74.1	70.1	59.8	69.1	68.9	72.9	74.2	67.9	53.9	76.4
2001	71.3	64.1	73.1	70.9	62.0	68.9	68.8	74.1	75.3	67.8	54.9	75.9

Note: Figures are standardised by the OECD.

Source: OECD. www.oecd.org

9

as well. Nevertheless, the efficiency side of the labour market under Labour looks quite healthy.

Setting the scene: equity

As noted earlier, the income gains made under Thatcher were not shared equally. Figure I.2 shows how the real incomes of the poorest fifth of the population barely grew at all under Thatcher whilst incomes at the top grew extremely rapidly. For children the picture was even starker. The incomes of the poorest fifth of households with children failed to grow at all over this period (see Dickens and Ellwood, Chapter 19). Under the Major administration, there were relative gains in income in favour of the poorest, but the level of income gain in this period was very low. So even though the poorest made some relative gain, their living standards grew only a little. Under the Blair government, real incomes have risen more strongly and all income classes have benefited, the top and bottom a little more than the middle. Since income growth at the bottom of the income distribution has risen only slightly faster than at the middle, relative poverty (which compares the incomes of the poorest to the middle), has fallen only modestly. Chapter 19 by Dickens and Ellwood explores the circumstances of families with children in more detail and here the picture is somewhat more positive. In sum, the increase in income inequality in Britain seen in the Thatcher years, has stopped but has not been substantially reversed.

The labour market under Labour

The profound shift toward more inequality, whether measured in terms of wages, income, jobs and returns to educational opportunities, was one of the most striking features of the Conservative years. Indeed many of the policies that Labour adopted, from the Working Families Tax Credit to the New Deal to the Minimum Wage were intended to address these problems. Yet many of the chapters in this volume suggest that despite these policies being in themselves successful, the effects have been modest and these inequalities have largely persisted.

Individuals can have unequal access to job opportunities because of where they live, or because of their age, gender, ethnicity or skill, and quite often because of a combination of these factors. Many of the same characteristics help explain differences in pay and educational opportunities. Yet Gregg and Wadsworth (Chapter 6) note that rising aggregate employment over the latest recovery disguises falling relative opportunities for less skilled workers. Disney and Hawkes (Chapter 4) show that rising employment among older workers has also left less skilled older workers behind. Gregg and Wadsworth (Chapter 2) show that good aggregate employment performance has done little to offset the trend towards increasing unequal division of work across households.

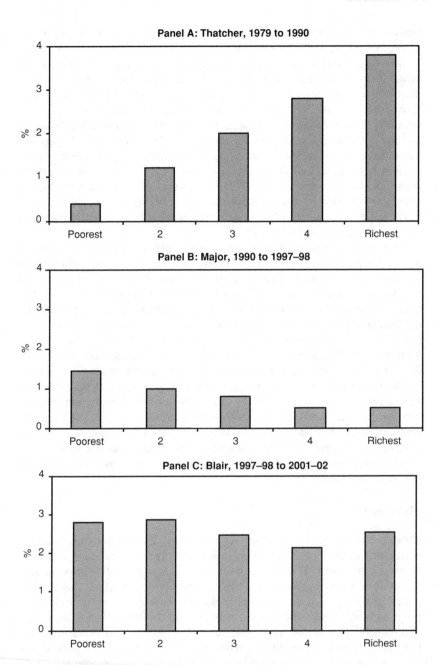

Figure I.2   Real yearly income growth by income quintile

Source: A. Shephard (2003) 'Inequality Under the Labour Government', Institute of Fiscal Studies Briefing Note No. 33.

Wadsworth's analysis (Chapter 8) of the economic position of ethnic minorities shows that recovery did little to improve their relative position in the labour market. Faggio and Nickell (Chapter 3) find that rising employment has done little to bring many inactive men back into the labour force. While Machin's chapter shows that wage inequality seems to have slowed sharply, the highest earners are still seeing the fastest rises in wages among men. Goos and Manning (Chapter 5) show that rising average wages disguise a simultaneous increase in both low paying and high paying jobs. Robinson (Chapter 15) shows that the gender pay gap has narrowed only marginally but not for women in part-time work. McIntosh (Chapter 16) shows that returns to vocational qualifications are falling increasingly behind those to academic qualifications. Dolton and McIntosh (Chapter 14) show that public sector pay is falling relative to private sector pay, particularly for better educated workers in the south of England.

While there are many things to worry about, there have been many positive effects stemming from the Labour administration's efforts. Gregg and Harkness (Chapter 7) show that the introduction of the New Deal for Lone Parents and the Working Families Tax Credit has had a significant positive impact on the employment position of lone parents. Dickens and Manning's analysis of the minimum wage (Chapter 13) concludes that around a million workers were helped by its introduction without any adverse employment consequences. Blundell, Reed, Van Reenen and Shephard (Chapter 1) conclude that the New Deal for Youth also appeared to have a small, but positive effect on employment opportunities for long-term unemployed youth. Metcalf (Chapter 11) is cautiously optimistic that the long-term decline of union membership has been halted. Green (Chapter 9) is similarly optimistic that the intensification of work effort has slowed. Dickens and Ellwood (Chapter 19) find that relative child poverty has fallen back since 1997, in part due to half a million children no longer living in a workless household, as shown in Gregg and Wadsworth (Chapter 2).

The future

Nine years of continuous recovery has proved insufficient to redress many of the labour market problems highlighted in this volume. There has been progress, but recovery is still not sustained or balanced enough to have brought many marginalised groups back into the workforce. It seems that further policy initiatives and an even tighter labour market are required. At some point there will have to be a debate concerning how much of the inequalities and relative poverty that have built up over the years is to be tolerated, and how many resources are to be devoted to dealing with the issue. Simply relying on aggregate growth and existing strategies will not be enough. Encouragingly, some of these issues raised in this book are currently being addressed. The government has realised that male inactivity is a problem and has extended its New Deal policies beyond the claimant unemployed to try and incorporate the many thousands of working age individuals on sickness related, rather than unemployment benefits, and the partners of unemployed claimants. The success of the Working Families Tax Credit among lone parents has encouraged the government to extend in-work welfare top-ups to childless individuals. The minimum wage has been uprated, though rather conservatively. It is, as yet, too early to tell whether these policies will have the desired impact. Perhaps the issues highlighted in this current volume could also form a guide as to where policy should go next.

Notes

1. Despite this, the government was rather quick to claim credit when the claimant count fell back below 1 million in 2001.
2. The massive pay rises awarded recently to chief executives and footballers, will not in themselves generate higher inflation because the number of individuals affected is small. The justification, behaviour and impression associated with these awards are, of course, very different matters.

References

Freeman, R. and Card, D. (2003), 'What Have Two Decades of British Economic Reform Delivered?', in R. Blundell, D. Card and R. Freeman (eds), *Seeking a Premier League Economy*, University of Chicago Press: Chicago.

Nickell, S. (2002), 'The Assessment: The Economic Record of the Labour Government Since 1997', *Oxford Review of Economic Policy*, Vol. 18, No. 2.

Part I:
Work, Unemployment and Inactivity

1

The Impact of the New Deal for Young People on the Labour Market: A Four-Year Assessment

Richard Blundell, Howard Reed, John Van Reenen and Andrew Shephard

Key findings

- Currently there are about 120,000 18–24 year olds participating in the New Deal for Young People (NDYP). About three-quarters of participants are male and they are much less skilled than the population as a whole.
- Evaluations of the NDYP in the first few years of the programme show that it has had a significant affect on raising the proportion of people leaving unemployment and finding jobs. The aggregate impact of the NDYP is to raise employment by about 17,000 a year. This is much smaller than the government's claimed figure of 375,000 which refers to *all* participants who found jobs.
- There does not appear to be a dramatic change in the low skilled UK youth labour market. The stock of longer-term unemployed has fallen, primarily because people have entered options such as education and training rather than finding jobs. The employment to population ratio for 18–24 year old men was virtually unchanged at 61 per cent between 1993 and 2001.
- Although the net amount of jobs created by the New Deal is probably small, so are the costs. The true costs are not as high as published details suggest, as benefits would have had to be paid to NDYP participants in any case. Hence the programme seems worth continuing on cost–benefit grounds.

Introduction

The New Deal programmes have been an integral part of the UK government's Welfare to Work strategy since 1998. In terms of its aims of helping participants

17

find jobs and boost their long-term employability, the government considers the New Deal to be a resounding success:[1]

> More than 375,000 long-term unemployed 18 to 24 year olds have found jobs through the New Deal for Young People (NDYP), while the New Deal for 25 Plus has helped over 110,000 older long-term unemployed people back into work.[2]

These numbers refer to the total amount of people participating on the programme and then subsequently finding jobs. Some of these people would have obtained jobs in the absence of the New Deal, so the real question is how many *extra* people have found jobs because of the New Deal? Even if there is a jobs benefit we then have to compare this with the social costs of maintaining the programme.

In fact, there *is* convincing evidence of a positive impact of the New Deal on employment *and* the benefits do appear to outweigh the costs. Looking at the youth labour market as a whole, however, there is little obvious sign of a large impact, even when focusing on the groups of individuals (young, less skilled men) who are most likely to benefit. This is probably because the number of jobs created is more in the region of 17,000 than 375,000. In other words the programme appears to be a success, but it has been a modest success at a modest cost.

What is the New Deal?

There are a bewildering number of 'New Deals'. Table 1.1 presents details of the main forms. We will focus almost exclusively upon the NDYP as this is the largest and best-studied New Deal programme.

The NDYP began in 12 'Pathfinder' areas in January 1998 before being introduced nationally in April 1998. All people aged between 18 and 24 who have been claiming Jobseeker's Allowance (JSA) for at least six months are required to take part. Initially, individuals enter a 'Gateway' period, where they are assigned a personal adviser who gives them extensive assistance with job search. If the unemployed person remains on JSA at the end of the Gateway period (formally, a *maximum* of four months), then they are offered up to four options:

- Entry into full-time education or training for up to 12 months for those without basic qualifications (without loss of benefits);
- A job for six months with a voluntary sector employer (paid a wage or allowance at least equal to JSA plus £400 spread over the six months);
- A job on the Environmental Task Force (paid a wage or allowance at least equal to JSA plus £400 spread over the six months);

- A subsidy to a prospective employer for six months, with training for at least one day a week (£60 a week plus an additional £750 training subsidy spread over the six months).

If an option is refused, the claimant is liable to suffer a benefits sanction. Initially, sanctions take the form of withdrawal of benefit for two weeks, and further refusals may result in repeated four-weekly withdrawals. Individuals returning to unemployment within 13 weeks after leaving an option go onto the 'follow-through' programme of job assistance, which is similar to the Gateway period. Figure 1.1 summarises the treatment process.

Figure 1.1   A simplified flow diagram of the New Deal programme

Figure 1.2 shows how the NDYP has built up over time. The programme was introduced in 1998 and it took about a year before the programme affected the entire stock of young people who had been unemployed for more than six months. At its peak in mid-1999 approximately 150,000 young people were enrolled on the NDYP. The proportion of men on the programme has consistently been much higher than that of women. Between 10,000 and 20,000 young people typically join and leave the NDYP each month.

The proportion of individual 'New Dealers' in options has fallen over time – in December 1998 about 34 per cent of participants were on options compared to 24 per cent in September 2002. This reflects the larger number of participants on the 'follow through' as they churn through the system.

The education/training option has consistently been the most popular New Deal option (see Table 1.2). The subsidised employment option has proved much less popular than was initially expected and it has become less used over time (in June 1999, 26 per cent of all participants were in subsidised employment, compared to 19 per cent in June 2002). Since the subsidy is quite generous (about 40–50 per cent of a typical New Dealer's expected wage) the low take-up may appear surprising. US wage subsidy schemes have also had low take-up and this appears to be largely due to the stigma associated

Table 1.1   A New Deal timeline

New Deal reform	Date	Related reforms
Prototypes for New Deal for Lone Parents (NDLP) begin in eight areas.	July 1997	
New Deal for Young People (NDYP) launched in 12 Pathfinder areas.	January 1998	
NDYP is extended nationally.	April 1998	Lone parent benefit is abolished.
The national New Deal 25 Plus (ND25+) programme commences.	June 1998	
	October 1998	Income Support (IS) for children under 11 is increased by £2.50.
Alternative provision of ND25+ piloted in 28 Units of Delivery.	November 1998	
New Deal for Partners (NDP) is piloted in three Pathfinder areas.	February 1999	
	April 1999	The National Minimum Wage (NMW) is introduced. The main rate is set at £3.60, with the youth rate at £3.00. A lower rate income tax of 10% is introduced. Both the family premium in IS and the child benefit for the first child is increased by £2.50.
New Deal for Musicians is launched.	August 1999	
NDP is rolled out nationally.	October 1999	Working Families Tax Credit (WFTC) is introduced to replace Family Credit. It is more generous than its predecessor, with a longer phase-out portion and greater support for childcare. IS for children under 11 is also increased by £4.70.
New Deal 50 Plus (ND50+) is piloted in nine Pathfinder areas.		
ND50+ is extended nationally.	April 2000	Increases in credits in WFTC and allowances in IS for children under 11. There is a 1% reduction in the basic rate of income tax to 22%.

June 2000		The young person's NMW is increased from £3.00 to £3.20.
October 2000		Increases of £4.35 in credits in WFTC for all children. The main NMW rate increases to £3.70. Increases of £4.35 in IS allowances for all children.
April 2001	There is considerable revision of the provision of New Deal for Long-Term Unemployed (NDLTU) following the pilots. Entry now occurs after receipt of Jobseeker's Allowance (JSA) in 18 of the last 21 months. Other reforms include a four-month Gateway period, and an Intensive Activity Period.	
June 2001	NDP is extended to cover partners of non-JSA benefits such as IS and Incapacity Benefit.	Increases of £5 in basic credits in WFTC.
July 2001	Personal Adviser meetings under NDLP are launched nationally.	
October 2001	Following the pilots, New Deal for Disabled Persons (NDDP) is extended nationally.	Main and development rates of the NMW increased to £4.10 and £3.50 respectively.
January 2002	Introduced tailored pathways for NDYP in 16 pilot areas. These are to test the impact of a more flexible option period.	
February 2002	The training option on NDYP is revised, so as to allow employers greater flexibility in the provision of training.	
April 2002	StepUP is piloted in six areas with high levels of unemployment. Designed for individuals who didn't find work whilst on the New Deal, it offers guaranteed jobs for up to a year.	Enhanced Children's Tax Credit for infants less than one year old is introduced.
October 2002	NDLTU pilots to be launched to provide assistance for those with repeat spells of unemployment. Additionally, 'Gateway to Work' will be introduced, providing assistance with job preparation.	
April 2003		Both NMW rates increase by a further 10p. WFTC replaced by the Working Tax Credit – for people in paid work, and the Child Tax Credit – for families with at least one child.

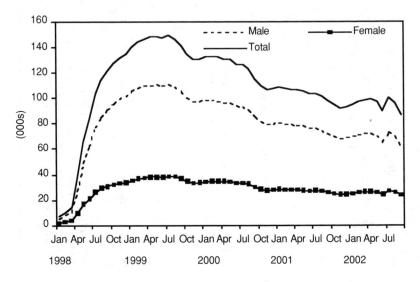

Figure 1.2 Number on New Deal for Young People at month end

Sources: National Statistics, *Labour Market Trends*, various years.

with programme participation. Since the NDYP affects a far wider range of young people than most US schemes, we would not expect such high levels of stigma. An alternative explanation is that employers are reluctant to deal with the bureaucracy accompanying the subsidy, especially given the requirement to allow participants a day a week in training.

Table 1.2 Distribution of New Deal participants by option

	Employment (%)	Education and training (%)	Voluntary sector (%)	Environmental Task Force (%)	Number in the New Deal
June 1999	25.8	40.4	17.7	16.1	149,900
June 2000	17.0	42.2	21.6	19.1	126,300
June 2001	17.1	39.5	23.5	19.6	102,700
June 2002	19.0	36.8	23.7	20.5	89,500

Sources: National Statistics, *Labour Market Trends*, various years.

The New Deal 25 Plus is a similar programme for older adults. It only comes into action when an adult has been on JSA for two years, and the allowances are slightly more generous. Figure 1.3 shows the numbers on this programme and reveals a similar profile to NDYP, although the stock of people has never reached much more than 80,000.

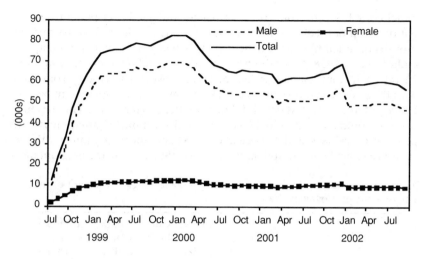

Figure 1.3   Number on New Deal 25+ at month end

Sources: National Statistics, *Labour Market Trends*, various years.

Evaluations of the New Deal for Young People

It is possible to examine the performance of the Gateway period of job assistance using publicly available micro data.[3] In order to estimate the impact of the New Deal we follow the analysis of Blundell, Dias, Meghir and Van Reenen (2001). We compared the improvement in labour market prospects of people going through the New Deal (the 'treatment group') with another group who are as similar as possible but who did not go through the New Deal (the 'comparison group'). The outcome we focus on is the probability of moving into a job if an unemployed person has been claiming JSA for six months.

Coming up with good comparison groups is the hardest part of any evaluation. Luckily the New Deal was piloted in some areas ahead of the national roll-out so one method we use is to compare 19–24 year olds[4] in the pilot areas ('Pathfinders') to similar 19–24 year olds in non-Pathfinder areas over the same period of time before and after the introduction of the NDYP. A second method is to examine an older age group with similar labour market characteristics who are ineligible for the New Deal. We chose to focus on 25–30 year olds who have been unemployed for six months as the alternative comparison group (the New Deal for the over 25s only affects people unemployed for over two years). After the national roll-out only the comparison across age groups is possible.

Table 1.3 contains the raw data on the outflow rates to jobs for these different groups. The data is taken from administrative records which follow a random 5 per cent of all individuals who have ever claimed JSA. The upper panel contains data from the pilot period and the lower panel from the national roll-out. For the pilot period, we consider those who reached six months on unemployment benefit (JSA) between 1 January 1998 and the end of March 1998 ('after the programme'). We follow them four months later (i.e. ten months after they become unemployed). This group is compared with the same age group who reached six months on unemployment benefit between January and March 1997 ('before the programme'). The national roll-out compares individuals who reached six months' unemployment between 1 April 1998 and 31 December 1998 ('after the programme') with the same age group between April and December 1997 ('before the programme').

Table 1.3 The impact of the New deal on people leaving the claimant count and entering into employment (raw data)

	Outflows by the end of the tenth month on Jobseeker's Allowance (%)		
	Before the programme	After the programme	Difference (after–before)
Pilot period			
(1) Treatment group: 19–24 year olds in Pathfinder areas	24.1	33	8.9
(2) Comparison group I: 19–24 year olds in all other areas	27.1	25	–2.1
(3) Implied impact of the New Deal (difference in differences of rows (1) – (2))			11
(4) Comparison group II: 25–30 year olds in Pathfinder areas	27.6	26	–1.6
(5) Implied impact of the New Deal (difference in differences of (1) – (4))			10.4
National roll-out			
(6) Treatment group: 19–24 year olds	25.8	28.1	2.3
(7) Comparison group: 25–30 year olds in Pathfinder areas	23	20	–3.1
(8) Implied impact of the New Deal (difference in differences of rows (6) – (7))			5.4

Notes: Data is from the JUVOS 5 per cent longitudinal sample of JSA claimants. Selected observations are all unemployed individuals completing a six-month spell on JSA over a predefined time interval (2nd to 4th quarters of 1997 and 1998 for the 'national roll-out' estimates, and the 1st quarters of 1997 and 1998 for the 'pilot period' estimates). Individuals followed up to the end of the tenth month on JSA to check whether they have found a job.

The first row of Table 1.3 shows that the young unemployed were almost 9 per cent more likely to obtain jobs in the after New Deal period. In the non-pilot areas young unemployed men were actually *less* likely to get jobs (a fall of 2.1 percentage points). So the impact of the New Deal (the 'difference in difference' in row 3) effect is a full 11 percentage points (i.e. an extremely large increase over the pre-programme average of 24 per cent). Row 4 uses a slightly older age group as a comparison (25–30 year old men with at least six months of unemployment). The implied New Deal impact (Row 5, 10.4 percentage points) is almost identical to when we used the first comparison group.

The similarity of the impact from both methods is reassuring as there are potential biases with both comparison groups. Using the older age group as a comparison might lead us to *overstate* the impact of the New Deal if employers are just substituting away from the older jobless towards the younger jobless without creating any new net employment. On the other hand, if the New Deal has improved the job prospects of 25–29 year olds who were not on the NDYP (e.g. through reducing wage pressure by making everyone search harder for jobs) then this will reduce unemployment for the older group. In this case comparing younger with older individuals would cause an *under-estimate* of the New Deal impact. If these biases were large we might expect them to cause the estimated impact to be quite different when using non-pilot as a comparison compared with within pilots. So these biases are either not too large (at least in the short term) or they more or less cancel each other out.

The lower panel of Table 1.3 examines data from the national roll-out (after April 1998). The magnitude of the New Deal effect is still positive, but about half the size of that estimated for Pathfinder areas. There is an increase of 5.4 percentage points compared to the pre-programme base of 25.8 percentage points (i.e. a 20 per cent (=5.4/25.8) increase in the outflow rate). This is due to the impact of the programme being much larger in the first quarter than in the subsequent quarters and leads us to suspect the long-run impact will be smaller than the short-run impact.

The raw estimates in Table 1.3 do not correct for changes in marital status, occupation, region, and past unemployment spells. Table 1.4 includes these extra controls, but they make relatively little difference to the raw numbers shown in Table 1.3. Row 3 of Table 1.4 illustrates that older individuals in the pilot areas do not appear to have had worse employment outcomes after the New Deal was introduced – if there was significant substitution we would expect to see their outflows to employment decline.

The impact of the New Deal incorporates the impact of both increased job search and the wage subsidy. Row 4 shows that 5.7 per cent of the impact of the New Deal could be purely due to the wage subsidy element (i.e. up to half of the overall impact). This means that there is some impact of better job search over and above any impact of the employers' wage subsidy. The impact of unsubsidised jobs is smaller in the subsequent quarters after the New Deal is introduced (compare rows (5) and (6)).

Table 1.4   Employment impact of the New Deal (correcting for characteristics)

	New Deal treatment group	Comparison group	Estimates based on Difference in Difference method
(1)	19–24 year olds living in Pathfinder areas	19–24 year olds living in all non–Pathfinder areas	11%
(2)	19–24 year olds living in Pathfinder areas	25–30 year olds living in Pathfinder areas	10.4%
(3)	25–30 year olds living in Pathfinder areas	25–30 year olds living in all other areas	1.6%
(4)	*Outflow into the employment option (affecting 19–24 year olds living in Pathfinder areas). Raw numbers from New Deal Evaluation Database*		*5.7%*
(5) Overall effect for the sample including the pilot period and the national roll-out (first three quarters the New Deal is operating in each region)	19–24 year olds	25–30 year olds	5.3%
(6)	*Outflows to subsidised jobs. Raw numbers from New Deal Evaluation Database*		*3.9%*

Notes: Estimates used the JUVOS 5 per cent longitudinal sample of JSA claimants. Selected observations are all unemployed individuals completing a six-month spell on JSA over a predefined time interval. All estimates from regressions including a set of other controls, namely marital status, sought occupation, region and some information on the labour market history (comprising the number of JSA spells since 1982 and the proportion of time on JSA over the two years that precede the start of the present unemployment spell). Number of observations range from 1,096 in row (2) to 17,433 in row (5). All estimates significant at the 10 per cent level or above, except for row (3).

Source: Blundell, Dias, Meghir and Van Reenen (2001).

We have conducted various checks on these results. Firstly, we examined whether the quality of job matches had deteriorated by using the outflow to jobs that lasted at least 13 weeks as the outcome variable. The effect (4.5 per cent) is very close to that for all jobs (5.3 per cent), so there is no evidence that New Deal jobs are of lower quality. Secondly, it may be that individuals are delaying their exits from unemployment prior to the New Deal in order to take advantage of the generosity of the programme. If this was the case one would expect to see a decline in outflows in the month before the programme starts. We could find no evidence of this in the data.

There have been other analyses of the impact of the New Deal that have used a more macroeconomic approach. In particular, Riley and Young (2001a) find that the NDYP has had a significant effect in reducing unemployment for the long-term unemployed in the 18–24 year old group, but not other groups. They find that youth unemployment fell by about 35,000 and youth employment rose by about 15,000. Van Reenen (2003) shows that the estimates of the micro-level evaluation imply an employment effect of about 17,000. The similarity of the 'micro' and 'macro' evaluations is unsurprising given that the empirical strategy (comparing younger versus older age groups) is essentially the same in both studies.

These direct effects on employment may underestimate the impact of the NDYP if there are 'economy-wide' effects that reduce wage pressure. For example, as people stay longer on the dole they may find it harder to compete with the employed and short-term unemployed for jobs. If the New Deal transforms long-term unemployed 'outsiders' into 'insiders' then wage pressure falls in the economy and the level of unemployment could fall for older groups, not just the 18–24 year olds.

Riley and Young (2001b) try to assess this but they obtain conflicting results – it is hard to separate the NDYP from the impact of the National Minimum Wage (introduced in 1999). On optimistic assumptions, Riley and Young argue that including the reduced wage pressure effect increases the New Deal's impact to 28,000 extra jobs a year by the start of 2002.

A (brief) comparison with evaluations from other countries

How do our findings compare with those from recent programme evaluations of mandatory job search associated with US 'welfare to work' reforms? Bloom and Michalopoulos (2001) survey 29 different initiatives where some people who were eligible for a programme were 'randomised' and then followed over time. This is as close as social science gets to a clinical trial where we follow those who receive a treatment versus those who receive a placebo. Eight of these schemes were job focused (rather than education/training focused) and mandatory for welfare recipients. These are closest in design to the New Deal. Each of these programmes had a significant and positive impact on employment, although the effect ranged from 10 per cent to 64 per cent with a median of 23 per cent. Since we found that the New Deal increased outflows by around 20 per cent (5 percentage points over a 26 per cent base), the UK impact is in the middle of the range of similar US welfare to work studies.

Unlike the US welfare to work reforms (where the affected groups are overwhelmingly females with children) the New Deal's main participants are men. Experiments involving unemployment insurance reforms may, therefore, be more relevant. Meyer (1995) discusses five randomised trials in the US and finds that increased job search assistance and monitoring significantly reduced the duration of unemployment claims. As with the New Deal it is unclear from these studies whether the 'carrot' of job assistance or the 'stick' of the tougher monitoring of job search played the most important role.

Both the welfare to work and unemployment insurance studies are across all adults, but a feature of the NDYP is that it is youth focused. Most evaluations of youth initiatives have been pessimistic, especially for young men. Our study gives more room for optimism, but it should be remembered that the participant group for most US youth training programmes are on average more disadvantaged than the British New Dealers.

Recent trends in the youth labour market: LFS evidence 1993–2001

The results in Tables 1.3 and 1.4 refer primarily to the impact of the Gateway in the initial 12 months of the NDYP programme. To assess the impact of the NDYP over a longer period, we use information from the UK Labour Force Survey (LFS) up to and including the year 2001. Because LFS has information on qualifications it allows us to examine trends for the labour market status of the group who we would expect to benefit most from the New Deal – less-qualified young men. The upper panel of Table 1.5 has the 18–24 year old group and the lower panel the 25–30 year old group. There is a clear fall in unemployment of the New Deal target group since 1998 (e.g. the proportion of those unemployed for over two years has dropped from 4.6 per cent to 1.6 per cent). But the proportion employed has not significantly risen, nor is it clear that there has been a break in trend or that the young have outperformed the older group.

If the New Deal had an impact much greater than is suggested by the economic evaluations because of significant increases in skills or through much reduced wage pressure, then we might expect to see larger changes. As it is, the size of the impacts discussed (say 17,000 jobs) would not be discernible in the overall figures. In other words, the picture in the youth labour market as a whole is consistent with the findings of the evaluations – no big change.

Conclusions

The fact that the jobs impact of NDYP is small does not mean that the programme is a waste of money. Table 1.6 shows the costs of the programme, but these exaggerate the true social costs, as a lot of the 'expenditures' are actually relabelled unemployment benefits. Van Reenen (2003) estimates that the social cost of each job is more in the region of £4,000, which is less than the social benefit (as measured by the average wage). The conclusion is that the New Deal appears to have been a success, but with much more modest achievements than is sometimes claimed.

Despite the low take-up, the employment subsidy has probably been more important in creating jobs than is commonly believed. Having a combination

Table 1.5 Low qualifications (GCSE grade D or below) men, 1993–2002

Panel A: young men (18–24)

	% in population of 18–24 men	Employment (%)	Unemployed under 6 months	Unemployed between 6 and 24 months	Unemployed over 24 months	Inactive	Full-time education or training
1993	26.1	56.9	7.9	12	8.1	11.7	3.5
1994	25.3	57.3	7.6	9.3	8.3	11.9	5.5
1995	24	58.3	8.8	9.4	6.6	11.4	5.6
1996	22.6	56.8	9	8.5	6.5	13.3	6
1997	22.1	58.6	8.5	7.3	4.6	12.4	8.6
1998	21.2	59.3	9.4	7	3.1	11.6	9.8
1999	20.6	60.5	8.7	5.6	2	13.4	9.9
2000	20.5	58.5	8.6	5.6	1.8	14.5	11
2001	19.9	58.8	9.3	5.3	1.6	14.6	10.3
mean	22.4	58.3	8.6	7.9	4.9	12.7	7.6

Panel B: older men (25–30)

	% in population of 25–30 men	Employment (%)	Unemployed under 6 months	Unemployed between 6 and 24 months	Unemployed over 24 months	Inactive	Full-time education or training
1993	28.3	68.2	5.1	8	6.6	10.2	1.6
1994	28.1	68.9	5.0	6.4	7.5	10.2	2.0
1995	28.0	69.0	4.6	6.4	7.0	10.9	2.0
1996	26.4	70.3	4.3	5.3	5.7	12.5	2.0
1997	25.3	73.6	4.4	4.1	4.5	11.6	1.8
1998	25.3	73.9	4.9	3.5	2.9	12.3	2.4
1999	23.6	76.0	4.0	3.0	2.5	12.0	2.5
2000	23.1	73.3	3.7	3.1	2.5	14.3	3.1
2001	23.2	72.4	4.6	3.2	2.4	15.2	2.3
mean	25.7	71.6	4.5	4.8	4.8	12.0	2.2

Notes: 1993–1997 before New Deal, 1999–2001 after New Deal, 1998 was a 'transition' year.

Source: LFS.

of carrot (job assistance) and stick (benefit sanctions) has some impact, but the balance of importance between the two is still unclear. As far as we know there is no convincing evidence on the impact of the options in raising human capital. Certainly there does not (yet) appear to be any discernible impact in the aggregate numbers of the youth labour market.

Table 1.6   Costs of the New Deal

| | Expenditure on the New Deals and Action Teams (£ millions) | | | | | |
	1998–99 Outturn	1999–00 Outturn	2000–01 Outturn	2001–02 Outturn	2002–03 Plans	2003–04 Plans
Running Costs:						
NDYP	98	88	119	89	87	85
New Deal 25 Plus	17	26	18	73	97	80
New Deal 50 Plus	–	2	11	5	6	6
New Deal for Lone Parents	17	27	29	37	70	87
New Deal for Disabled People	1	7	7	6	12	12
New Deal for Partners	1	5	10	6	14	17
Action Teams	–	–	5	20	27	27
Other current expenditure:						
NDYP	162	282	293	212	230	232
New Deal 25 Plus	17	71	42	134	160	175
New Deal 50 Plus	–	–	3	3	10	10
New Deal for Lone Parents	1	12	14	9	72	88
New Deal for Disabled People	0	15	7	6	46	47
New Deal for Partners	–	–	1	2	12	12
Action Teams	–	–	6	24	31	31
Annually managed expenditure:						
NDYP allowances*	–	–	–	–	37	38
New Deal 25 Plus allowances*	–	–	–	–	45	45
New Deal 50 Plus employer credits	–	1	42	66	103	103

Notes: Table shows total expenditure by DWP on the New Deals and Action Teams, including Windfall Tax expenditure. All figures rounded to the nearest million. * indicates allowance payments to NDYP and New Deal 25 Plus participants. These allowances were previously paid from other current expenditure.

Source: 2002 Department for Work and Pensions Departmental Report, Appendix 3. (Available at http://www.dwp.gov.uk/publications/dwp/2002/dwpreport/index.asp)

Notes

1. On-line information about the New Deal is available at www.newdeal.gov.uk
2. HM Treasury Pre-Budget Report 2002, paragraph 4.18.
3. These numbers are based on an analysis of the Joint Unemployment and Vacancies Operating System (JUVOS) data, which contain information over time for a sample of 5 per cent of those claiming unemployment-related benefits in the UK. For more details on the analysis see Blundell, Dias, Meghir and Van Reenen (2001).
4. We drop 18 year olds because there has been a large increase in the participation rate in full-time education for this group in recent years.

References

Bloom, D. and Michalopoulos, C. (2001), *How Welfare and Work Policies Affect Employment Income: a Synthesis of Research*, MDRC: New York.

Blundell, R., Dias, M., Meghir, C. and Van Reenen, J. (2001), 'Evaluating the Impact of a Mandatory Job Search Assistance Program: the New Deal for Young People Gateway in the UK', Institute for Fiscal Studies Working Paper, WP01/20.

Heckman, J., Lalonde, R. and Smith, J. (2000), 'The Economics and Econometrics of Active Labour Market Policies', in O. Ashenfelter and D. Card (eds), *Handbook of Labor Economics*, Volume III, North Holland: Amsterdam.

Meyer, B. (1995), 'Lessons from the U.S Unemployment Insurance Experiments', *Journal of Economic Literature*, vol. XXXIII, pp. 91–131.

Riley, R. and Young, G. (2001a), 'Does Welfare to Work Policy Increase Employment: Evidence from the UK New Deal for Young People', National Institute for Economic and Social Research Discussion Paper No. 183.

Riley, R. and Young, G. (2001b), 'The Macro-economic Effect of the New Deal for Young People', National Institute for Economic and Social Research Discussion Paper No. 184.

Van Reenen, J. (2003), 'Active Labor Market Policies and the British New Deal for Unemployed Youth in Context', in R. Blundell, D. Card and R. Freeman (eds), *Seeking a Premier League Economy*, University of Chicago Press: Chicago, forthcoming.

2
Workless Households and the Recovery

Paul Gregg and Jonathan Wadsworth

Key findings

- By 1996 the distribution of work across households was more unequal than at any time in the previous 25 years; such that one in five households of working age had no employed adult present.
- Economic recovery after 1996 has reduced the share of households where no one is in work.
- Single parent households have been the main beneficiaries.
- However, the long-term increase in unequal allocation of work across households appears only to have halted over the recovery but has not yet been put into reverse.

Introduction

In 1997 the new Labour government inherited an economy where nearly one in five households containing working age adults had no-one in employment. Some 4.6 million adults and 2.5 million children were living in these workless households, and the majority of them were dependent on welfare payments. These numbers had not improved, and had indeed worsened, since recovery began in 1993 despite almost four years of steady growth. Two noticeable trends help explain these patterns. First, there are more single adult households. Young adults are leaving the parental home earlier than in the past, but delaying marriage or separating more frequently. More single adult households means households are either in work or not, and so there is less chance that work can be shared within households. This trend therefore has the potential to make the distribution of work across households more uneven. Second, married women with children have gone out to work in increasing numbers, but not from households where male (largely older and less skilled) employment was lost during the big recessions of the early 1980s and 1990s. Even so, around half of the rise in workless households from the mid-1970s to the mid-1990s was not explained by these two trends, but from other factors affecting the growing propensity for households either to have no earners or all adults working (see Gregg, Hansen and Wadsworth, 1999).

The incoming Labour administration recognised the problem and began to monitor the situation and to introduce a raft of policy responses. The New Deal programmes, reaching out to others than just the unemployed, the Working Families Tax Credit, the National Minimum Wage and other financial inducements all stemmed from an analysis that many households with no earner had little incentive to work for the low wages on offer. Hence the policy emphasis on raising the relative returns to working, tackling barriers on moving into work, and giving encouragement and help to search for work. In what follows we assess developments in workless household numbers over the past five years and assess whether any progress has been made.

Did things get better?

The short answer is that things stopped getting worse. Figure 2.1 tracks movements in the workless household rate and the proportion of working age individuals without a job (the non-employment rate), back to the mid-1970s.[1] It is apparent that the share of individuals without a job is approximately the same in 2002 as it was in 1975. This is not true for the jobless rate measured across households. Subject to some cyclical variation, the proportion of households with no one in work grew steadily over the same period, reaching nearly 20 per cent of all working age households by the mid-1990s. Since 1996, both the individual jobless count and the number of workless households has declined, the latter by around 400,000, some 3 percentage points. The improvement has been most marked among families with children, where nearly 500,000 fewer children are now in workless households than in 1996. However, despite the most sustained recovery for decades, the most recent low point in the workless household count is still three times as large as that observed in the mid-1970s and 50 per cent higher than the previous low observed at the end of the recovery in the late 1980s. One in six households is still jobless, amounting to some 4 million adults and 2.1 million children (see Table 2.1).

If the same proportion of people are jobless as in the mid-1970s but the workless household numbers are much higher, this suggests that there has been a shift in how work is distributed across households. Gregg and Wadsworth (2002) suggest that it is possible to compare the actual household rate with what the rate would be if everyone had the same chance of being in

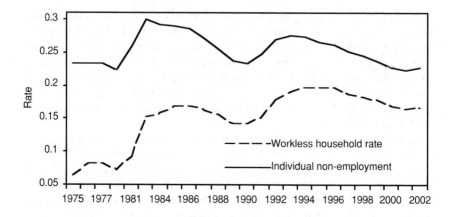

Figure 2.1   Distribution of work across households, 1975–2002

Source: LFS.

Table 2.1   Workless households in Britain

	Workless households (working age)		Households where all adults work		Working age adults in workless households		Children <16 in workless households		Employment rate
	(000s)	(%)	(000s)	(%)	(000s)	(%)	(000s)	(%)	
1993	3,200	18.7	9,900	58.2	4,400	13.8	2,400	20.8	72.7
1996	3,400	19.3	10,500	60.7	4,600	14.2	2,600	21.5	74.6
1998	3,200	17.9	11,100	63.0	4,200	13.1	2,400	20.0	76.5
2000	3,000	16.9	11,400	65.2	3,900	12.3	2,100	17.9	77.3
2002	3,000	16.8	11,800	65.7	4,000	12.2	2,100	18.3	77.3

Notes: Child data not available before 1981. Employment rate excludes students and households with retired heads. Numbers rounded to nearest 100,000.

Source: LFS.

work whilst allowing for any changes in the average number of adults who comprise a household. So if 25 per cent of adults are out of work then we might expect that 25 per cent of one-adult households and 6.2 per cent of two-adult households (.25 multiplied by .25) would be workless. If we observe rates higher than these, then work is not randomly distributed but rather there is 'polarisation' and this polarisation rate gives a measure of the excess numbers of workless households. On this basis, Figure 2.2 suggests that during the 1970s, a random allocation of work predicts the actual distribution of work across households quite well so there was little polarisation. By the mid-1990s, however, the workless household rate had moved increasingly out of line with the individual workless rate, so that in 1996 the excess of workless households stood at nearly 7 percentage points, or 50 per cent above what it would be if the chances of being in work were randomly assigned (see Table 2.2).

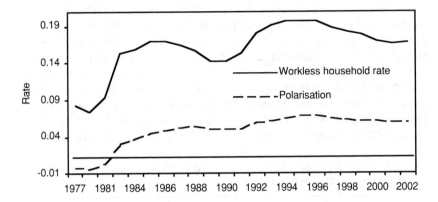

Figure 2.2   Excess in workless household

Source: LFS:

Table 2.2   Polarisation and workless household rates

	Workless Household Rate	Polarisation (% point excess)	Polarisation adjusted for cycle	Relative polarisation (% excess)
1993	18.7	+ 6.1	22.3	+ 47
1996	19.3	+ 6.8	26.0	+ 53
1998	17.9	+ 6.2	25.4	+ 52
2000	16.9	+ 6.1	26.9	+ 56
2002	16.8	+ 5.9	25.9	+ 54

Source: LFS, authors' calculations.

Since 1996 the number of workless households has fallen and the measure of polarisation has fallen back a little. However, Figure 2.2 also shows that polarisation usually tends to ease back in a recovery. If we adjust for the economic cycle then the level of polarisation of work has been unchanged since 1996. In other words, given the strength of the recovery the fall in the numbers of workless households shows neither relative improvement nor further deterioration. There are still around 1 million more workless households now than would be the case in the absence of polarisation, as was the case in the 1970s.

This excessive number of workless households is also much higher in the UK than in other OECD countries. Access to comparable data is not often as easy as in Britain, but we have obtained data that allow us to repeat these calculations for Australia, the US, Spain, Germany and France (Table 2.3). Britain had the highest workless household rate in 1996, despite having the second lowest non-employment rate. As a result Britain has the highest degree of polarisation. Australia was not far behind. Spain had fewer workless households than Britain despite only having just over half its adult population in work and hence had negative polarisation. Since 1996, the workless household rate in Britain has fallen closer to those in Germany and France, though polarisation remains much higher. Both polarisation and the workless household rate have fallen in the US. In France, polarisation has risen, despite a recovery in employment over the period. Note the strong employment recovery in Spain has helped reduce the numbers of workless households, but polarisation has actually become less negative. This means that the recovery in Spain has not benefited workless households as much as other households.

Table 2.3   Workless households, non-employment and polarisation in Australia, Britain, the US, Spain, Germany and France

	Australia	GB	US	Spain	Germany	France
Workless household rate						
1996	15.7	19.3	12.4	16.2	16.5	16.7
2000	16.1	16.9	10.7	12.3	16.3	16.9
Non-employment rate						
1996	26.5	25.4	24.2	44.0	29.8	31.5
2000	26.8	23.0	22.1	36.0	27.3	29.5
Polarisation						
(% point excess)						
1996	4.4	6.8	1.5	–3.0	–0.8	1.8
2000	4.6	6.1	1.0	–2.1	0.4	2.8
Polarisation in households						
with children						
1996	6.6	9.1	1.7	–8.4	–3.0	–4.4
2000	5.9	7.5	0.5	–7.1	–1.9	–3.2

Notes: Latest Australian data refer to 1998. Data exclude students and refer to households with working age occupants.

The unequal distribution of work across households affects households with children to a much larger extent in Britain and Australia than elsewhere. Indeed in the mainland European countries, families with children are less likely to be workless than would be expected given the prevailing employment rate and the number of adults in the family. Polarisation among households with children does however appear to have improved in Britain, Australia and the US since 1996, but worsened in Spain, France and Germany (although it remains much lower in these countries than elsewhere).

Table 2.4 gives workless household and polarisation rates in Britain according to number of adults and the presence of children. Jobless rates among single parent households and single adults without children are much higher than we would expect if everyone in the population had the same chance of being in work. As a result, polarisation rates are much higher for these groups. Chapter 7 shows how Britain is unusual among OECD countries in having very low levels of employment among lone parents. Although polarisation amongst single adults without children is less, this group is much larger than single parents and so is as important in explaining the high numbers of workless households in Britain.

Since 1993, and especially after the current government took office, the situation of lone parents has improved and workless rates among two-adult households with children have also fallen sharply. This should help reduce the overall rate of polarisation. However, there are now more single adult households, both single parents and those without children, in the population. Since polarisation depends on both the workless rate *and* the share of each group in the population, this has counteracted the improvements within single parent and couples with children. Moreover, the improvement for families with children has not been matched among other household types. It would seem that the next targets for policy should be these other household types.

Table 2.4 Workless households and polarisation by presence of children and number of adults

	1 adult		2 adults		3 adults	
	Child	No child	Child	No child	Child	No child
Workless rate						
(share)						
1993	61 (7)	35 (22)	10 (32)	11 (25)	5 (5)	4 (9)
1996	60 (9)	35 (25)	9 (29)	11 (26)	7 (3)	3 (8)
1998	57 (9)	31 (26)	7 (28)	10 (27)	5 (3)	4 (8)
2000	50 (10)	31 (25)	6 (30)	9 (25)	4 (4)	3 (7)
2002	49 (10)	30 (25)	6 (30)	9 (25)	3 (4)	3 (7)
Polarisation						
(% point excess)						
1993	34	8	3	3	3	2
1996	33	8	2	4	0	2
1998	32	7	1	4	4	2
2000	27	8	1	4	3	2
2002	26	8	1	4	2	2

Note: Share of each type in household population in brackets.

Source: LFS, authors' calculations.

The incidence of worklessness

The policy responses to high levels of worklessness depend in part on the reason why the individuals who comprise the household are not in work. Non-employment is not a homogeneous category and the reasons individuals give for their jobless state may offer insights as to the likely source of any problems. We know that it is harder to get individuals back into work if they have dropped out of the labour force, whether caused by early retirement (see Chapter 4), or movements onto sickness benefit (see Chapter 3), than if they remain unemployed. As male inactivity has continued to rise over the last five years, so this form of upward pressure on workless households has continued.

Table 2.5 suggests that the composition of workless households manifests itself in different forms. In the 1980s the most common group was the unemployed. The proportion of workless households that contains an unemployed worker has fallen sharply, even since 1996. Most workless households are now economically inactive. Single parents and households with adults in their 50s make up a substantial proportion of the total, but the

Table 2.5   Composition of workless households

	1 adult	2 adults	3+ adults	Total
Workless households containing at least 1 unemployed person				
1996	24	44	69	31
2000	19	28	58	22
2002	17	25	53	19
Workless households containing a single parent				
1996	33			23
2000	31			23
2002	33			24
Workless households containing everyone over 55				
1996	25	17	1	22
2000	28	25	1	27
2002	28	23	1	26
Workless households containing other categories				
1996	18	39	31	24
2000	22	48	42	29
2002	23	52	48	30

Notes: Numbers are percentage of households with at least one unemployed occupant, lone parent not unemployed, all occupants aged 55 and over. Other category is the residual.

Source: LFS.

biggest increase has been amongst households that are neither unemployed, single parents or older workers. This group covers younger people claiming long-term sickness and disability benefits (highlighted in Chapter 3).

Conclusion

It seems that the recovery and government policy have halted the rise in the workless household rate. The workless household rate has fallen by around 3 percentage points over the last six years, affecting some 600,000 adults and some 500,000 children. This break in the seemingly upward trend towards more workless households is to be welcomed. However, adjusting for the strength of the recovery, there has been no improvement in the workless household position since 1996. Despite improvements in the employment position among lone parents and couples with children over and above what the recovery would predict, there have been continued shifts in family composition toward single adult households that have countered these improvements. There is still one in six households of working age that is workless, three times the rate observed in the 1970s and worklessness still disproportionately affects households with children to a much greater extent in Britain than in other countries. Moreover, there has been less sign of any improvement among households without children, so it would seem that policy now also needs to be focused in this area.

Note

1. We exclude full-time students and households where the head is above retirement age. This means we focus on households likely to be dependent on welfare payments aimed at working age people. It is also why our numbers differ slightly from published sources.

References

Gregg, P., Hansen, K. and Wadsworth, J. (1999), 'The Rise of the Workless Household', in P. Gregg and J. Wadsworth (eds), *The State of Working Britain*, Manchester University Press: Manchester and New York.

Gregg, P. and Wadsworth, J. (2002), 'Why We Should (also) Measure Worklessness at the Household Level: Theory and Evidence from Britain, Spain, Germany and the United States', CMPO Bristol Working Paper No. 02/053.

3
The Rise in Inactivity Among Adult Men

Giulia Faggio and Stephen Nickell

Key findings

- Inactivity rates among working age men over 25 have risen by a multiple of around four since the mid-1970s. Among prime-age men (aged 25–54), inactivity rates have risen even more (over five times) over the same period. By contrast, unemployment rates are roughly the same now as they were in the mid-1970s and inactivity rates among women have fallen significantly.
- Rises in the inactivity rate of prime-age men in the bottom skill quartile make up the majority of the increase in overall prime-age male inactivity since the mid-1970s. As a consequence, between 50 and 60 per cent of inactive prime-age men are now in the bottom skill quartile.
- Around 70 per cent of inactive prime-age men report themselves as having a limiting health problem. For older men, this number is around 50 per cent.
- In the 1970s, a mere 10 per cent of prime-age men reporting a limiting health problem were inactive. By the late 1990s, the proportion had risen to around 40 per cent. Since the 1970s, there has been a significant rise in the overall proportion of men reporting a limiting health problem. Much of the rise in prime-age male inactivity can be accounted for by these two facts. By contrast, among older men, around half the rise in inactivity since the 1970s is accounted for by increasing inactivity among those without any reported limiting illness. Many of these would be occupational pensioners.
- The level of inactivity among prime-age men is particularly concentrated among those who are both low skilled and suffering from a chronic health problem or disability. Over time as inactivity rose, this concentration got much worse.

• Important factors underlying these changes are the significant weakening of the low skill labour market and the operation of the invalidity benefit system.

Introduction

In *The State of Working Britain*, published in 1999,[1] there is an analysis of both unemployment and inactivity. Since that time the basic numbers have changed little and a description of the new policies introduced by the Labour government is available in Nickell and Quintini (2002). However, what is not available is a comprehensive analysis of the continuous rise in inactivity among adult men over the last 30 years and this is the topic of this chapter. In what follows, we present an overview of the rise in male inactivity noting the contrast with the fall in female inactivity over the same period. A particular point which emerges is the significant extent to which the rise in male inactivity is concentrated among the low skilled. We then analyse the close connection between inactivity among men and the incidence of long-term sickness and disability. Indeed, we find the connection to be so close that for prime-age men (aged 25–54), the rise in inactivity since the 1980s has come about more or less exclusively because of the increase in the numbers of those with a limiting illness or disability and the increasing proportion of this group who are inactive. Finally, we offer an explanation for what has happened. The driving force has been the substantial shift in labour demand away from low-skill workers which has outrun the shift in labour supply in the same direction. This particularly disadvantaged those low skilled workers who were suffering from an actual or potential limiting illness or disability.[2] When combined with the operation of the invalidity benefit system, the outcome was a dramatic rise in inactivity for this group.

The overall picture

The first question is why restrict ourselves to looking at inactivity among men? The answer is because inactivity rates among adult men have risen dramatically since the early 1970s whereas those for adult women have been falling. While the latter is to be expected as more and more married women go out to work,[3] continuing the trend since 1950, the former is more surprising. As we can see from Table 3.1, not only did male inactivity rise during the recessions of the early 1980s and 1990s, it continued to rise when the labour market was booming in the late 1980s and the late 1990s. So while male unemployment is now back to where it was in the 1970s, male inactivity has risen around fourfold.

In Table 3.1, we present information from both the General Household Survey (GHS), and the Labour Force Survey (LFS). There are two different definitions of unemployment and inactivity on display, and these are described in the notes to the table. By and large, the broad patterns generated in Table 3.1 are much the same whichever definitions are used. In what follows, therefore, we do not intend to spend time analysing the consequences of the different definitions at every point in our investigation.

Table 3.1   Inactivity and unemployment rates (%), 1972–2002

| | Inactivity rate (%) | | | | | | Unemployment rate (%) | | |
| | Men (25–64) | | | Women (25–59) | | | Men (25–64) | | |
	GHS	LFS	LFS (ILO)	GHS	LFS	LFS (ILO)	GHS	LFS	LFS (ILO)
1972–76	3.9	2.8		40.2	39.4		3.6	4.7	
1977–78	4.8	4.7		36.7	37.4		3.9	4.4	
1979–81	6.2	5.8		35.6	37.7		6.1	5.9	
1982–86	8.9	10.5		35.5	35.2		9.7	9.1	
1987–91	9.9	11.3		29.6	30.2		7.5	7.5	
1992–96	12.2	11.4	12.5	28.0	26.5	28.1	10.1	9.7	9.0
1997–99	14.3	12.8	13.8	25.9	25.2	26.8	5.3	6.0	5.4
2000–01	14.8	13.2	14.1	24.7	24.2	25.1	3.8	4.8	4.2
2002		13.3	14.3		23.8	24.7		4.9	4.3

Notes: (1) The inactive are those who are not working and not unemployed. LF unemployed are those without a job who are (a) looking for work in the reference week or (b) prevented from seeking work by temporary sickness or holiday or (c) waiting to start a job or (d) waiting for the results of a job application. ILO unemployed are those without a job who are available to start work in two weeks and (a) have looked for work in the previous four weeks or (b) are waiting to start a job. (2) The GHS uses the LF definition up to 1996, the ILO definition in 1998, 2000. The LFS series uses the LF definition. The LFS (ILO) series used the ILO definition.

Inactivity rates among prime-age and older men

In Table 3.2, we see that inactivity rates have risen substantially not only for older men but also for those of prime age. The patterns of increase are, however, different. For older men, the rise in inactivity is concentrated in the 1970s and 1980s, particularly following the early 1980s recession, but stopped in the 1990s. By contrast, for the prime-aged, inactivity rates continue rising up to the present day, despite the relatively buoyant labour market of the last seven or eight years. As a consequence, for this group, inactivity rates are now far greater than unemployment rates. This is a complete reversal of the situation in the 1970s. Interestingly enough, inactivity rates for prime-age men have risen significantly in most OECD countries since the 1970s with Germany being the most notable exception, the German rate having risen by less than one percentage point (from 5.1 per cent in 1979 to 5.9 per cent in 1998).

Given the shift in the demand for labour against the unskilled since 1980 (see Nickell and Bell, 1995, for example), we might expect bigger increases in inactivity among the unskilled. This has indeed happened as we can see in

Table 3.2 Inactivity rates of men (%), 1972–2002

| | Men aged 25–54 | | | Men aged 55–64 | | |
	GHS	LFS	LFS (ILO)	GHS	LFS	LFS (ILO)
1972–76	1.6	1.1		11.9	9.1	
1977–78	2.1	2.0		14.2	14.2	
1979–81	2.6	2.5		18.7	18.2	
1982–86	3.4	4.7		28.3	31.1	
1987–91	4.0	5.7		32.4	33.1	
1992–96	5.9	5.7	6.9	37.7	35.3	36.0
1997–99	7.9	7.2	8.3	39.9	36.0	36.6
2000–01	8.1	7.4	8.5	38.9	35.2	35.7
2002		7.5	8.6		34.5	35.0

Notes: As in Table 3.1.

Table 3.3 Inactivity rates for men by skill (%), 1972–2002

| | Men aged 25–54 | | | | Men aged 55–64 | | | |
| | | GHS | | LFS | | GHS | | LFS |
	Low skill	Other	Low skill	Other	Low skill	Other	Low skill	Other
1972–76	2.2	1.4			12.7	11.6		
1977–78	2.9	1.8			14.9	14.0		
1979–81	3.5	2.3	4.3	1.9	20.7	18.0		
1982–86	5.8	2.6	7.4	3.8	30.9	27.4	33.0	30.5
1987–91	8.1	2.6	9.6	4.4	36.6	31.0	37.8	31.5
1992–96	11.7	4.0	13.4	3.1	42.4	36.1	43.4	32.6
1997–99	15.4	5.4	17.7	3.7	50.6	36.3	47.4	32.1
2000–01	15.8	5.5	18.1	3.8	45.4	36.7	48.0	30.9
2002			18.8	3.7			47.6	30.1

Notes: (1) As in Table 3.1. (2) 'Low skill' is the bottom skill quartile based on educational qualifications. Until the early 1990s, those in the bottom skill quartile are a subset of those without qualifications. So the 'low skill' numbers refer to the mean for those with no qualifications. Later, those without qualifications are less than 25 per cent of prime-age men. So the bottom quartile also includes some proportion of the next education group, i.e. those with some GCSEs. So now, the 'low skill' numbers refer to a suitably weighted average of those without qualifications and those in the next education group. 'Other' represents those outside the bottom skill quartile.

Table 3.3. For older workers, the difference between the low skilled (bottom skill quartile) and the rest is not so great, at least in part because some in the higher skill groups have access to good early retirement packages. Among the prime-aged, however, the low skilled are three or four times more likely to be inactive than the remainder. As a consequence between 50 and 60 per cent of inactive prime-age men are now in the bottom skill quartile. Furthermore, the relative situation of the low skilled has worsened substantially since the 1970s. Indeed, this effect is so strong that of the overall rise in prime-age male inactivity since 1970s, some 50 to 70 per cent is down to the rise in inactivity in the bottom skill quartile.[4] Additionally, using LFS definitions, since the early 1980s there has been *no* increase in prime-age inactivity among those outside the bottom skill quartile whereas the inactivity rates of the low skilled have risen over 2.5 times.

Inactivity and disability

Inactive men over the age of 25 report themselves as being in one of four major categories: full-time student; looking after family; early retired; sick or disabled. In the prime-age group, around 70 per cent of the inactive report themselves as sick or disabled. In the older age group, the equivalent figure is over 50 per cent with another 35 per cent being early retired.[5] So, disability is a key factor in understanding the rise in male inactivity. To pursue this, we must first find out how many people report themselves as chronically ill.

In Table 3.4, we see that just under 20 per cent of men aged 25–64 report themselves as having a limiting long-standing illness (LLSI) and around 18 per cent report a limiting health problem or disability (LHPD). This difference appears to be systematic perhaps because in the case of LLSI, the illness limits 'things people normally do' whereas in LHPD, the illness limits 'the kind of work the person does'. The former is apparently a slightly broader category at least among the prime-aged, so for this group the numbers with LLSI are somewhat higher than those with LHPD. The key facts which emerge from Table 3.4 are first that the proportion reporting LLSI has not risen systematically since the late 1970s. Second, the numbers reporting LHPD rose slowly

Table 3.4   Percentage of men affected by chronic illness

	Men aged 25–64		Men aged 25–54		Men aged 55–64	
	LLSI	LHPD	LLSI	LHPD	LLSI	LHPD
1972–76	15.0		11.2		28.1	
1979–81	18.7		14.7		32.8	
1982–86	18.2	12.7	14.0	8.7	33.2	27.1
1987–91	19.0	14.8	14.8	10.4	35.0	31.8
1992–96	20.0	16.5	16.2	12.2	35.5	34.3
1997–99	20.0	17.0	16.6	13.3	33.6	36.6
2000–01	18.9	18.5	15.0	14.6	32.9	37.3
2002		18.1		14.1		36.3

Notes: (1) As in Table 3.1. (2) LLSI refers to a limiting long-standing illness. This is reported in the GHS, where people are asked if they suffer from a long-standing illness that limits things which they would normally do. LHPD refers to a limiting health problem or disability. This is reported in the LFS and refers to a health problem or disability which affects the kind of work the person does. (3) The GHS failed to ask a consistent question of this type in 1977–78. The LFS question was changed in 1997 and we have made a slight adjustment to the data post-1997 to generate a consistent series.

but systematically throughout. The different patterns of incidence observed for LLSI and LHPD may perhaps arise because LLSI is less responsive to a decline in labour demand than LHPD, which directly refers to work. Either way, what is clear is that the proportionate rise in illness or disability in the 1980s and 1990s is smaller than the rise in inactivity.

Turning to skill based and regional variations in illness or disability, the basic result for skills is that prime-age men in the bottom skill quartile are around twice as likely to suffer from a limiting illness than the remainder. This differential has grown systematically since the 1970s, when it was closer to 35 per cent. For older men, the differential is smaller, at around 50 to 70 per cent, but again it has risen strongly since the 1970s. Across regions, the differences are much more modest. For prime-age men, the differential between the low and high employment regions is between 15 (LLSI) and 30 (LHPD) per cent. For older men the differential is a bit bigger with the low employment regions having a proportion with limiting illness or disability which is about 36 per cent higher than in high employment regions.

Inactivity among men with a limiting illness

As we have already noted, around 70 per cent of inactive prime-age men report sickness or disability as the reason for their inactivity. Unsurprisingly, this is consistent with around 71 to 75 per cent of this same group reporting an LLSI or an LHPD. Among older workers the numbers are a little lower at just over 60 per cent, probably because there is a significant group of healthy early retirees among the over 55s. Recall that some 35 per cent of the inactive 55–64 year old men report early retirement as opposed to sickness or disability as the cause of their inactivity (in the LFS).

So, in the light of this, is the typical person with an LLSI or an LHPD inactive? The short answer is no. As we can see from Table 3.5, among prime-age men, the majority of those with a limiting illness or disability are economically active. However, whereas in the 1970s a mere 10 per cent of this group were inactive, by the late 1990s this number had risen to around 35 per cent (LLSI) or 43 per cent (LHPD). Inactivity among prime-age men without an LLSI has also risen but among those without an LHPD, there has been no significant change since the early 1980s. If we use these data plus changes in the incidence of long-standing illness in the working age population (Table 3.4), we can work out what proportion of the dramatic rise in inactivity among prime-age men is 'explained' by the rise in inactivity among those with a limiting illness or disability. The answer is that around 70 per cent of the rise in prime-age male inactivity since the 1970s can be accounted for by rising inactivity among the increasing numbers with an LLSI and that more or less *all* the rise since the 1980s can be accounted for by rising inactivity among the increasing numbers with an LHPD. So what proportion of these increases can be accounted for by rises in the incidence of chronic illness and what proportion by rises in inactivity among those who are chronically sick? The answers to this question are different, depending on whether we use the LLSI numbers from the GHS or the LHPD numbers from the LFS. In the former, nearly all the rise since the 1970s is due to an increase in inactivity rates among those with an LLSI, with less than one-fifth accounted for by the rising incidence of chronic illness. In the latter case, about half of the increase in inactivity is down to rising rates among those with chronic illness (LHPD) with the other half being accounted for by the rising incidence of LHPD. Why we have these differences between the GHS and the LFS is not clear.

Table 3.5   Inactivity rates among men (%)

| | Men aged 25–54 | | | | Men aged 55–64 | | | |
| | With | | Without | | With | | Without | |
	LLSI	LHPD	LLSI	LHPD	LLSI	LHPD	LLSI	LHPD
1972–76	10.0		0.4		32.0		4.0	
1979–81	11.9		0.7		39.7		8.4	
1982–86	15.9	28.8	1.2	1.9	53.4	66.6	16.4	18.4
1987–91	19.2	28.5	1.3	1.5	59.1	65.0	18.6	16.6
1992–96	26.3	36.3	1.8	1.5	66.0	68.6	23.2	17.7
1997–99	33.8	43.1	2.8	1.9	64.6	72.8	29.6	18.5
2000–01	34.5	41.8	3.2	2.0	70.9	70.2	25.1	18.7
2002		43.6		2.1		70.2		18.3

Notes: See the notes to Tables 3.1 and 3.4. LLSI is a limiting long-standing illness. LHPD is a limiting health problem or disability.

Among older workers, the situation recorded by the GHS is different with around half the rise in inactivity since the 1970s accounted for by rising inactivity among those without any reported limiting illness. This expanding group would tend to report themselves as inactive because of early retirement rather than because of sickness or disability. They would consist mainly of occupational pensioners taking early retirement, an option widely available, particularly in public sector occupations (e.g. teachers, doctors, police, civil servants).

Inactivity, disability and differentials by skill

Table 3.3 showed us that prime-age men in the bottom skill quartile are now around three or four times more likely to be inactive than the remainder of the prime-age male population. This difference is more or less entirely explained by two facts. First, those in the bottom skill quartile are more likely to report a limiting illness or disability than the rest. This explains just over half the difference. The remainder is due to the fact that among prime-age men who do report a limiting illness or disability, those in the bottom skill quartile are more likely to be inactive.

Pursuing the interaction between disability and skill further, we report in Table 3.6 the extent to which inactivity is concentrated among those who are both low skilled and chronically sick or disabled. (Chapter 6 shows that male inactivity rates are also much higher among less skilled men in low employment regions than among less skilled men in high employment regions.) Thus, while this group is less than 6 per cent of the prime-age male population, it now contributes nearly 3 percentage points to the total inactivity rate of 8.1 per cent. This contribution is actually higher than that of the chronically sick and disabled in the top three quartiles of the skill distribution who comprise nearly 10 per cent of the prime-age male population. Furthermore, the results in Table 3.6 indicate that this degree of concentration is considerably higher now than in the late 1970s. Indeed if we use data from the LFS, this degree of concentration is even more marked. So that of the rise in prime-age male inactivity from the early 1980s, nearly two-thirds is accounted for by the increase in inactivity among those in the bottom skill quartile with a limiting health problem or disability.

Table 3.6   The concentration of inactivity among the low skilled and chronically sick: age 25–54

| | All | Percentage of male population who are inactive | | | |
| | | Low skill | | Other | |
		Chronically sick/disabled	Well	Chronically sick/disabled	Well
1979–81	2.6	0.76	0.20	1.10	0.49
1982–86	3.4	1.05	0.42	1.30	0.60
1987–91	4.0	1.51	0.48	1.48	0.57
1992–96	5.9	2.26	0.56	2.24	0.88
1998	7.9	2.70	0.95	3.07	1.22
2000	8.1	2.88	1.00	2.65	1.60
Change					
(1979–81 to 2000)	5.5	2.1	0.8	1.6	1.1
		Percentage of male population in each group			
1979–81	100	4.5	20.5	10.2	64.8
2000	100	5.8	19.2	9.2	65.8

Notes: (1) These data are based on the GHS and so use the LLSI definition of chronic illness (see Table 3.5). (2) 'Low skill' refers to those in the bottom skill quartile, 'Other' to those outside this group (see Table 3.3). (3) If LFS data are used, the rise since the mid-1980s is even more concentrated among those in the bottom skill quartile with chronic illness.

Some explanations

One fundamental change underlying the facts set out above is the dramatic weakening of the market for unskilled labour in the UK since the late 1970s. Throughout the 1980s and into the 1990s there has been a strong shift in demand in favour of skilled workers and against unskilled workers in the UK. This change has come about because of the rapid expansion in the production and export of low-skill intensive goods by the developing countries (Wood, 1994) and because technical change has been biased in favour of the skilled (Berman et al., 1998). The consensus view is that the latter effect is dominant (Machin et al., 1999).

At the same time as this shift in demand, the UK has seen a shift in supply in the same direction, that is there are more skilled and fewer unskilled workers in the population of working age. Unfortunately for the unskilled, the shift in demand has outpaced the shift in supply (Nickell and Layard, 1999). On top of this, the UK had a particularly large group of very unskilled workers in the first place, relative to the rest of northern Europe.[6]

It is important to recognise that this shift in demand against the unskilled is fundamentally a within-industry phenomenon. That is, this change has *not* occurred because of a shift in demand away from industrial sectors with low skill intensity towards those with high skill intensity. The vast majority of the change has occurred because of a shift in demand away from the unskilled within *all* industrial sectors, manufacturing and services alike (Machin, 1995). Of course, because, over the same period, employment in the production sector contracted and that in the service sector expanded for other reasons, a majority of the unskilled who lost their jobs will have come from the production sector. But even had the production sector not contracted and the service sector not expanded, there would still have been job losses among the unskilled.

These fundamental economic changes generated a severe weakening of the unskilled labour market, the symptoms being a falling wage relative to the skilled and unskilled jobs becoming much harder to find. This would be a particular problem in the low employment regions. A consequence of all this would be a rise in the non-employment rates of low skill workers. This has indeed happened, but the question arises as to why this rise in non-employment has been so heavily focused on inactivity as opposed to unemployment? For example, the unemployment rate among those without qualifications fell from 19 per cent in the early 1980s to around 12 per cent in the late 1990s whereas the inactivity rate among the same group rose by a multiple of around three.

To answer this question, first consider another. Given the weakening labour market for the low skilled, which group would one expect to be particularly badly hit? A plausible answer is that it would be the group who have an additional disadvantage, namely those who suffer from a long-term illness or disability which limits the sort of work they can do.

The story would then proceed as follows. Back in the early 1970s, even the men in this group with low skills did not tend to withdraw from the labour force. Around 87 per cent of men in this category were economically active at that time. However, they did find it harder to get work. Back in the 1970s, those with a long-term illness or disability were three times as likely to be unemployed as the remainder of the workforce. So once the low-skill labour market started to weaken, those unskilled men with a chronic illness or disability were particularly badly hit. Because the low skill group found it much harder to get work, those operating the social security system found it much easier to shift them onto Invalidity Benefit (IVB, now Incapacity Benefit). Thus, some individuals who were hard to place in work were advised by the Employment Service to claim IVB (National Audit Office, 1989). Furthermore, doctors, whose certification was required for IVB entitlement, were influenced by their assessment of the probability of patients finding a job (Ritchie et al., 1993).[7]

These last might be termed 'push' factors into inactivity. 'Pull' factors include the fact that invalidity benefits were considerably higher than those available to the unemployed. Furthermore, this gap increased from the mid-1980s to the mid-1990s before falling back in the later 1990s. This occurred because of the operation of the Additional Pension system, an earnings related supplement to IVB. Another factor on the 'pull' side is the fact that once in the IVB system, the pressure to take up work is minimal. For example, Beatty and Fothergill (1999) report that in their survey of working-age men who had not worked for six months, only 5 per cent of those reporting themselves as long-term sick were looking for a job. The upshot of all this was that the number of male IVB claimants doubled from the early 1980s to the mid-1990s. Furthermore, since the harder it is to find work, the more likely are those with a limiting illness or disability to end up in the IVB system. The discrepancy in inactivity rates between high and low employment regions is sustained and worsened given that it is significantly harder to find work in the low employment regions. This story seems to be a plausible explanation of some of the facts noted above.

However, this is not the whole story. First, there have been significant increases in the incidence of chronic illness or disability, particularly among the low skilled. When combined with the behaviour of the Employment Service described above, this suggests that some individuals, after losing their jobs, were moved onto Invalidity Benefit and only then reported themselves as suffering from a limiting health problem. Whether this was commonplace cannot, however, be confirmed from the data reported here. Second, we can see from Table 3.6 how inactivity rose significantly among the chronically sick or disabled even outside the bottom skill quartile. It would be difficult to explain this by the weakening of the low skill labour market and suggests the operation of labour demand or supply effects for the chronically sick at all skill levels.

The current policy strategy

The present strategy to try and reverse the processes described above is three pronged. First, there are relatively generous in-work benefits for disabled individuals, the Disabled Person's Tax Credit which replaced the Disability Working Allowance in October 1999. Second, there is the New Deal for the Disabled and more generally the Job Centre Plus system. However, this New Deal is entirely voluntary. Third, on the medical side, the strategy is to make it harder for individuals to enter and to stay in the Incapacity Benefit system. The general idea is to make work relatively more rewarding and to provide help to obtain work which is tailored to individual needs. While much of this strategy is relatively new and is still evolving, so far there is little evidence that it is having a significant impact on the numbers. Arguably more effective carrots and sticks for potential employers are also required to make a serious dent in the problem alongside some degree of compulsion in the New Deal.

Conclusion

Working age men have been systematically withdrawing from the labour force in the UK since the early 1970s. At present, around 8 per cent of prime-age men (25–54) and 35 per cent of older men (55–64) are classified as inactive and these numbers are roughly four times their levels in the early 1970s. Inactive men are heavily concentrated in the bottom skill quartile with the notable exception of the group of early-retired, occupational pensioners. In the main, the increase in inactivity among prime-age men is due to the fact that there has been some increase in those suffering from a limiting health problem or disability (now around 13 per cent of the total) and members of this group have increasingly withdrawn from the labour force. Among older men, however, the situation is different. Around half their rise in inactivity since the 1970s is among men who report no limiting illness, in the main occupational pensioners.

Leaving aside the expansion of this last category, a major force driving these changes has been the collapse in demand for unskilled workers since the late 1970s. Underlying this collapse has been the rapid expansion of the production and export of low-skill intensive goods by developing countries and the bias of technical change in favour of the skilled. This shift in demand against the unskilled has outpaced the shift in supply, undermining the labour market for the unskilled. The problems generated by this have been accentuated by the fact that the UK has a particularly large group of very low-skill workers.

Symptoms of the weakening low skill labour market are a falling wage relative to the skilled and a shortage of unskilled jobs, particularly in low employment regions. So why did this lead to a huge rise in inactivity among the low skilled rather than in unemployment, which is at the same level now as in the late 1970s? The answer is that the individuals who were hit worst were those who had an additional disadvantage, namely suffering from a long-term illness or disability. This group, who mostly used to work, found themselves pushed and pulled towards a life on invalidity benefits. The push was provided by the Employment Service and the medical gate-keepers of the benefit system. The pull was generated by the generosity of invalidity benefits relative to unemployment benefits. The end result is a very large group of inactive invalidity benefit recipients. And once in this group, it is very difficult to get out. Some policy changes have been introduced to encourage exit from this group, but they have yet to have much impact.

Notes

1. See Gregg and Wadsworth (1999).
2. A potential limiting illness or disability may be thought of as one which emerges following job loss, when the individual concerned is diverted onto the invalidity benefit system.
3. The fall in inactivity among women has been concentrated among married women, particularly those with young children. In fact inactivity rates among single women have risen, notably among single parents whose numbers have also increased. Some, but not all, the issues which are important here are similar to those for men described in this chapter.
4. 50 per cent is the number generated using GHS data, 70 per cent is derived using LFS data, where the definitions are a bit different (see Table 3.1).
5. These numbers are from the LFS. The categories are mutually exclusive in the sense that individuals select the (one) category into which they fall. Of course, in practice, some of the sick or disabled will also have retired early.
6. The results of the OECD Literacy Survey (OECD, 1997) indicate that some 22 per cent of the population of working age in the UK is at the lowest level of literacy (close to illiteracy) compared with around 10 per cent in the typical northern European country (Germany, Netherlands, Sweden).
7. See Huddleston (2002) for further analysis. It is worth noting that most of the inactive who are chronically sick or disabled are claiming Incapacity Benefit (Invalidity Benefit prior to 1995) and by 2001, over 50 per cent of these claimants were suffering from mental or behavioural disorders (mostly depression) or diseases of the musculoskeletal system (mostly back pain). In 1979 the equivalent proportion was below 25 per cent (UK Social Security Statistics).

References

Beatty, C. and Fothergill, S. (1999), 'Incapacity Benefit and Unemployment', Centre for Regional Economic and Social Research, Sheffield Hallam University, July.

Berman, E., Bound, J. and Machin, S. (1998), 'Implications of Skill Biased Technological Change: International Evidence', *Quarterly Journal of Economics*, Vol. 113, pp. 1245–79.

Gregg, P. and Wadsworth, J. (eds) (1999), *The State of Working Britain*, Manchester University Press: Manchester.

Huddleston, T. (2002), 'Explaining the Growth in the Number of People Claiming Incapacity Benefits', Department of Work and Pensions.

Machin, S. (1995), 'Changes in the Relative Demand for Skill in the UK', in A. Booth, and D. Snower (eds), *Acquiring Skills*, Cambridge University Press: Cambridge.

Machin, S., Van Reenen, J. and Desjonqueres, T. (1999), 'Another Nail in the Coffin: Or Can the Trade Based Explanation of Changing Skill Structures be Resurrected?', *Scandinavian Journal of Economics*, Vol. 101, pp. 533–54.

National Audit Office (1989), *Invalidity Benefit: Report by the Comptroller and Auditor General*, HMSO: London.

Nickell, S. and Bell, B. (1995), 'The Collapse in Demand for the Unskilled and Unemployment Across the OECD', *Oxford Review of Economic Policy*, Vol. 11(1), pp. 40–62.

Nickell, S. and Layard, R. (1999), 'Labour Market Institutions and Economic Performance', in O. Ashenfelter and D. Card (eds), *Handbook of Labor Economics*, Vol. 3, North Holland: Amsterdam.

Nickell, S. and Quintini, G. (2002), 'The Recent Performance of the UK Labour Market', *Oxford Review of Economic Policy*, Vol. 18(2).

OECD (1997), *Literacy Skills for the Knowledge Society*, OECD: Paris.

Ritchie, J., Ward, K. and Duldig, W. (1993), *GPs and IVB*, DSS Research Report No. 18, HMSO: London.

Wood, A. (1994), *North-South Trade, Employment and Inequality*, Clarendon Press: Oxford.

4

Why Has Employment Recently Risen Among Older Workers in Britain?

Richard Disney and Denise Hawkes

Key findings

- From late 1998 to late 2002, employment among those aged 50 and over increased by 650,000. Their employment *rate* also rose, by 2 percentage points. This is in sharp contrast to the downward trend in the two decades prior to the mid-1990s.
- This growth was disproportionately concentrated among people in their 50s rather than their 60s, women rather than men and, on balance, among more highly educated workers.
- The buoyant economy of the period is a major reason for the upturn – there is a particularly strong association between the growth of GDP and the employment rate of people aged in their 50s (relative to older workers).
- On the demand side, demographic change and the shift to a service sector-based economy may reduce the likelihood of future precipitate falls in employment of older workers of the kind that was experienced in the early 1980s.
- On the supply side, falling equity markets and tighter regulations concerning ill-health related retirement in public pension programmes may have led people to postpone retirement. There is no clear evidence that reforms to the public disability insurance programme have had any effect on employment rates.
- Other policies, such as the voluntary code of practice on age diversity and New Deal 50 Plus may have had small effects on employment but mostly serve to keep the issue of employment of older workers on the public agenda.

Introduction

In common with most other OECD countries the employment of men and women aged 50 and over in Britain has declined markedly since the early 1970s. A variety of explanations – both supply- and demand-based – have been adduced for this decline (Blundell, Meghir and Smith, 2002; Campbell, 1999; Disney, 1999; Banks et al., 2002). These arguments include: that older workers have lacked the requisite skills in the face of technological change, faced forms of institutional discrimination, have been disproportionately located in declining sectors of economic activity, and have been induced into retirement by a combination of social security and occupational pension incentives.

In the last few years, however, there seems to have been a change in the economic fortunes of this age group, as illustrated in Table 4.1.

Table 4.1   Numbers of employed men and women aged 50 and over, Q4 1998 – Q4 2002

	Aged 50 to SPA (000s)	Above SPA (000s)	Total (000s)
Men			
1998 Q4	3,325	263	3,588
2002 Q4	3,603	306	3,903
Change	+278	+43	+315
Women			
1998 Q4	2,213	522	2,735
2002 Q4	2,485	588	3,073
Change	+272	+66	+338
Total change	+550	+109	+653

Note: Data from LFS. SPA = state pension age (currently 65 for men, 60 for women).

The table shows that, at the end of 2002, roughly 7 million people aged 50 and over were employed in Britain, of which about 56 per cent were men. This represents an increase of 653,000 since 1998, with the increase equally shared between men and women. Even allowing for supply changes, with the 'baby boom' generation just entering their 50s in the late 1990s, this reflects a significant increase in the employment *rate*. Employment rates among men aged 50–64 increased by 2 percentage points during the period 1998–2002. This is in contrast to men and women under 50 where, despite an increase in employment, there were no significant increases in employment *rates*.

Is this increase a genuine increase, reflected across all data sets? Is it a temporary phenomenon, associated with the upturn phase of the business cycle in the latter part of the 1990s, or is it the start of a new trend, reversing the apparently secular decline of the previous 25 years? Have government policies such as the 'Welfare to Work' strategy, the cutback in disability benefits, and anti-age discrimination initiatives played any part in it? This chapter investigates these issues, focusing on recent trends and recent policies. Much of the background analysis on general inducements to retire and the factors underpinning the demand side of the labour market can be found in Disney (1999).

Employment trends amongst older workers

Employment trends

Figure 4.1 provides a time series of employment rates from 1986 to 2000–02 drawn from two sources: the Labour Force Survey (LFS), which is regularly used in government publications when describing employment rates, and the Family Expenditure Survey (FES), which is a long-running sample survey of households. The group for which we compare alternative data sets in Figure 4.1 is 50–54 year olds; an age group that will actively be considering the timing of retirement.

One striking feature of the data is the convergence of employment rates among men and women in this age group. Taking the LFS numbers, the

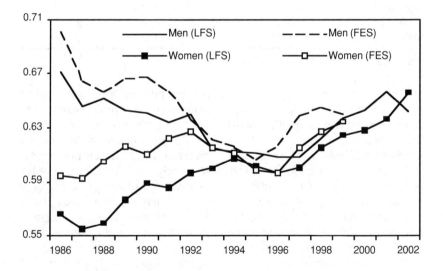

Figure 4.1 Employment rates for men and women aged 50–54

Notes: The FES data are smoothed given smaller sample size so that information for 2000 (the latest available year) is lost. 'Raw' employment rates in the FES for 50–54 year olds in 2000 are: men=0.635, women=0.625.

Sources: Authors' own calculations from LFS and FES.

employment rate among these men is almost now back to mid-1980s levels, whilst that of women is rising steadily over the period. Neither trend is so clear-cut in the FES, although there has definitely been a turnaround in older workers' fortunes from the mid-1990s. Among older women the slight tendency to earlier retirement as each cohort ages, akin to the trend among men, has been more than offset by each successive cohort in this age range having a higher overall rate of economic activity.

Economic activity by age and schooling

Table 4.2 describes employment rates for different age groups of men and women, using the LFS, comparing 1990, the peak of the last economic cycle, with 2002.

Table 4.2   Peak to peak employment rates (%), 1990–2002

	50–54	55–59	60–64	65 and over
Men				
1990	64	57	39	5
2002	64	56	36	4
Women				
1990	59	47	20	3
2002	66	51	23	3

Source: LFS.

For men, the data suggest that employment rates by 2002 among older workers had been restored to those at the previous cycle peak.[1] It should be noted, nevertheless, that of every five men in their 50s, two are not working. The very low male employment rates after age 65 illustrate the importance of 65 as a retirement age for men, as it is the age at which men are first entitled to a state old-age pension. This is so even though, since the abolition of the 'earnings test' in 1989, the direct tax system contains no disincentives to working after 65 (60 for women).[2] For women, there is evidence of a steady rise in employment rates among those aged 50 and over, largely arising from the 'cohort effects' described earlier. The decline in employment at state pension age for women (age 60) is not so dramatic.

Figure 4.2 examines another trend of some interest – the rise in self-employment among older workers. The data for age group 55–59 are chosen by way of illustration – trends for 50–54 year olds are very similar but there is less evidence of any trend for those aged 60 and over. The two data sources agree that there has been a rise of around 50 per cent, or 5 percentage points, in the self-employment rate among older men since the mid-1980s (in contrast to men at other ages). This pattern contrasts with the overall self-employment

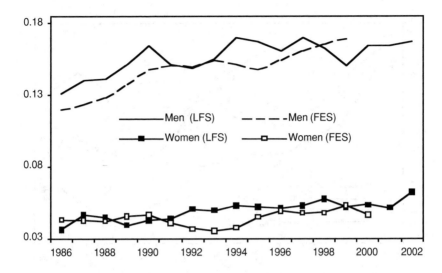

Figure 4.2   Self-employment rates for men and women aged 55–59

Notes: The FES data are smoothed given smaller sample size so that information for 2000 (the latest available year) is lost. 'Raw' self-employment rates in the FES for 55–59 year olds in 2000 are: men=0.165, women=0.062.

Sources: Authors' own calculations from LFS and FES.

rate which has been falling for a few years now. Self-employment rates among older women are much lower and show little change over time.

The increase in self-employment may arise as a result of higher levels of redundancy (both voluntary and involuntary), particularly in newly privatised sectors and contracted-out sectors, which has led to the growth of 'buying in' of labour services and other forms of consultancy. Whether there is any evidence of changes in benefit eligibility and 'Welfare to Work' policies playing a part is considered later in this chapter.

The final piece of descriptive evidence concerns the composition of employment. The data for men differentiates between workers with educational qualifications beyond school leaving age (which we term, at the risk of simplification, 'skilled') and those who left school at the earliest school leaving age ('unskilled'). The data are from the FES, since there are no LFS data on a comparable basis for the period. Figure 4.3 illustrates the employment rates of men aged 50–54 and 55–59, for our two groups termed 'skilled' and 'unskilled'.

The data illustrate rather different trends for the different groups. 'Skilled' men aged 50–54 exhibit a slower secular decline in their employment rate.

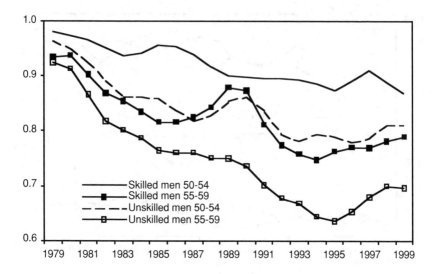

Figure 4.3   Employment rates among skilled and unskilled older men, 1979–99

Source: FES.

But there is much greater volatility in employment rates of 'unskilled' men aged 50–54, with sharp declines in recessions in the early 1980s and early 1990s and recoveries in the improved economic conditions of the mid to late 1980s and late 1990s. Indeed by 1988–89, parity in employment rates had been restored although this had not yet taken place in the second upturn of the late 1990s.

Comparing 50–54 year olds alone might suggest that unskilled employment among older workers is disproportionately affected by adverse demand shocks, while skilled workers are less affected. But examination of the 55–59 category suggests that we cannot generalise this finding – 'skilled' 55–59 year old workers have almost the same time path of employment rates as 'unskilled' 50–54 year olds, while 'unskilled' 55–59 year olds exhibit a more rapid, secular, decline in economic activity, at least until the 1990s. This suggests that there are two potential dimensions to vulnerability to demand shocks (the business cycle): lack of skill, and age. Younger, more skilled workers may be the most immune to fluctuations, and older unskilled workers the least affected (although even this group sees some improvement in the late 1990s). Investigations of 'older workers' that do not differentiate workers by age and skill level may miss something.[3]

Explanations: the demand side

Secular trends

The demand factors behind the long-term decline in employment rates of older workers are well established. Over time, the demand for skilled workers appears to have increased faster than the demand for less skilled workers in OECD countries. Older people have less formal qualifications (such as level of educational attainment) than younger people. Although older workers on average embody greater on-the-job training than younger workers, skills depreciate with age. So older workers are more vulnerable to technological change in favour of skills than are younger workers.

There are other features of the UK economy that have contributed to this decline in employment of older workers. Because older workers have fewer 'modern' skills, such as computer-familiarity, and were historically concentrated in declining sectors of the economy, such as manufacturing (Campbell, 1999), they have been more vulnerable to adverse macroeconomic shocks in the traded sector of the economy (such as exchange rate rises). Moreover, insofar as semi-skilled and unskilled jobs involve greater physical effort, there is evidence that age reduces physical functional capacities and increases the likelihood of early retirement in such jobs.

Why do older workers not seek alternative jobs that involve less effort, responsibility or hours, especially if their existing career jobs are stressful, physically or mentally? Changing careers late in the working life is risky – as Hurd (1996) points out, jobs involve 'packages' of fixed hours, wages and overhead costs. The shorter time horizon to retirement when hiring new workers makes younger workers (so long as they can be retained) a better investment than older workers if there are substantial fixed costs (such as training or hiring costs) involved. Disney, Hawkes and Heden (2000) show for the UK that occupations in the LFS that offer training are much less likely to hire older people. Moreover, leaving a career job for alternative employment is likely to induce substantial cuts in both wages and, perhaps, pension rights – which are an increasingly important consideration as the worker ages (Gustman and Steinmeier, 1993). So there is a strong incentive for older workers to retire directly from full-time work into economic inactivity rather than to seek alternative, less onerous, employment in order to extend their economically active life.

Are there any factors that might reverse the long-term trend? First, the long-run shift of the economy towards the service sector may benefit older workers. Some service sector jobs may require interpersonal skills that are accumulated with experience and also require less in the way of physical functional capacities. Moreover, the gradual ageing of the population increases the demand for services utilised by older people, and older workers may benefit from these shifts in spending patterns.[4]

Second, the stereotype of the 'career job' culminating in retirement may also be ending. Gregg and Wadsworth (1999) provide evidence of a decline in 'long-term jobs' in the UK economy since the 1970s. This trend could be associated with greater flexibility, such as 'bridge' jobs to retirement, spells of self-employment interspersed with employment, and so on. This might or might not be to the benefit of older workers who want to prolong their time in the workforce but would prefer to shift out of their existing jobs because they are too physically onerous or taxing in other respects. However, to the extent that greater 'flexibility' in the labour market is associated with training and re-training, and other fixed costs, the barriers to older workers described previously remain. Moreover, in one important dimension, the labour market in the UK seems to be no more 'flexible' than before. Average hours of work have *increased* in the UK through the 1980s but have eased back a little more recently, both for men and women (see Chapter 9). If older people prefer fewer hours of work, these long hours may be a deterrent to continuing in paid work, although, without young children, older workers may be more amenable to 'non-standard' working hours such as shift working.

Third, given demographic trends, there will in future be fewer young workers with which to compete (although, of course, correspondingly larger numbers of older workers to compete against). This ought to lead employers to rethink their behaviour towards age, whatever the institutional and legal environment. Well-publicised cases of service sector employers explicitly recruiting among older people may be part of a new trend, or simply illustrate the exceptions to continued myopic thinking among other employers.

Cyclicality

Notwithstanding long-run trends, a major factor behind the rise in employment rates of older workers was the relatively fast growth of the UK economy in the late 1990s. Older workers may be particularly vulnerable in recessions but also respond positively to booms by deferring retirement or indeed returning to work from unemployment or long-term sickness. But does this cyclical response of older workers' employment vary across age, skill and gender?

To examine this proposition, we run simple regressions of employment rates by age–gender–skill groups on annual GDP growth in constant prices for 1978–2000. The object of this exercise is to see whether the sensitivity of the relationship (if any) between this cyclical measure and employment of older workers varies across groups. Table 4.3 describes the results of this straight-forward basic exercise. There are positive correlations between employment rates and GDP growth as expected: if the growth rate doubles, for example, employment of skilled men aged 50–54 rises by 22 per cent. The age group 50–54 exhibits similar responsiveness to GDP growth as those skilled men aged under 50. The responsiveness (correlation) then declines monotonically with age – although there is still a significant relationship for all age groups.

Those defined as 'skilled' in terms of schooling, are marginally more responsive than the 'unskilled' to economic conditions. Finally, men's employment rates are more responsive to GDP growth than those of women. There is also some evidence (not shown) that, for younger age groups, the responsiveness depends on whether GDP growth is positive or negative, with some suggestion that employment rates are more responsive to GDP falls than to rises.

These results imply that the upturn in the economic cycle since the mid-1990s has played a large part in the recovery in employment rates of older workers, but that this effect dampens with age and is slightly stronger for men with better educational qualifications. As economic growth has slowed after 2001, we might anticipate a slowing of the improvement in the economic activity of older workers.

Table 4.3   Effect of real GDP growth on employment rates by age, 1978–2000

Age	'Skilled'					'Unskilled'				
	<50	50–54	55–59	60–65	>65	<50	50–54	55–59	60–65	>65
Men										
Δreal GDP	0.23	0.22	0.20	0.13	0.03	0.21	0.20	0.18	0.12	0.02
Women										
Δreal GDP	0.19	0.18	0.14	0.06	0.01	0.16	0.16	0.13	0.05	0.01

Note: 'Skilled' are those who left full-time education after the minimum school leaving age.

Source: LFS.

Explanations: the supply side

Changes in occupational pension schemes and early retirement provisions

One feature of pension provision in the UK has been the importance of retirement incentives within occupational pension schemes. These arise from two features: opportunities for early retirement on grounds of 'ill health' and from the specific incentives concerning choice of retirement date within 'defined benefit' pension plans.

Most occupational pension schemes offer some form of 'early retirement' package for people who become permanently incapacitated or seriously ill before 'normal' retirement age, and these packages have been extensively utilised. In the public sector in the late 1990s, ill health accounted for 39 per cent of all retirements in the police service, 39 per cent in local government and 22 per cent in the civil service (HM Treasury, 2000). Within the fire service, rates of ill-health retirement varied from 11 per cent in some authorities to 93 per cent in others. This form of early retirement grew rapidly in the 1980s and 1990s and, as the figures for the fire service indicate, exhibited disparities in levels that could not be explained simply by underlying trends in illness in the population.

The growing prevalence of ill-health retirement in the private sector has not been so dramatic. Even so, as the Cabinet Office Performance and Innovation Unit (2000) suggested, private sector managers saw ill-health related retirement as an increasingly attractive way of 'downsizing' workforces in the late 1980s and 1990s – the payment of pensions were 'off budget', pension funds were in general running significant surpluses at that time, and there were fiscal incentives for individuals to take retirement packages.

These incentives have been eroded. The changed tax treatment of pension funds coupled with changes in the accounting treatment of pension liabilities, and the reduction in the value of pension funds arising from the collapse in equity markets, have made it tougher to finance such generous early retirement 'packages'. These financial pressures are not so direct in the public sector, where several pension plans are either partially or wholly unfunded. But HM Treasury (2000) and the Cabinet Office report both recommended that stronger efforts be made to deter early retirement in the public sector. These included linking Service Delivery Agreements from 2000 to target reductions in rates of early retirement across sectors, active measures in each sector for redeployment rather than retirement, greater consistency in medical procedures and examinations, and investigation of the postponement of 'normal' retirement beyond the (then) current effective age of 60. Mandatory retirement ages have in fact been abolished but it is hard to get good evidence on whether there is a changing 'culture' in the public sector towards later retirement – government websites are currently devoid of information as to whether SDA targets on ill-health related retirement have been implemented, let alone achieved.

In the private sector, there have been other changes to pension plans. Since 1978, most occupational pension schemes have been 'defined benefit' (DB) – that is, benefits depend on some formula related to years of service and salary (typically final salary or an average of years close to final salary). Such plans give a strong incentive for individuals to retire at or around the time that their final salary is likely to peak (subject to life expectancy), as described in Disney (1999). Since around 2000, however, many companies have switched new employees (and in some cases, existing plan members) into 'defined contribution' (DC) schemes, where benefits depend solely on contributions to, and returns on, plan members' funds, taking advantage of more lenient contracting-out rules after 1988. The reasons for this transition are straight-forward – with falling equity markets, members rather than funds bear the investment risk in DC plans, the tax privileges of occupational pensions have been eroded, and tougher regulations on matching assets to liabilities are by-passed.

How does this shift from DB to DC plans affect retirement decisions? There is a plausible argument that the *incentives* in DC plans may encourage deferral of retirement, since the fund value accumulates with every year that retirement is postponed whereas, after a time, with a plausible age–earnings profile, individuals lose out from not retiring through a DB plan. Offsetting this is the wealth effect by which higher fund values may induce earlier retirement (Blundell, Meghir and Smith, 2002). A combination of falling values of fund investments, coupled with employees bearing a greater share of investment risk, suggests that retirement decisions may be deferred in the future. So, both for financial reasons and because of a tightening of early retirement 'windows' in company pension plans, early retirement through occupational pensions may be becoming less prevalent.

Disability benefits

For those not covered by occupational pension schemes, the only route in recent years into retirement before state pension age has been through the disability benefit scheme (Disney, 1999). Numbers of claimants increased rapidly in the 1970s and 1980s and policies were introduced in the mid-1990s with a view to halting this exodus. The main changes under legislation introduced in 1995 were (i) to debar new claimants from receiving the main disability benefit, Invalidity Benefit (IVB), beyond state pension age; (ii) to cut some benefit rates and to make the replacement for IVB, Incapacity Benefit, taxable (unlike IVB and the state pension); and (iii) to toughen up the eligibility tests for disability benefits.

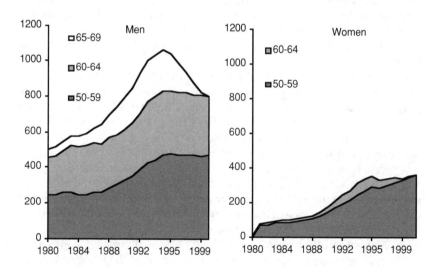

Figure 4.4 Number of claimants of Invalidity and Incapacity Benefit: aged 50 and over, 1980–2000

Source: Banks et al. (2002).

Figure 4.4 examines the impact of these changes on older male and female claimant numbers. It is clear that there is a fall in claimant numbers after 1995, but that this stems almost wholly from phasing out claims of IVB above state pension age over the five-year period. The increase in claimants among men aged 50 or more, but below state pension age, has abated but there seems to be no decrease in the growth of claims among older women of working age. In fact econometric evidence in Disney, Emmerson and Wakefield (2003) finds no evidence of an impact of the 1995 legislation on economic activity among older people of working age. The reduction in the increase in claims among older men of working age may again be related to the more buoyant demand for labour in the late 1990s.

Anti-age discrimination policies

The Cabinet Office report (2000) suggested that attitudes to older workers 'have made an important contribution to the problem of falling employment rates among older people, and that a government strategy to address the problem' is needed (p. 52). Surveys of employers in the late 1990s, cited by this report, suggested that employers were reluctant to employ older workers, who were believed to be resistant to change, lacked ambition and were unwilling to cope with the pressures of technological and market change. On the other hand, as suggested above, some respondents argued that older workers had experience and knowledge lacked by younger workers. Moreover, large companies (especially privatised utilities) that had downsized rapidly had suffered 'corporate memory loss' resulting in many aspects of the business having to be re-learnt from scratch (train operators and Railtrack being obvious examples).

It is of course hard to distinguish stereotyping of older people, which may illustrate age discrimination, from genuine age-related differences in productivity and skills. Since 1999, issues associated with age discrimination have been handled through the voluntary Code of Practice on Age Diversity launched by the Department for Education and Employment (DfEE). It aims to tackle age discrimination by setting out the standard for non-ageist approaches to recruitment, training and development, promotion, redundancy and retirement. By raising awareness of age discrimination and the benefits of age diversity in the work place, it is argued, the trend towards early retirement can be reduced. The Code of Practice was updated in December 2002 and has been promoted by the government-backed Age Positive Campaign.

An evaluation of the Code of Practice by National Opinion Polls (2001) found that, although larger employers were aware of the Code of Practice this was not the case for the medium and small employers. The report argued that there was a need to promote the Code of Practice to smaller firms (this has subsequently been the aim of the revision to the Code of Practice), and that the Age Positive Campaign should be extended to the general public rather than aimed merely at professional bodies, trade associations and linked government organisations. It was also suggested that eventually the Code would need to become law.

A legislative approach to age discrimination is now forthcoming since the European Council of Ministers adopted the Employment Directive on Equal Treatment (on the basis of Article 13 of the EU Treaty). This requires that all EU member states introduce legislation prohibiting direct and indirect discrimination on the grounds of age, sexual orientation, religion and belief, and disability. The anti-age discrimination component of the legislation must be introduced by 2006. Equal treatment in employment and vocational training is already being implemented under the Employment Directive (EU Council Directive 2000/78/EC) and it will be interesting whether the association between training offers across occupations and disproportionate hirings of younger workers described in Disney, Hawkes and Heden (2000) will be taken as evidence of informal discrimination.

It is hard to evaluate whether the voluntary approach has had any impact. Not only is the extent of 'heightened awareness' open to doubt, from the evidence of employer attitudes, but it is difficult to prove that awareness generates action. For this reason, many bodies have advocated the more legalistic approach that underlies the European Union's stance. Nevertheless, even here, it is hard to predict what the employment effects of legislation will be without recourse to some 'natural experiment' in which some groups of workers are subject to anti-age discrimination legislation and others are not. This 'experiment' is present in the US where, although Federal legislation has been in place on anti-age discrimination since 1968, there are substantial variations across states and across time in discretionary additional legislation and in the enforcement of the legislation.

The impact of such legislation on older workers is, however, rather complex. If workers are paid according to their productivity at every stage of the lifecycle, and there are no mandatory retirement ages, and employers can observe productivity, then there should be no reason not to hire older workers. Only an employer who actively discriminated against older workers would refuse to hire, and this would be illegal.

However, a more subtle reasoning is as follows. Some employers may 'backload' remuneration by having a steeper gradient of pay with age than is consistent with productivity at each age (and also perhaps providing a company pension plan). This is an incentive device to retain more efficient workers or to induce greater efficiency. But with rising pay over the lifetime, employers will want ultimately to get rid of workers – mandatory retirement. If such long-term contracts are costlessly negotiable, legislation that requires firms to retain older workers beyond the age at which they would want to get rid of them would flatten lifetime age–earnings profiles. However, if negotiating such contracts is hindered because firms may arbitrarily renege on them (i.e. by getting rid of older workers whose current total remuneration exceeds their current productivity), then anti-age discrimination may *steepen* the age–earnings profile whilst maintaining employment levels of older workers. Neumark and Stock (1999) use the cross-state and time variation in legislation across states of the US to argue that this is precisely what has happened in practice. If this is true (and it is possible that 'long-term contracts' of this kind are increasingly rare in the 'flexible labour market'), then the mere presence of anti-age discrimination legislation may have positive effects for the employability of older workers. At present in the UK, however, there is little clear-cut evidence of employment effects stemming from the existing Code of Practice.

Welfare to Work policies

New Deal 50 Plus is part of the Government's Welfare to Work strategy. It was launched in nine areas in October 1999 and extended nationally in April 2000. It is a voluntary scheme available to those over 50 who have been on Jobseeker's Allowance, Income Support, Incapacity Benefit or Severe Disablement Allowance for six months or more. The aim of the programme is to help people aged 50 or over back into employment, by personal advice and help with job search. If the recipient finds a job with an income of less than £15,000 they receive a tax-free employment credit of £60 a week for a full-time post (at least 30 hours) and £40 for a part-time post (at least 16 hours) for up to 52 weeks. This employment credit is also paid to those entering self-employment. In addition a training grant of up to £750 can be paid to those receiving an employment credit. £600 of this can be received in the first year of employment to be used to support back-to-work training. The remaining £150 will be paid into an Individual Learning Account after 12 months in work.

In February 2002, the Cabinet Office announced that, in the first 22 months of the New Deal 50 Plus programme, more than 60,000 people over 50 had gone into work. However, as in evaluations of other Welfare to Work programmes, it is important to know the counterfactual – how many of the target group would have found work in the absence of the programme and what is the aggregate employment impact of the programme. An evaluation of New Deal 50 Plus, undertaken by the Institute for Employment Studies (e.g. Atkinson, 2001) used largely qualitative data from New Deal 50 Plus participants and employment service/benefits agency staff.

A primary finding of this evaluation was that both the clients and the advisers considered the employment credit to be the key reason for participation in New Deal and consequently finding a position because the employment credit enabled the client to accept a lower paid job. A concern raised by the advisers – that once the employment credit expired, many programme participants would leave their job – was not apparent in the studies of participants. Once in employment the New Deal 50 Plus participants did not appear to change jobs. A second finding focused on the lack of take-up of the training grant. In most cases clients reported that they had not known of this part of the scheme. Other than this qualitative and rather subjective study, there seem to have been few other analyses undertaken. Indeed, whilst *Labour Market Trends* publishes figures concerning New Deal 18–24 and New Deal 25 Plus, comparable figures for New Deal 50 Plus are not reported. In the absence of quantitative evidence, it is hard to escape the conclusion that much of the re-employment of New Deal 50 Plus participants has arisen from the favourable demand conditions. Perhaps the main purpose and rationale of the programme so far has been to create a recognition, in Whitehall as much as anywhere, that disadvantaged workers need not simply be young, or single mothers.

Conclusion

There has been a significant reversal in the trend towards lower employment rates among older workers since the mid-1990s, although the magnitude of the change differs across data sets. Moreover, the aggregate increase for older workers conceals significant differences across old workers differentiated by gender, age and educational qualification. Men close to state pension age with less educational qualifications have been less affected than men closer to 50 with skills. Higher participation of later cohorts is driving up employment rates among women, especially among those with more schooling.

There are undoubtedly some longer-term factors that have slowed the previous decline in employment rates among older workers. The collapse of manufacturing industry in the early 1980s and the downsizing of workforces associated with privatisation will not occur on such a large scale simply because both these sectors are so much smaller. Moreover, demographic changes to the composition of the labour market and, possibly, changes in employer attitudes, may have played a part. Of much more significance has been the upturn in the economic cycle that took place in the late 1990s. Workers in their 50s, in particular, have benefited from the improved economic conditions, which may or may not be long-lasting.

On the supply side, the difficulties of private pension funds associated with falling equity markets, and tightening of the regulations governing early retirement in public pension programmes, may have played a part. There is no clear cut-evidence that the reforms of the public disability programme have had any large-scale effect. Finally, the Code of Practice on Age Diversity, the Age Positive Campaign and New Deal 50 Plus may have had impacts, but these may be through their symbolic importance and the association with relatively favourable demand conditions, rather than through the measures themselves. In the short run, at least, the recovery in employment rates among older workers is going to depend in large part on the future state of the economy.

Notes

1. The FES tends to report higher employment rates in the 1980s and early 1990s than the LFS, so that the recovery of employment rates to previous peaks looks more impressive in the LFS. The FES has a smaller sample size and is subject to greater measurement error, but the structure and sample size of the LFS has changed over time.

2. Indeed there is evidence of a small but significant increase in hours worked among those who continue to work after state pension age after its abolition (Disney and Smith, 2002).

3. For 60–64 year olds, the decline in employment rates from around 70 per cent in 1979 to 43–44 per cent in 1999 is common to both 'skilled' and 'unskilled' men, suggesting that age dominates skill in the vulnerability of the oldest group in the labour force. Conversely, for *younger* groups (i.e. aged less than 50), there is again greater cyclicality in employment rates among 'unskilled' than 'skilled' men, but with a smaller overall fall in the former's employment rates over the period. This confirms the general points made in the text. For women, the disparate trends are reflected in an *increase* in employment rates among 'skilled' 50–54 year olds, while employment rates remain roughly constant for the 'unskilled', as well as slightly more volatility. (Data are available from the authors on request.)

4. This argument should not be oversold, however. The assertion that changes in the composition of demand will be matched by changes in the composition of *employment* remain largely unproven, and there are some clear cases, such as the demand for nursing and residential care, where increased longevity will almost certainly be associated with growing demand for younger, largely female, workers, rather than older workers.

References

Atkinson, J. (2001), 'The New Deal 50 Plus: Evidence from Client Surveys', *Labour Market Trends*, 109, November, pp. 523–5.

Banks, J., Blundell, R., Disney, R. and Emmerson, C. (2002), 'Retirement, Pensions and Saving Adequacy: A Guide to the Debate', *Briefing Note* 29, Institute for Fiscal Studies: London. Download at: http://www.ifs.org.uk/pensions/bn29.pdf

Blundell, R., Meghir, C. and Smith, S. (2002), 'Pension Incentives and the Pattern of Early Retirement', *Economic Journal*, 112, March, C153–C170.

Cabinet Office Performance and Innovation Unit (2000), *Winning the Generation Game*, The Stationery Office: London.

Campbell, N. (1999), 'The Decline of Employment Among Older Workers in Britain', CASE Paper 19, STICERD, London School of Economics.

Disney, R. (1999), 'Why Have Older Men Stopped Working?' in P. Gregg and J. Wadsworth (eds), *The State of Working Britain*, Manchester University Press: Manchester, pp. 58–74.

Disney, R., Emmerson, C. and Wakefield, M. (2003), 'Ill-Health and Retirement in Britain: A Panel-Data Based Analysis', Institute for Fiscal Studies Working Paper 03/02, London.

Disney, R., Hawkes, D. and Heden, Y. (2000), 'Declining Job Opportunities For Older Workers in Britain: the Role of Job-Specific Characteristics', University of Nottingham. Download at: http://www.nottingham.ac.uk/economics/staff/details/richard_disney.html

Disney, R. and Smith, S. (2002), 'The Labour Supply Effect of the Abolition of the Earnings Rule for Older Workers in the United Kingdom', *Economic Journal*, 112, March, C136–C152.

Gregg, P. and Wadsworth, J. (1999), 'Job Tenure, 1975–98', in P. Gregg and J. Wadsworth (eds), *The State of Working Britain*, Manchester University Press: Manchester, pp. 109–26.

Gustman, A. and Steinmeier, T. (1993), 'Pension Portability and Labour Mobility: Evidence From the Survey of Income and Program Participation', *Journal of Public Economics*, 50, pp. 299–323.

HM Treasury (2000), *Review of Ill Health Retirement in the Public Sector*, London, Download at: http://www.hm–treasury.gov.uk/documents/public_spending_and_services/evidence_and_analysis/pss_ea_illhealth.cfm

Hurd, M. D. (1996), 'The Effect of Labor Market Rigidities on the Labor Force Behavior of Older Workers', in D. A. Wise (ed.), *Advances in the Economics of Aging*, Chicago University Press for National Bureau of Economic Research: Chicago, pp. 11–58.

Neumark, D. and Stock, W. A. (1999), 'Age Discrimination Laws and Labor Market Efficiency', *Journal of Political Economy*, 107, 5, pp. 1081–125.

5

McJobs and MacJobs: The Growing Polarisation of Jobs in the UK

Maarten Goos and Alan Manning

Key findings

- There has been a large rise in the number of well paid jobs (MacJobs) in the UK over the past 25 years but also a rise in the number of badly paid jobs (McJobs). 'Middling' jobs have been disappearing.
- The most likely cause of these trends is technology with machines and computers replacing jobs that can be mechanised. The worst paid jobs (e.g. cleaning) cannot be done effectively by machines so employment in these occupations tends to rise.
- The growing polarisation of jobs cannot be explained by the changing structure of the labour force.
- Policies to increase pay among the low paid, and immigration seem likely to be most effective at dealing with the problems caused by the increasing polarisation of work.

Introduction

Over the last 25 years inequality in Britain has increased. The gap in wages between rich and poor has widened, the employment rates of the skilled and unskilled have diverged and there is greater polarisation of work across households (see previous edition of *The State of Working Britain*, Gregg and Wadsworth, 1999). In their writings about these subjects, economists have emphasised the role played by 'skill-biased technical change', the idea that technical change is biased in favour of skilled workers and against the less skilled. As the demand for skill has increased, the resulting fall in the demand for the unskilled has led to a fall in their relative wages and their employment rates.

One should not conclude from this that 'skill-biased technical change' inevitably causes problems like the rise in inequality that we have seen. If the increase in the demand for skills is matched by a similar increase in the supply of skills there is no reason to expect an increase in inequality to be the result. And, for much of the 200-odd years since the beginning of the Industrial Revolution, this is what seemed to happen: big rises in the demand for skills, big rises in the supply of skilled workers and not much happening to inequality. Since skilled jobs tend to be 'better' than less skilled jobs both in terms of the wages they pay and the content of the work, this also means that the number of 'bad jobs' has been falling, the number of 'good jobs' rising. The solution to our current predicament is simple: in the words of Tony Blair, 'education, education, education' to help the supply of skills catch up with demand. The government may not meet its targets on educational attainment, but at least it is pushing in the right direction.

The views of labour economists diverge from those of the man or woman in the street at this point. Your mother probably thinks that, while there may be more good jobs around than before in the professions, computing and information technology (the MacJobs), there are also more bad jobs in fast food, shops and personal services (the McJobs). These 'McJobs' offer low wages, and few prospects. To many labour economists this view makes no sense: the number of bad jobs can't be rising because the (relative) wages of the low skilled are falling and falling wages means falling demand according to the conventional wisdom. It follows that the problem for the low skilled is not an excess of bad jobs but a lack of jobs. This chapter shows, however, that there is something in the popular view.

To assess whether there are more good or bad jobs around, one first needs a definition of a job. The most natural definition to use is to define a job as an occupation: for example in the Labour Force Survey (LFS), the occupation variable is derived from the question 'what was your main job in the week ending Sunday?' We also include industry as, for example, being the manager of a McDonald's store is likely to be very different from being the manager of a bank (though the difference is probably less than it used to be). But, it is occupation rather than industry that plays the most important role in what follows.

Once we have defined a job we also need to define a 'good job' and a 'bad job'. We take a simplistic approach to this question: we rank jobs according to the average level of wages in that job so that 'good' means well paid and 'bad' means badly paid. This is not meant to connote the true 'worth' of any job: caring for old people is a 'good' job in the sense that the people who do it are to be admired but a 'bad' job on our definition because it is so badly paid.

Our ranking of jobs is undeniably crude: there are some jobs that pay particularly high wages to compensate for dangerous working conditions that we will mistakenly categorise as better than they really are. And there are other jobs with a particularly easy life that pay relatively low wages which we will mistakenly categorise as worse than they really are. But, our ranking probably gives the right impression: managerial and professional occupations are good jobs, cleaners and unskilled jobs are bad jobs.

The data used in this chapter come from two sources, the New Earnings Survey (NES) and the LFS. Both have advantages and disadvantages relative to the other. The LFS is a more representative sample than the NES but is smaller (so allows less precise estimation of the numbers in different jobs) and does not have wage information until 1993. We disaggregate jobs into 90 occupations and ten industries though our results are robust to using other definitions of a job. Examples of 'jobs' in this definition are a 'waiter in a restaurant' or a 'computer analyst in finance'. Note that not all occupation–industry combinations exist – for example, there are no nurses working in construction or air traffic controllers working in hospitals. Of the possible 900 jobs 766 actually exist in the LFS and 757 in the NES data.

Figure 5.1 presents the basic result. The top panel of Figure 5.1 uses data from the LFS, the bottom panel from the NES. We group jobs into the 'lowest 10 per cent', the 'second-lowest 10 per cent', up to the 'top 10 per cent' based on their average wage (measured as the median) in 1979. In technical jargon, these are called deciles, the first decile being the bottom 10 per cent etc. Both the LFS and the NES show the same pattern – a large growth in the share of employment in the top two deciles, but also a growth, albeit smaller, in the share of jobs in the bottom decile. So Figure 5.1 shows that there has been a strong increase in the number of workers in good jobs but also that there has been a significant increase in the number of low paid jobs with 'middling' jobs being in decline. Though the increase in the number of workers with bad jobs has been less relative to the increase in workers with good jobs, employment polarisation into low paid and high paid work is clear from Figure 5.1. It is this process of job polarisation that is the central theme of this chapter.

What are these fast growing jobs? Table 5.1 lists the two largest jobs in the bottom and top three deciles and their change in employment using the LFS. The most prevalent jobs in the lowest quality decile are sales assistants and check-out operators, together with cooks, waiters and bar staff. Between 1979 and 1999 the number of workers employed in these occupations increased from about 1.2 million to 1.9 million. Also the number of nurses, hospital ward assistants and care assistants has increased over the last 25 years despite their relatively low wages. The number of workers in jobs paying about the economy-wide average has decreased instead. For example, the number of routine process operatives (3rd decile) or machine operators (8th decile) fell between 1979 and 1999. As can be seen from Figure 5.1, this must be true for most jobs in the 3rd to 8th quality deciles (many of which were in manufacturing and production). Most of the occupations in the top two deciles

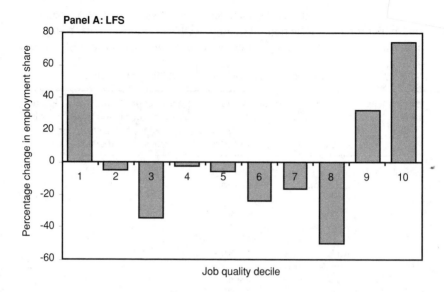

Notes: Data are taken from the LFS allowing for 90 occupations in 10 industries. Changes are measured between 1979 and 1999.

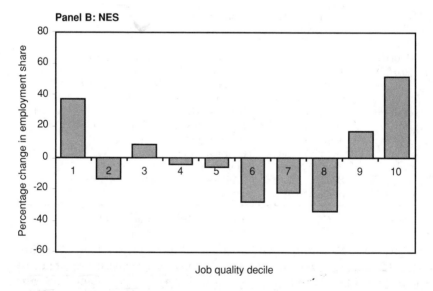

Notes: Data are taken from the NES allowing for 90 occupations in 10 industries. Changes are measured between 1976 and 1995.

Figure 5.1   Percentage change in employment share by job quality decile

are professional occupations like managers or engineers. Note that job cell sizes are smaller for jobs in the highest quality deciles, also reflected in the relative high number of jobs in these deciles reported in the last column of Table 5.1.

Table 5.1   Characteristics of selected jobs in different job quality deciles

Job quality deciles	Two largest jobs within selected deciles		Number of workers in 1979 (000s)	Number of workers in 1999 (000s)	Number of jobs
	Occupation	Industry			
Lowest decile	Sales assistants, check-out operators	Retail distribution	926	1,449	21
	Cooks, waiters, waitresses, bar staff	Hotels and catering	270	483	
2nd decile	Nurses, hospital ward assistants, care assistants	Medical and health services	240	758	65
	Counter clerks, cashiers	Retail distribution	133	150	
3rd decile	Textiles, garments and related trades	Manufacturing of textiles	381	172	71
	Routine process operatives	Manufacturing of textiles	225	116	
8th decile	Machine setters and repairers	Manufacturing of metal goods	533	267	65
	Machine operators	Manufacturing of metal goods	246	104	
9th decile	Service officers	Public services	217	313	144
	Production managers	Manufacturing of metal goods	113	125	
Highest decile	Engineers and technologists	Manufacturing of metal goods	123	186	100
	Health professionals	Sanitary services	90	207	

Note: Data are taken from the LFS allowing for 90 occupations in 10 industries.

Because workers in the best jobs are less concentrated, Table 5.2 lists the 'top 10' jobs by employment growth. As one might expect, here are many jobs involving new technology in business services and finance. It is also noteworthy that there is evidence here of the 'managerial' epidemic that has swept Britain in the past 25 years with very rapid growth of workers in managerial positions. All of these jobs are 'good jobs' from the top end of the pay distribution. But it is not only good jobs that are in the 'top 10':

Table 5.2   Top 10 jobs by employment growth

Occupation	Industry	Real median wage in 1979	Employment in 1979 (000s)	Employment in 1999 (000s)	% change in employment
All	All	3.10	22,653	27,231	
Engineers and technologists	Banking, finance, insurance, business services and leasing	5.34	25	212	749
Computer analysts/ programmers	Banking, finance, insurance, business services and leasing	5.67	20	167	717
Financial institution and office managers	Public administration	4.28	17	142	716
Literary, artistic and sports professionals	Banking, finance, insurance, business services and leasing	4.28	13	90	605
Specialist managers	Banking, finance, insurance, business services and leasing	5.26	64	352	453
Managers and administrators (not otherwise specified)	Public admin, sanitary services, education	4.02	29	152	428
Specialist managers	Transport and communication	4.88	17	85	404
Merchandisers and telephone sales persons	Retail distribution	2.15	12	54	364
Matrons, house parents, welfare, community and youth workers	Public admin, sanitary services, education	3.27	52	236	350
Security guards	Banking, finance, insurance, business services and leasing	2.62	21	92	343

Note: Data are taken from the LFS allowing for 90 occupations in 10 industries.

further down the list one finds 'merchandisers and telephone sales persons' in 'retail distribution', and 'security guards' in 'banking, finance, insurance, business services and leasing'. These are 'bad jobs'. The domination of 'good jobs' in the 'top 10' reflects the fact that, as can be seen from Figure 5.1, there is some tendency for the growth in the best jobs to be larger than the employment growth in the worst jobs. But, if one moved outside the 'top 10' one would also find rapid growth in the numbers of low-paid workers in restaurants, shops and medical and health services.

Table 5.3 presents the 'bottom 10' jobs in which there have been the largest declines in employment. There are two sorts of occupations that dominate here: craft jobs and clerical jobs in non-service industries.

Table 5.3   Bottom 10 jobs by employment growth

Occupation	Industry	Real median wage in 1979	Employment in 1979 (000s)	Employment in 1999 (000s)	% change in employment
All	All	3.10	22,653	27,231	
Glass product makers, musical instrument makers	Production of glass products, musical instruments	2.848	50	13	–75
Metal machining, fitting and instrument making trades	Energy and water supplies	4.087	48	13	–74
Numerical clerks	Production of metals, mineral products and chemicals	2.958	46	14	–69
Secretaries, personal assistants, typists, word processor operators	Manufacture of metals, mineral products and chemicals	3.017	35	11	–68
Metal machining, fitting and instrument making trades	Production of metals, mineral products and chemicals	3.603	94	32	–66
Rail, crane, fork lift operatives	Manufacturing of metal goods	3.277	61	23	–63
Builders and related occupations	Construction	2.972	33	13	–60
Cabinet, box and pattern makers	Manufacturing of metal goods	3.534	32	13	–60
Electricians	Communication	3.411	142	58	–60
Financial associate professionals	Manufacturing of metal goods	4.382	28	11	–59

Note: Data are taken from the LFS allowing for 90 occupations in 10 industries.

We have presented results for total employment of men and women, using 90 occupations and 10 industries. But, we would arrive at the same qualitative conclusion whether we define employment in terms of bodies or total hours, however we disaggregate occupation and industry and whether we combine men and women or consider them separately. There is some evidence that employment polarisation is more marked for men than for women (because women have made inroads into some of the better jobs) and that it is slightly less marked when one looks at hours rather than employment (because more of the growth in the worst jobs has been in part-time employment). One might also be worried about the rankings of jobs changing over time. But, such changes are relatively minor – what are good jobs now were, for the most part, good jobs 25 years ago and the same is true for bad jobs.

Whichever way we look at it, there is a growing polarisation of jobs in the UK: there are more good 'MacJobs' and more bad 'McJobs'. The data show there have been strong increases in the number of high paid jobs but also significant increases in the number of low paid jobs over the last 25 years. Craft and clerical occupations in non-service industries are disappearing while the importance of low and high paid service jobs has increased.

The natural questions to ask are: Why is this happening? What are the consequences? What, if anything, should be done about it? Let us consider these questions in turn.

The roots of increasing job polarisation

A natural place to start is to consider the impact of changes in technology on employment. If technical change is biased towards more skilled workers in better jobs, 'skill-biased technical change' increases the average quality of jobs. As a statement about the average quality of jobs, this conclusion is undoubtedly right: our data also suggest that the average job quality is increasing, but this net effect hides the increased polarisation towards both good and bad jobs.

Many current discussions of the impact of technical change on employment and wages focus on the role played by computers and technology. But, it is important to realise that many of these changes occurred *before* the widespread application of computer technology. As Card and diNardo (2003) argue, there is a tendency to think that innovations in computer technology are older than they really are. For example, more advanced graphical interface operating systems only gained widespread use with the introduction of Microsoft's Windows 3.1 in 1990. Use of the Internet grew very rapidly only after the introduction of Netscape's Navigator program in 1994. The sharper rise of wage inequality in the 1980s should point to more important technological innovations very early in the computer revolution, such as the introduction of the IBM PC in 1981. Whether or not you believe the 1990s were more innovative than the 1980s, comparisons of relative timing are subject to substantial leeway in interpretation, depending on the lags in the adoption of new technologies.

Technical change tends to increase productivity in manufacturing more than elsewhere. As productivity rises in manufacturing, the relative costs and prices of manufactured goods fall, but not by enough to make demand for manufactured goods rise as fast as the rise in productivity. As a result, the share of manufacturing in total employment falls. This differential in productivity growth between manufacturing and services was identified a long time ago by Baumol (1967) and can explain why there is a long-run decline away from jobs (often skilled craft jobs) in manufacturing towards relatively labour-intensive sectors that include 'good' professional and managerial jobs but also 'bad' personal service jobs like restaurant and retail work.

The 'computer revolution' has given an extra twist to these long-running trends. Autor, Levy and Murnane (2001) show that workers doing routine manual or information processing tasks are easily substituted for capital. In contrast, jobs involving non-routine tasks only have limited opportunities for substitution or are even complements in production. For example a waiter's job cannot be easily done by capital (perhaps excepting sushi bars) and asking a robot to clean your house is a recipe for disaster. Also, computers cannot easily substitute for the job of an engineer. But machines and computers can do the work of routine process operatives or machine operators or of book-keepers.

So far, the discussion has focused solely on the impact of changes in technology on the pattern of labour demand. But, there might also be changes in the pattern of labour supply. The two most dramatic changes in labour supply are the increased educational attainment of the labour force and the increased labour market participation of women.

Figure 5.2a plots the percentage of workers with an A-level or higher degree by job decile in 1979 and Figure 5.2b the change in the percentage over the period 1979–99. Figure 5.2a shows that, not surprisingly, the more educated are concentrated in the best jobs. As these jobs are increasing in number, more educated workers are needed to fill them. But the actual rise in the educational attainment of the population far exceeds that needed to fill the increasing number of good jobs: Figure 5.2b shows that there are more educated people in the worst jobs now than there used to be. Some, but by no means all, of these jobs are being done by students whose employment has increased a lot in recent years.

Besides an increase in the supply of more educated labour, women have increased their attachment to the labour market over the past 25 years. Figure 5.3a plots the fraction of female workers by job decile in 1979 and Figure 5.3b the change in each decile. Figure 5.3a shows that women are heavily over-represented in the worst jobs. So if women are more likely to enter low paid jobs, an increase in the supply of female labour might be able to explain

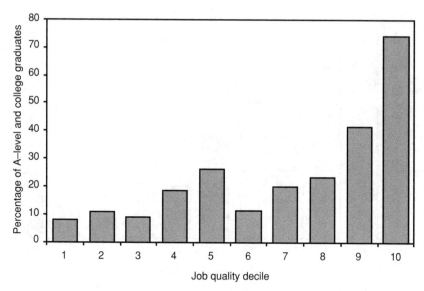

Figure 5.2a   Percentage of A-level and college graduates by job quality decile

Note: Data are taken from the LFS allowing for 90 occupations in 10 industries in 1979.

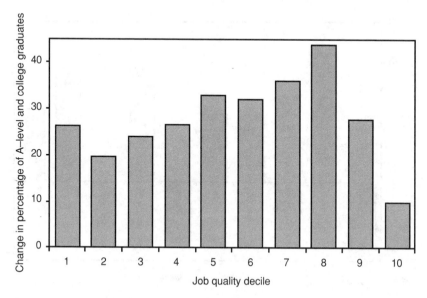

Figure 5.2b   Change in percentage of A-level and college graduates by job quality decile

Notes: Data are taken from the LFS allowing for 90 occupations in 10 industries. The changes are measured between 1979 and 1999.

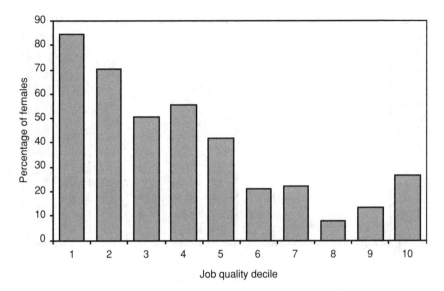

Figure 5.3a   Percentage of females by job quality decile

Note: Data are taken from the LFS allowing for 90 occupations in 10 industries in 1979.

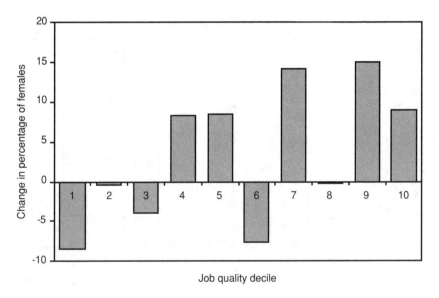

Figure 5.3b   Change in the percentage of females by job quality decile

Notes: Data are taken from the LFS allowing for 90 occupations in 10 industries. The changes are measured between 1979 and 1999.

part of the increase in the number of bad jobs. But, when one quantifies these effects of increased supply they are insufficient to explain what is happening. This is also intuitively clear from the fact that women are getting better jobs today than they did 25 years ago: Figure 5.3b shows that the percentage of women in the worst jobs has been falling and the percentage in the best jobs rising as women have made inroads into the better-paid occupations.

The consequences of increased job polarisation

One of the consequences of increased job polarisation is that it is likely to be associated with an increase in wage inequality. Suppose the wage distribution within jobs remains the same but there are more workers in high paying jobs and low paying jobs. The gap between the top and the bottom of the wage distribution will change. How large is this effect? As a measure of the gap between the well paid and the average we use the gap between the earnings of the top 10 per cent and the average (median). As a measure of the gap between the badly paid and the average we use the gap between the average (median) and the earnings of the bottom 10 per cent. Figure 5.4 compares what actually happened over the period 1976–95 with what would have happened if the only change in the wage distribution were that caused by the increased

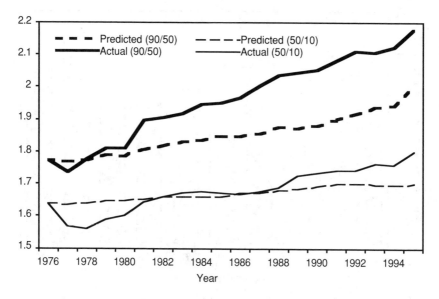

Figure 5.4   How much of actual wage dispersion can be explained by job polarisation?

Notes: Data are taken from the NES allowing for 90 occupations in 10 industries. The vertical axis measures the ratio of the different percentiles of the actual and predicted wage distribution.

polarisation of work. Something like 60 per cent of the rise in wage inequality at the top of the distribution can be explained by increased job polarisation and 40 per cent of the rise at the bottom. So job polarisation is an important factor in understanding the rise in wage inequality though it does not explain everything and some other factors must have been at work.

The most important other factor is that the gap in average wages between the best and the worst jobs has been rising. Figure 5.5 plots the growth in average wages over the period 1976–95 by job decile. One can readily see that wage growth has been greatest in the best jobs and lowest in the worst jobs. This will act to increase the extent of wage inequality. When one quantifies the importance of job polarisation together with increased differences in average pay between jobs, one can explain over half of the actual changes in the wage distribution.

It is easy to understand why wage growth at the top is high in terms of a simple demand and supply model beloved of economists. If the demand for skilled workers increases faster than their supply, employment and wages in good jobs increase. But what is happening at the bottom end of the distribution is harder to understand using a supply and demand model. As argued above, the nature of technological change is a plausible explanation

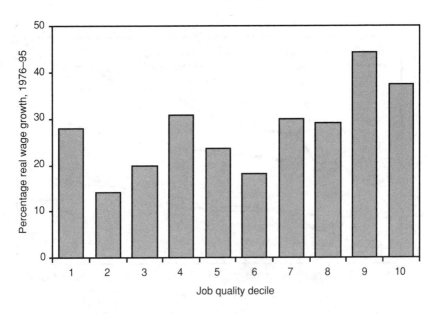

Figure 5.5   Relationship between Real Wage Growth and job quality decile

Notes: Data are taken from the NES allowing for 90 occupations in 10 industries. Wage growth is measured between 1976 and 1995.

for the increasing number of bad jobs. But, if the demand for workers in these jobs is rising, why have their wages not increased relative to the average as Figure 5.5 shows?

. One explanation is that institutions have changed in such a way as to lead to a fall in wages at the bottom of the wage distribution. Evidence from the US suggests that the evolution of unionisation and the minimum wage can explain a lot of what is happening to the bottom half of the wage distribution there. The UK has also seen a marked decline in unionisation (see Chapter 11), a decline in minimum wages (though they were never very strong and still are not – see Chapter 13) and the indexation of welfare benefits to prices not to wages – see Gosling and Lemieux (2003) for an overview. Perhaps these changes can account for the rise in wage inequality in the bottom half of the distribution.

Another consequence of increasing job polarisation is an increased amount of over-education. Although the growth in the best jobs requires an increased number of educated workers to fill them, the actual increase in the number of educated workers has been far in excess of that necessary. To some extent, this is the result of increased educational requirements within jobs but it is also occurring in jobs where we do not think this is very important. This is not to say that increasing educational attainment is a mistake: it is necessary to fill the ever-increasing numbers of good jobs and the rising returns to education suggest that we do not have a general over-supply of educated workers. But, there is an inevitable tension between increasing the educational attainment of the whole population and the change in the structure of employment that results in an increasing level of employment in jobs where formal educational qualifications are not that necessary.

What can be done about it?

It seems likely that we are going to see an increasing polarisation in jobs in the future as the reasons for it seem unlikely to disappear in a hurry. We are going to need increasing numbers of people to do ever-increasing numbers of good jobs but also to do increasing numbers of bad jobs. But, are the effects of this inevitably bad?

We do need more education to fill the increasing number of good jobs. But, 'education, education, education' is not enough as, on its own, it will result in increasing numbers of educated people trapped in bad jobs. We also need to do something about the increasing number of bad jobs.

One of the reasons that these jobs are bad is that they are badly paid. It seems unlikely that cleaning toilets will ever be a high-status occupation (though the reasons why not are a sad reflection on our culture) but one can act to mitigate the gap in pay between bad jobs and good jobs. The minimum wage is the simplest way to put a floor to wages, though the level at which the UK's National Minimum Wage (NMW) has been set has only had a minimal effect on wage inequality. Although the Low Pay Commission thought they were setting a minimum wage at a level that was going to benefit 9 per cent, Chapter 13 suggests that, in fact, 5 per cent (and perhaps fewer) of adult workers were affected by the NMW and suggests that even this might be an over-estimate. Subsequent increases in the NMW have done little to reverse this.

There is the possibility that a higher minimum wage might reduce demand for workers in bad jobs. But, this is not necessarily a problem as long as these workers can fill the better jobs, and the existence of many over-qualified workers suggests that this is possible. Other policy tools can also be used in conjunction with the minimum wage to make 'bad' jobs more remunerative. The Working Families Tax Credit helps to raise the take-home pay of those in low paid jobs.

One other policy tool is immigration. An increasing fraction of those in the UK without any educational qualifications (who are likely to fill the bad jobs) are immigrants. More immigration might provide a ready source of workers for the 'bad' jobs. Immigration policy tends to look more favourably on skilled workers to help fill the increasing number of good jobs. But, perhaps we also need more unskilled immigrants to do the bad jobs. To some extent this is already the pattern: immigrants' qualifications are more polarised than those of the native-born (see Chapter 8).

Some find the prospect of deliberately importing unskilled immigrants to do our dirty work distasteful. We must ensure (through the minimum wage) that they are not exploited. But the discomfort that the liberal conscience often feels when confronted with the sight of immigrants doing the bad jobs often has more to do with the guilt felt at the pampered lifestyle we are accustomed to leading and has little to do with what is best for the immigrants.

Another alternative is the view that the bad jobs still have to be done (e.g. toilets need to be cleaned) and we should all do our share at some point in our life-cycle. One could interpret this as a form of 'community service'. To some extent this is already happening: more and more of the bad jobs are being done by students who, in later life, will go on to be in the good jobs. But there could perhaps be further moves in this direction.

Conclusion

There is an increasing polarisation of jobs in the UK. There are more 'good' jobs around, in managerial, professional and technical occupations, but also more 'bad' jobs, in shops, bars, restaurants and caring. The 'middling' jobs of craft and clerical workers are disappearing, the casualties of technological progress. It seems likely that this process will continue so it cannot be ignored. Unchecked it will lead to widening inequality in our society. Over the past 25 years the consequences of this increased polarisation of work have been compounded by a rising gap in average pay between the good and the bad jobs.

What can be done about this? We need to do something to narrow the gap between good and bad jobs. The 'gap' is partly a pay gap but also a status gap. The pay gap can be addressed by policies like the minimum wage though it needs to be raised for it to have anything more than a token effect. In a recent book, Toynbee (2003) illustrates pay is not just a matter of income but also of respect, status and personal worth. Indeed, the status gap is problematic too in a society in which the correlation of status with pay is increasingly strong.

To fill the increasing number of good jobs, we need to continue to strive to increase the educational attainment of our workers. But, perhaps we also need immigration of less-skilled workers to meet the increased demand for workers in 'bad' jobs. What is clear is that current policies are, at best, only going to deal with some aspects of these changes but not others.

References

Autor, D. H., Levy, F. and Murnane, R. J. (2001), 'The Skill Content of Recent Technological Change: An Empirical Exploration', NBER Working Paper No. 8337, June.

Baumol, W. J. (1967), 'Macroeconomics of Unbalanced Growth: The Anatomy of Urban Crisis', *American Economic Review*, 57, pp. 415–26.

Card, D. and diNardo, J. (2003), 'Skill-Biased Technological Change and Rising Wage Inequality: Some Problems and Puzzles', *Journal of Labor Economics*, 20, pp. 733–83.

Gosling, A. and Lemieux, T. (2003), 'Labour Market Reforms and Changes in Wage Inequality in the United Kingdom and the United States', in R. Blundell, D. Card and R. Freeman (eds), *Seeking a Premier League Economy*, University of Chicago Press: Chicago.

Gregg, P. and Wadsworth, J. (eds) (1999), *The State of Working Britain*, Manchester University Press: Manchester.

Toynbee, P. (2003), *Hard Work*, Bloomsbury Press: London.

6

Labour Market Prospects of Less Skilled Workers Over the Recovery

Paul Gregg and Jonathan Wadsworth

Key findings

- Unemployment among the less skilled has fallen sharply since 1993 but much of this has been because of rising inactivity rather than improved employment. Rising inactivity during a strong employment recovery is unusual and should be a major cause for concern.
- Less than half of all women without formal qualifications are in work and there has been no improvement relative to other women over the course of the recovery.
- Among less skilled men, only youths appear to have made any improvement in their relative labour market position over the recovery. One-third of men without formal qualifications are now inactive.
- Labour market prospects of less skilled workers did improve in the areas of Britain where demand was strongest. It appears that a local employment rate in excess of 75 per cent is needed before any improvement for the less skilled takes place.
- Whilst average real wages of the less skilled did rise over the recovery, real wages of other workers grew slightly faster, so the average pay of the less skilled fell further behind. Recovery and the National Minimum Wage appear to have been insufficient to generate an improvement in the relative pay prospects of less skilled workers.

Introduction

One of the enduring problems of the British labour market is the relative disadvantage, whether measured by pay or access to jobs, experienced by workers with a low level of educational attainment. There has been a large-scale rise in the overall level of educational attainment in recent years, which should serve to reduce the supply of less skilled workers, especially those with no formal qualifications. As long as the supply of less skilled workers falls faster than demand, this should help their employment chances. In recovery, this is typically what happens. As the labour market tightens and labour becomes scarcer, demand conditions for the more marginalised groups tend to pick up, so that there is a degree of convergence of employment rates. This is evident for young workers or some ethnic minorities (see Chapter 8). If, however, there are more fundamental barriers to employment of the less skilled, such as poor levels of literacy and numeracy, which discourage employers from using such labour, then there may be little improvement in their prospects, even in the tightest labour markets. This chapter looks at whether the latest recovery has reached the less skilled and asks how tight labour markets need to get before their prospects improve. We find that only when the employment rate in a region goes above 75 per cent do the less skilled begin to do as well as, or better than, other workers.

The less skilled

In order to define a less skilled group, we use two definitions: a) those with no formal qualifications and b) the bottom 30 per cent of the education cohort in each year. The first definition follows a fixed qualification group, whilst the second follows a fixed percentage of the population which, since the share of the population with no qualifications is falling fast,[1] makes it easier to compare like with like over time.

When comparing economic performance across groups, it is possible to look at the absolute (percentage point) gap in unemployment or employment rates or to use the ratio of these rates (the relative difference). If these two methods always moved in the same direction over time, there would be little need to worry. However, the relative and absolute measures sometimes move in different directions. So when looking at the unemployment rate, for example, the absolute gaps between the less skilled and others tend to be larger in downturns while the relative gaps are larger in upturns. There is no definitive answer on whether absolute or relative measures are preferable and so in what follows we use both. In general, we find that the deteriorating economic position of the low skilled is common to both approaches over the recovery.

Employment

Table 6.1 gives the aggregate change in unemployment, employment and inactivity over the course of the recovery. The good news is that the unemployment rate has fallen for the low qualified as a whole and for those with no qualifications. Moreover, the percentage point gap between male less skilled workers and that for other men narrowed, though the (relative) percentage gap did not. The bad news is that much of the decline in unemployment for the less skilled, much more than for other workers, can be accounted for by labour force withdrawal rather than by increased employment. As a result neither the absolute nor relative employment gaps for workers with no qualifications have improved over the recovery. For the larger low qualifications group, male employment and inactivity gaps do however appear to have stabilised.

Table 6.1   Unemployment, employment and inactivity rates by education over recovery

	No quals.	Low quals.	Other	% point gap: no quals. – other	% difference: no quals. v. other	% point gap: low quals. – other	% difference: low quals. v. other
Men							
Unemployment							
1993	19.9	18.4	9.7	+10	+205	+9	+90
1997	17.0	13.9	6.0	+11	+183	+8	+133
2002	11.7	9.3	4.1	+7	+185	+5	+130
Employment							
1993	63.2	65.8	83.1	–20	–24	–17	–21
1997	59.4	66.0	85.4	–26	–30	–19	–23
2002	59.2	69.3	86.4	–27	–31	–17	–20
Inactivity							
1993	21.2	19.4	8.0	+13	+165	+11	+144
1997	28.4	23.3	9.2	+19	+209	+14	+155
2002	33.0	23.6	9.9	+23	+233	+14	+138
Women							
Unemployment							
1993	10.2	9.7	6.6	+4	+55	+3	+48
1997	8.2	7.7	4.9	+3	+67	+3	+58
2002	7.1	4.1	3.5	+4	+103	+3	+85
Employment							
1993	52.8	54.7	74.0	–21	–29	–19	–26
1997	47.7	54.6	76.1	–28	–37	–21	–28
2002	46.9	55.6	79.2	–32	–41	–24	–30
Inactivity							
1993	41.2	39.4	20.8	+20	+98	+19	+89
1997	46.4	40.8	20.0	+26	+132	+21	+103
2002	49.5	40.6	17.9	+31	+177	+23	+126

Notes: Low quals. group comprises bottom 30 per cent of education distribution in each year, excluding students. Unemployment is expressed as percentage of the labour force. Employment and inactivity expressed as a percentage of the population of working age, excluding students.

Source: LFS, authors' calculations.

For women all the less skilled differentials, whether employment, unemployment or inactivity, on both the relative or absolute basis got worse over the recovery. This general picture of deterioration is even more acute for those without formal qualifications. The employment rate of women without qualifications has fallen below 50 per cent and the rate for men is now below 60 per cent. The similarity of the trends over time between the no and low qualifications groups means that we focus hereafter only on the low qualification group.

The less skilled are generally older and so these aggregate statistics disguise different patterns across age groups. As Figure 6.1 shows, employment and inactivity gaps between the less skilled and others tend to be higher for workers below the age of 50, though the levels of employment are much lower and

Table 6.2 Employment rates in recovery by age and education

	Low quals.	Other	% point gap: low quals – other	% Difference: low quals v. other
Men				
Age 16–24				
1993	57.2	77.2	–20	–26
1997	58.9	82.6	–24	–29
2002	63.9	83.2	–19	–23
Age 25–49				
1993	72.5	88.7	–16	–18
1997	73.1	90.9	–18	–20
2002	76.2	92.4	–16	–18
Age 50+				
1993	57.0	69.5	–12	–18
1997	58.9	72.6	–14	–19
2002	60.7	74.6	–14	–19
Women				
Age 16–24				
1993	39.6	73.6	–34	–46
1997	39.6	74.7	–35	–47
2002	41.7	78.9	–37	–47
Age 25–49				
1993	56.7	74.9	–18	–24
1997	55.8	77.5	–22	–28
2002	56.1	80.1	–24	–30
Age 50+				
1993	54.2	66.6	–12	–19
1997	53.5	69.4	–16	–23
2002	56.1	73.4	–17	–24

Note: Figures exclude students.

Source: LFS, authors' calculations.

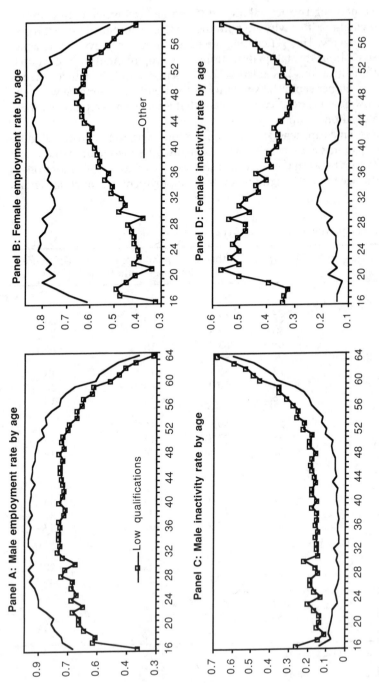

Figure 6.1 Employment and inactivity rates by qualifications and gender, 2002

Source: LFS.

inactivity higher for the over 50s. So the poor economic performance of the less well educated is even more acute among the young. Table 6.2 does suggest however that both employment rates and the employment gap narrowed more for younger less skilled men than older less skilled men, particularly during the latter half of the recovery. This may be helped by the introduction of the New Deal for Young People around this period, though less of an improvement is apparent for younger less skilled women. Despite the New Deal (see Chapter 1), nearly one in four less skilled young men and one in five young women are still unemployed. Older less skilled workers, especially women, have lost ground compared to other older groups. Unemployment has fallen and economic inactivity among the less well educated increased for all age groups.

So why don't the less skilled appear to have benefited much from recovery this time? It is possible that the recovery was not sustained, balanced or strong enough to provide enough demand for the less skilled. One way of assessing this hypothesis is to compare the lot of the less skilled across areas of the country with differing economic performance. If the level of economic performance matters, then we would expect the less skilled to do better in areas with higher overall employment. In Table 6.3 we therefore compare the situation of less skilled workers living in the high employment, South-East of England (outside London) and East Anglia with those in the low employment areas of Tyne & Wear, Merseyside and Strathclyde over the recovery. We also include a middle category of Greater Manchester and the rest of Northern England outside the urban conurbations.

Although these areas of the country had very different employment rates in 1993, the signs of recovery were apparent in all regions. Indeed employment rose more in the low employment areas than elsewhere. Low skilled workers however did much better in the labour markets that were initially tighter.[2] Table 6.3 shows that employment rates for all the less skilled groups are higher in the tight labour markets of the South-East than in the depressed urban conurbations. The employment gap between the disadvantaged groups and the area average is also smaller in the tighter labour markets.

Moreover, the employment gap between the less skilled and others narrowed much more in the high employment areas than in the depressed areas as job market conditions improved after 1993. Despite overall employment growing faster in the more depressed regions, employment among less skilled men in these areas actually fell. For less skilled women employment rates did not fall, but there was a decline for less skilled women in the low employment areas relative to other women in the same areas and also a decline relative to less skilled workers living in the prosperous South. By 2002, only 25 per cent of less skilled men living in social housing were in work in the depressed urban conurbations, sharply down from 1993. In contrast, the employment rate for similar groups in the South-East was around 65 per cent.

Table 6.3 Area economic performance and employment rates of less skilled

	High employment areas			Middle employment areas			Low employment areas		
	1993	2002	% point change	1993	2002	% point change	1993	2002	% point change
Area employment rate	76.6	81.1	+3.5	70.9	73.5	+3.6	64.6	70.3	+5.7
Men									
Low quals.	73.9	79.5	+5.6	61.6	62.4	+0.8	52.8	51.6	-1.2
Low quals. 25–49	79.6	84.9	+4.7	69.8	70.6	+0.8	58.9	53.5	-5.4
Low quals. council housing	57.6	65.0	+7.4	38.7	35.7	-3.0	32.2	25.3	-6.9
Women									
Low quals.	59.1	64.8	+5.7	52.4	50.8	-1.6	46.1	50.3	+4.2
Low quals. 25–49	61.8	64.5	+2.2	55.7	53.7	-2.0	47.8	50.2	+2.4
Low quals. council housing	41.7	45.5	+3.8	32.0	29.1	-2.9	29.8	32.9	+3.1

Note: High employment areas are South-East (not London) and East Anglia. Middle employment areas are North of England, North and East Yorkshire and Greater Manchester. Low employment areas are Tyne & Wear, Merseyside and Strathclyde. Low quals. comprise bottom 30 per cent of education qualifications in each year. Council housing includes housing associations.

Panel A: Employment rates of less skilled men by area

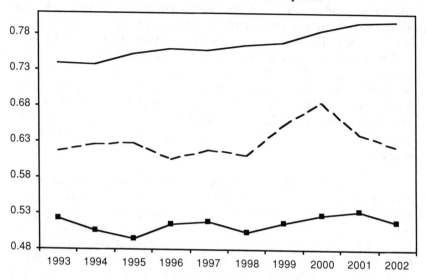

Panel B: Inactivity rate of less skilled men by area

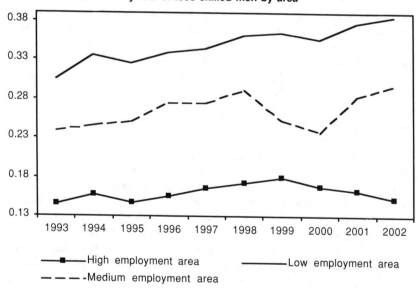

Figure 6.2 Employment, unemployment and inactivity of less skilled by area labour market performance

Source: LFS.

Figure 6.2 shows that this divergence in performance occurred throughout the recovery, with the low employment areas seeing stagnation in employment among the low skilled, whilst employment of the less skilled rose in the tight labour markets. These patterns suggest to us that the overall level of demand for labour matters for the prospects of the less skilled. Aggregate employment rates over 75 per cent seem to be needed before jobless rates of the less skilled begin to fall faster than the population on average. Unfortunately the recovery has not been sustained enough or balanced enough to achieve this outside eastern and southern England excluding London.

Wages

Over the 1980s the less skilled experienced declining employment and deteriorating wages relative to other workers (see also Chapter 12). The previous section indicates that employment prospects have continued to deteriorate, but can the same be said of wage prospects for the less skilled? Since the less skilled are over-represented in the stock of low paid workers, it might be thought that the introduction of the National Minimum Wage (see Chapter 13) would help to narrow wage differentials. Table 6.4 outlines changes in hourly wages for less skilled workers, adjusted for inflation, relative to others over the course of the recovery. The average (median) wage gap between the less skilled and other employees is around 30 per cent. This gap is similar for women and men, though the overall level of wages for women is of course much lower. Whilst average real wages of the less skilled did rise over the recovery, real wages of other workers grew slightly faster, so the average pay of the less skilled fell somewhat further behind. Recovery and the National Minimum Wage appear to have been insufficient to prevent any improvement in the relative wage prospects for most less skilled workers. There are exceptions to this general pattern. Average real wages of less skilled young men appear to have narrowed relative to others in their age group over the recovery, as have wages of older less skilled women. In general however, wage inequality appears to have worsened.

Table 6.5 undertakes a similar exercise to that used in Table 6.3, now comparing wage growth of less skilled workers across regions with differing levels of labour market tightness. Once again it is apparent that less skilled workers do much better in the tightest labour markets. Average real wages of less skilled workers are higher and grew faster in the higher employment areas of the South than in the depressed urban conurbations. Indeed wages of less skilled women in the South grew faster than average wages of others in the region, so that the wage gap narrowed. Average wages among less skilled men in the South rose less than the average rate of increase over the period in that region. In the urban conurbations, there was little change in average real wages for less skilled men. This again suggests that the level and incidence of demand matters for the labour market prospects of the less skilled. There appears to be a continued deterioration of demand for less skilled labour everywhere except in the tightest labour markets, where expansion does appear to bring disproportionate gains in employment and wages for the less skilled.

Table 6.4   Real hourly pay over recovery by gender and education

	No quals.	Low quals.	Other	Ratio: no quals./other	Ratio: low quals./other
Men					
Total					
1993	6.20	6.40	9.00	–32	–29
1997	5.90	6.20	8.80	–33	–30
2002	6.30	6.70	9.90	–36	–32
Age 16–24					
1993	3.90	4.00	5.00	–22	–20
1997	3.80	4.00	4.80	–21	–17
2002	4.70	4.80	5.70	–18	–16
Age 25–49					
1993	6.60	6.70	9.80	–33	–32
1997	6.10	6.40	9.50	–36	–33
2002	6.60	7.00	10.70	–38	–35
Age 50+					
1993	6.30	6.40	9.70	–35	–34
1997	6.10	6.40	9.40	–35	–32
2002	6.50	6.80	10.30	–37	–34
Women					
Total					
1993	4.50	4.60	6.60	–32	–30
1997	4.40	4.60	6.60	–33	–30
2002	4.90	5.20	7.60	–36	–32
Age 16–24					
1993	3.70	3.90	4.90	–24	–20
1997	3.40	3.60	4.60	–26	–22
2002	4.30	4.30	5.40	–30	–30
Age 25–49					
1993	4.50	4.60	7.10	–37	–35
1997	4.40	4.70	7.00	–37	–33
2002	4.90	5.10	8.10	–40	–37
Age 50+					
1993	4.50	4.60	7.10	–37	–35
1997	4.50	4.70	7.30	–38	–36
2002	4.90	5.30	7.80	–37	–32

Notes: Figures exclude students. Median wages expressed in January 2002 prices.

Source: LFS, authors' calculations.

Table 6.5   Area economic performance and relative earnings of less skilled workers

	High employment areas			Middle employment areas			Low employment areas		
	1993 £	2002 £	% change	1993 £	2002 £	% change	1993 £	2002 £	% change
Area average real hourly wage	7.50	8.60	+15	6.50	7.30	+12	6.70	7.20	+ 7
Men									
Low quals.	6.50	7.40	+14	6.20	6.30	+2	6.30	6.30	0
No quals.	6.30	6.80	+8	6.10	6.10	0	6.20	6.30	+2
Women									
Low quals.	4.70	5.60	+19	4.30	4.90	+14	4.50	5.10	+13
No quals.	4.60	5.40	+17	4.40	4.70	+7	4.40	4.90	+11

Notes: See Table 6.4. Hourly wages measured in January 2002 prices, rounded to nearest 10p. Averages are median wages.

Source: LFS, authors' calculations.

What jobs do less skilled workers get?

Table 6.6 indicates that the stock of jobs taken by the less skilled after a spell of unemployment or inactivity is concentrated in retail, hospitality and man-

Table 6.6   Sectoral distribution of new hires 2001

	Total All new hires	All new hires	From non-employment Less skilled new hires	Men	Women
Manufacturing	16	13	16	24	10
Selling	16	17	22	18	25
Hotels/rests.	6	6	10	7	12
Finance	17	17	11	11	12
Education	8	10	6	2	10
Health	11	11	10	2	16
% Female	51	55	55		
% Part-time	28	42	48	20	71
% Temporary	23	34	28	34	24
Median hourly wage	5.90	5.00	4.60	4.90	4.40
% in new job 3 months later	–	8	5	6	4

Notes: Authors' calculations use matched quarterly panels pooled over eight quarters 2000–02. Excludes students.

Source: LFS, authors' calculations.

ufacturing. There is also a relatively higher share of part-time jobs, but not temporary jobs, compared with other workers. Among the less skilled, women fill many more part-time jobs than men. Wages in jobs taken by the less skilled are also relatively low, typically paying 50–90 pence above the minimum hourly wage.

Conclusion

Since 1993 Britain has experienced a sustained and geographically widespread improvement in employment levels. However, the less skilled have only begun to benefit meaningfully from this recovery in areas where the employment rate was in excess of 75 per cent when the recovery began in 1993. In the tightest labour markets employment and wages of the less skilled have risen. While aggregate employment growth can therefore improve the relative position of the least skilled, job creation has not yet been sustained sufficiently or balanced enough across regions for the least skilled to have benefited disproportionately. Rather than just relying on a general expansion of employment it seems that continued efforts are needed to increase employment opportunities across the major British cities, Northern England, Scotland and Wales. There is also a need to understand why it is that employment and wages of men have deteriorated so markedly in the more depressed areas.

Notes

1. The share of the working age population with no formal qualifications was 30 per cent in 1993, falling to 15 per cent in 2002.
2. The share of less skilled is higher in the low employment areas, at around 35 per cent, compared with the high employment areas, at around 29 per cent.

7
Welfare Reform and the Employment of Lone Parents

Paul Gregg and Susan Harkness

Key findings

- Employment rates for lone parents in the UK in the early 1990s were extremely low, when compared with those in other countries or with married women in this country, at just over 40 per cent.
- Since 1993 the employment of lone parents has risen by 11 percentage points to reach 53 per cent in 2002. This is more than twice the increase in employment for the population as a whole.
- The rate of increase in employment was notably faster after 1998 when government policies aimed at raising employment levels of lone parents, the New Deal for Lone Parents (NDLP) and the Working Families Tax Credit (WFTC) came into effect.
- Analysis presented here suggests that these policies raised the proportion of lone parents who were working at least 16 hours (the level needed to receive WFTC) by just over 7 percentage points, affecting 120,000 lone parents.
- The number of hours worked by those lone parents already working appears to have been largely unaffected by the policy changes.

Introduction

By 1996, very low employment rates among single mothers helped explain why the UK had the highest proportion of children living in workless households among OECD countries and one of the highest incidences of child poverty (see Chapters 2 and 19). These low employment rates, alongside a large rise in the number of children living in lone parent families, contributed towards the sharp increase in child poverty over the 1980s and 1990s. In 2002 there were around 1.7 million lone parents, accounting for nearly one in four British families with children, compared to 0.5 million in the early 1970s. In 1997, the incoming Labour government initiated a series of policy reforms aimed at reducing child poverty and raising lone parents' employment. Over the last 30 years the employment of married mothers in the UK rose dramatically, especially for those with young children. Yet the employment rate of lone mothers was lower in the early 1990s than it was in the late 1970s, at just over 40 per cent.

The UK is almost alone among OECD countries in having such low employment rates for lone mothers. Figure 7.1 shows that only Ireland, Poland and Australia have lower rates of employment of single mothers than the UK. In countries such as the US, Canada, Italy, Sweden, Finland and Portugal lone parent employment rates were all above 65 per cent. Figure 7.2 contrasts the employment rates of single mothers with those of married mothers within each country for the year 2000. The 24 percentage point gap between employment for lone parents and other mothers in the UK is greater than for any other OECD country. In around half the countries single parents are *more* likely to work than married mothers. This employment gap has not always existed. In contrast to rising employment of married mothers over the last 30 years or so, employment rates of lone parents have declined over time. Figure 7.3, using data from the General Household Survey (GHS, three-

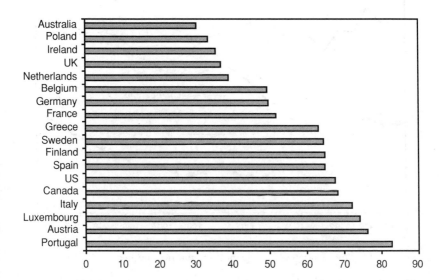

Figure 7.1   Lone parents' employment rates

Source: *OECD Employment Outlook*, 2001.

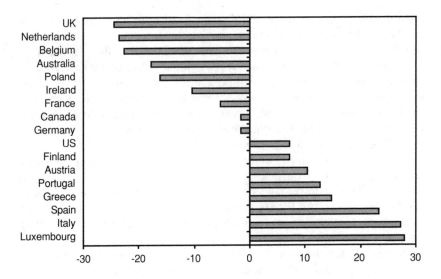

Figure 7.2   Employment gap between single and married mothers

Source: *OECD Employment Outlook*, 2001.

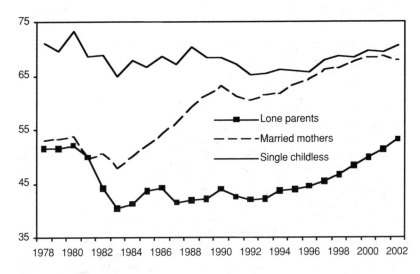

Figure 7.3   Employment rates of single mothers, married mothers, 1978–2002

Note: In order to overcome the problem of small sample sizes among lone parents, three-year moving averages are used in the GHS data.

Source: GHS (1978–91) and LFS (1992–2002).

year averages from 1977–79 to 1991–93) and Labour Force Survey (LFS, from 1992–2002), shows how employment rates have changed for single and married mothers and single childless women, between the late 1970s and 2002.[1] Married mothers' employment rates were only marginally higher than those of lone parents in the late 1970s. While employment rates of lone parents fell and then stagnated in the 1980s, for married mothers, employment rates grew steadily from around 1984. By the mid-1990s employment rates of single childless women and married mothers were broadly similar. Since 1992, however, the employment rate among lone parents has risen sharply from 42 per cent to 53 per cent (see Figure 7.3). This acceleration in lone parents' employment rates substantially narrowed the differential with other women by 2002. In this chapter we aim to identify how much of the relative employment gain by lone parents can be attributed to policy reforms.

Evidence on the impact of welfare reform in Canada and the US

Prior to 1997 there was clear evidence, mainly from North America, on the sensitivity of lone parent employment to financial incentives and on the potential role of personal advisers in raising employment levels. In the US, the Earned Income Tax Credit (EITC), which was introduced in 1975 as a minor programme but substantially expanded from the mid-1990s, has been the subject of substantial academic scrutiny. These studies have unanimously found that the EITC led to an increase in single parents' employment (Eissa and Leibman, 1996; Blank, Card and Robins, 1999). While the WFTC has been compared with the EITC, evidence from experimental policy evaluations was also at least as influential in the WFTC's development. Of particular relevance was the evidence from experimental policy trials aimed at raising employment and incomes of lone parents undertaken in a number of pilot locations. The most influential of these were the Canadian Self-Sufficiency Project (SSP), the Minnesota Family Investment Program (MFIP), the Milwaukee New Hope Project, and the California Gain programme. The evidence from the first two of these experiments showed that a twin track strategy of improved financial incentives to 'make work pay' together with a case managed welfare system to encourage activation, job search and ease transition problems around welfare systems and childcare, was most effective in increasing employment. Blank, Card and Robins (1999) provide a summary of earlier findings suggesting that such a twin track approach can lead to more substantive employment gains than individual policies when introduced alone.

Welfare reform in the UK

Welfare reforms in the UK have focused on improving financial incentives to work, through the WFTC, and introducing case managed welfare systems for lone parents aimed at raising their employment, under the NDLP and later the Job Centre Plus programme. Although the package of reforms that have been introduced were largely modelled on North American policy experiments, many elements of the package of reforms differed radically from those seen in the US after 1996. In the UK, the generosity of both in- and out-of-work benefits has been increased substantially for families with children and there have been no time limits on receipt of welfare payments. Participation in job search and training or other support programmes has remained entirely voluntary. Thus, unlike in the US where in-work benefits were introduced primarily as a strategy for reducing the welfare caseload, in the UK the dominant aim has been to raise incomes for those both in and out of employment. This is reflected in the government's commitment to reduce the numbers of children living in relative poverty by a quarter by 2004–05. A specific target, of achieving an employment rate of 70 per cent by 2010, has also been set for lone parents.

Welfare policy towards lone parents has undergone rapid change since 1997, with the introduction of the NDLP in April 1998 and the replacement of Family Credit (FC) with WFTC from October 1999. However, lone parents have been the focus of considerable policy change since 1988 when FC was first introduced. Table 7.1 highlights the major policy reforms since FC was first introduced in 1988. In 1992, the number of hours that needed to be worked to be eligible for in-work credits was cut from 24 to 16. In 1994 a childcare disregard was introduced so that the amount lone parents could earn before the credit was withdrawn was increased by up to £40 a week, and in 1995 an extra 30-hour credit was introduced. However, evidence suggests that the childcare disregard was never widely used and the 30-hour credit had little impact on the decision of whether to work or not although it may have had some influence on the choice of hours worked at the margin.

From April 1998 a more substantial set of reforms was introduced. First the NDLP, which was piloted in the autumn of 1997, was rolled out nationally. In the first year, only benefit claimants where the youngest child was over five were invited by letter to voluntarily attend a meeting to discuss employment. Those with younger children could volunteer to join the programme. From May 2000 this age restriction was lowered to three. In April 2001, Work Focused Interviews (WFI) began for lone parents under the Job Centre Plus programme. These made attendance to discuss work options with an adviser compulsory while there is still no requirement to seek work. Again there is a roll-out strategy and this process is expected to be complete by 2004 when it will cover all lone parents.

Compared to FC, the WFTC both raised the maximum benefit payable to working lone parents and reduced the rate at which the tax credit was withdrawn. This increased generosity and the slower withdrawal of benefits meant that the WFTC was available much further up the earnings distribution. The impact of these changes on the budget constraints faced by a typical

Table 7.1   Reform of welfare systems affecting lone parents 1988–2002

Year	Reform
1988	**Family Credit** introduced to replace Family Income Supplement (FIS). Must be employed 24+ hours and taper 70 per cent.
1992	*July*: Minimum hours reduced to 16.
1994	*October*: Childcare charges could be offset against earnings up to £40.
1995	*July*: 30 hours extra credit introduced.
1997	**NDLP Phase 1**: *July 1997 to October 1998*. Launched in eight pilot areas. Lone Parent Supplementary rates abolished for new claims – worth CHB £6.30 IS £5.20.
1998	**NDLP Phase 2**: *April to October*. National roll-out. All lone parents making new claims for IS (flow claimants) whose youngest child was aged over five years three months were invited to participate in NDLP. Lone parents with children under the age of five years three months did not receive an invitation letter but were able to participate if they wished. **NDLP Phase 3**: *October* onwards. The full national roll-out of NDLP commenced as Phase 3. Invitation letters sent to all those lone parents whose youngest child was aged over five years three months, who had made a claim for IS prior to April 1998 (stock claimants), as well as those making new IS claims (flow claimants). Phase 3 of NDLP was *originally* actively marketed to all lone parents on IS whose youngest child was five years three months or over (i.e. in full-time education).
1999	**Working Families Tax Credit**: *October*.
2000	**NDLP**: From *May 2000*, the target group was expanded to include all lone parents with a youngest child aged three years and over. Lone parents on IS with younger children who asked to join the programme were welcome to do so.
2001	*April*: **Roll-out of Work Focused Interviews (WFI)** – stock lone parents whose youngest child is aged 13–15. New claimants whose youngest child is aged five years three months or above. *July*: **Adviser Discretion Fund** – discretionary award of up to £300, for use on anything which will help a lone parent in finding a job or, if successful, accept a job offer. *November*: **NDLP** widened to all lone parents on low incomes.
2002	**WFI**: *April 2002*. Stock lone parents whose youngest child is aged 9–12; new claimants whose youngest child is three years or above.

lone parent family is illustrated graphically in Figure 7.4. In the specimen household, a lone parent would cease to be eligible for tax credits at £15,000 in 1997, whereas under the 2001 regime this point was reached at around £22,500. Under FC childcare costs (up to a maximum value) were deducted from income in order to calculate the credits. However, under WFTC a fraction of childcare costs (70 per cent of costs up to £120 a week) were added to the basic credits. Further, these extra credits no longer counted as income for the calculation of Housing Benefit (HB) entitlements. This meant that all lone parents working part-time could now benefit from claiming for childcare

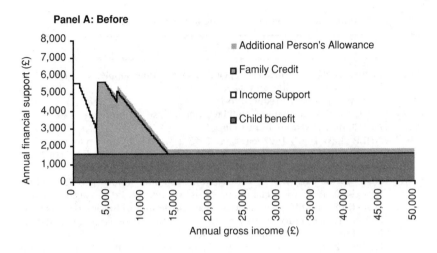

Notes: Assumes live-alone parent, two children under 11, no housing costs or childcare costs. Entitlement for WFTC reached at £3,400, or 16 hours work/week at the minimum wage. Values uprated to April 2002 prices.

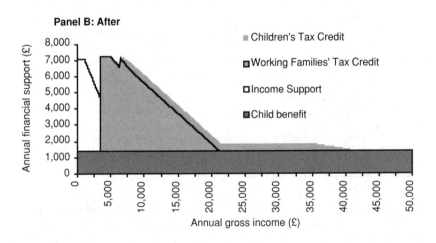

Figure 7.4   Support package before and after welfare reform

Notes: Assumes live-alone parent, two children under 11, no housing costs or childcare costs. Entitlement for WFTC reached at £3,400, or 16 hours work/week at the minimum wage. Values uprated to April 2002 prices.

Source: Brewer and Gregg (2003).

costs whereas before their earnings may well have been too low (below the applicable amount) to get any extra help. Those with childcare costs who were also eligible for HB also saw particularly large improvements in the returns to working.

From 2000 the generosity of Income Support (IS) payments to workless lone parents also grew at a rate broadly in line with WFTC credits. Improved work incentives, resulting from the improved generosity of the scheme and the lower rate of taper alongside greater help with childcare costs, were therefore the main drivers for change. Table 7.2 gives some examples of how the financial returns to work changed from 1997 to 2001. The regimes are compared for two hours options, 16 and 35, for an individual with potential earnings of £4.20 an hour (or just above the 2001 National Minimum Wage). The comparisons are adjusted for price changes over time and so are real changes. A lone parent with two children under 11 working at just 16 hours

Table 7.2   The effect of the reforms on the weekly income gain to work for parents with children

| | Gain to work (£) | | | |
| | 16 hours | | 35 hours | |
	1997	2001	1997	2001
Not on Housing Benefit				
Lone parent	63	71	107	130
Primary earner in a couple with children	26	50	79	99
Single person, no children	13	13	72	79
On Housing Benefit				
Lone parent	43	43	65	80
Primary earner in a couple with children	20	21	42	49
Single person, no children	2	8	2	31
With childcare of £50/week when in work				
Lone Parent	13	56	92	115
Second earner in a couple with children: no childcare costs, first earner on £300 a week	67	30	127	93

Notes: Table measures difference between zero-income benefit income and income after taxes and benefits in work. Assumes two children under 11 and full take-up of all entitled benefits, hourly wage of £4.20, rent of £50 a week where indicated, in-work childcare costs of £50 a week where indicated (slightly more than the average of those lone parents currently claiming the Childcare Tax Credit). All values expressed in 2002 prices.

Source: Brewer and Gregg (2003).

in a near minimum wage job gains only modestly from the reforms. However, at longer hours (or, by extension, higher wages) the new returns to work are larger. At 35 hours the reforms add £23 to net income. However, if the claimant lone parent rents a property and is thus also eligible for HB these gains are reduced to just £15 a week for full-time work and are virtually zero for part-time work, since the extra credit income results in lower HB entitlements. On the other hand, the new Childcare Tax Credit covers childcare costs even at low part-time wages and results in large extra gains to working relative to 1997. These childcare payments are exempted from HB entitlement calculations. So the package is a mixed bag with extra income from working being largest for those with higher weekly earnings and for those on lower earnings who pay for formal childcare.

Changes in welfare receipt

In 2002 there were around 1.7 million lone parents in the UK, of whom half (850,000) were on IS. The upper panel of Figure 7.5 charts the number of lone parents claiming the main welfare payment for non-working lone parents, IS (or its pre-1988 equivalent, Supplementary Benefit). There was a fivefold increase in the number of claimants in receipt of income support between 1971 and 1996, which reflects both falling employment and the increasing incidence of lone parenthood. Since the mid-1990s, however, the number of lone parents dependent on IS has sharply declined. This is perhaps surprising given that from 1999 onwards there has been a substantial increase in the generosity of IS payments with the average value of payments increasing by over 30 per cent in real terms between 1998 and 2002.

As the numbers of lone parents dependent on income support has declined, the numbers receiving in-work benefits has grown rapidly (Figure 7.5, lower panel). In May 2002, 706,000 lone parents were in receipt of WFTC. This is double the number in receipt of Family Credit in 1997, and nine times the numbers receiving FC in 1988. This rapid rise in the number of lone parents claiming in-work benefits has corresponded with a substantial increase in the generosity of the award). In 2002, over one-fifth of lone parents on WFTC (160,000) also received help with childcare costs with average value of £39.46. This was a fivefold increase in the numbers receiving assistance with childcare compared to 1998. In 2002, approximately 10 per cent (83,740) of those on IS were participating in the New Deal for Lone Parents. The government claims a significant success rate for the New Deal, with 52 per cent of those leaving the NDLP taking up employment, although many of these may have left welfare in the absence of the New Deal.

Lone parents' employment began to recover in the early 1990s, such that by spring 2002 the employment rate stood 11 percentage points higher than it had in 1992, at 53 per cent.[3] To assess the impact of policy it is necessary to strip out the impact of the economic cycle and compositional changes

Panel A: Income support recipients

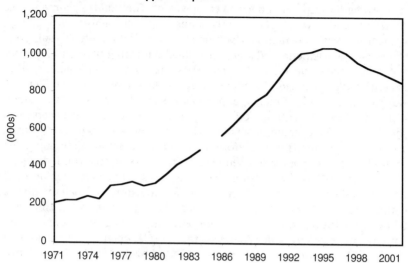

Panel B: Family Credit/Working Families Tax Credit recipients

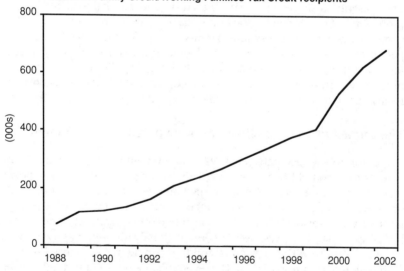

Figure 7.5 Lone parents claiming income support and Working Families Tax Credits

Note: Great Britain (excludes NI), figures for May.

Source: Working Families Tax Credit Statistics Quarterly Enquiry, May 2002.

among lone parents. To do this we take a 'difference-in-difference' approach to assessing the impact of policy on employment. This builds a counterfactual of what would have happened in the absence of policy reform by making a comparison with a benchmark population. The ideal counterfactual group *should not* have experienced any policy shocks affecting their employment, but *should* have the same characteristics that affect employment, have experienced the same local labour market shocks and reacted in an identical way to them. The benchmark group therefore should share as many common features as possible with the focus group; the only difference between them should be in their experience of policy. The 'difference-in-difference' approach asks how lone parents were performing in terms of employment compared to this benchmark population before and after the policy reforms took place.

Lone parents have two defining characteristics, having children and not having a resident partner, and hence there are two natural comparator groups: couples with children and single individuals without children. However, while comparisons with couples are interesting, this group has not been entirely unaffected by policy change as the WFTC is open to all families with children. Singles without children are unaffected by the WFTC, although two further 'New Deal' programmes may have affected the employment of single childless people (the New Deal for Young People and the New Deal 25 Plus). However, as these schemes cover only a tiny fraction of this group we match lone parents to single adults. We match on characteristics that affect the probability of employment (including age, education and region) and then compare the performance of lone parents to this counterfactual group in the period before and after reform. Any change in the relative employment of lone parents is taken as our measure of the effect of policy change. Any gain in employment relative to the control group after 1998, over and above the relative gain made prior to policy change, is our measure of policy impact.

The impact of welfare reform on lone parents' employment

According to the LFS, between 1992 and 2002 employment rates of lone parents rose from 42 to 53 per cent. This rise began before the new policy regime came into effect in 1998, but sped up thereafter with the annual rate of increase rising from 0.75 percentage points a year before 1998 to 1.65 points a year afterwards. There have been two other key developments over the period. First, there has been a compositional shift among lone parents away from those with very young children (single, never married women with children aged zero to two). However, this has occurred throughout the decade at a broadly constant rate of just under 1 percentage point a year so the impact when comparing different points in time should be small. Second, there was a decade-long sustained rise in employment in the population as a whole from 1992. Our simple difference-in-difference calculation accounts for this change in the labour market performance of lone parents relative to the rest of the population (see Table 7.3). The first set of numbers reported here (top panel) are not conditional on characteristics and serve only as an indicator of changing relative performance. Lone parents saw a rise in employment nearly 6 percentage points higher than the rest of the population after 1998. As lone parents were making relative gains prior to 1998, a simple difference-in-difference calculation suggests that policy reform since 1998 raised lone parents' employment relative to the population average by around 4.6 percentage points. The middle panel tells the same story but this time compares lone parents to women in couples with children. Again this is just an unconditional comparison of relative performance across the two groups. Lone parents had seen slower employment growth than other mothers prior to 1998 but have posted a 5 percentage point relative gain since 1998. However, as previously discussed, couples with children may have been affected by policy reform, as second earners in couples where the main earner is on a relatively low wage now have seen reduced incentives to work.

From now on we concentrate on comparisons with singles without children as this group is least affected by the tax and benefit reforms, and which Gregg and Harkness (2003) have shown provide a good historical benchmark.

Table 7.3 (bottom panel) shows how lone parents have fared when compared to all single women without children. This shows a somewhat smaller raw difference-in-difference estimate than when the whole population or just couples with children are used as a comparison. These estimates make no attempt to identify single people with similar characteristics as lone parents. We do this next by constructing a counterfactual population from our sample of single women without children. We match lone parents on a set of characteristics that influence employment rates, including age, education, housing tenure and region of residence.[4] Results from the matched samples are reported in Table 7.4. The matched estimates suggest that since 1998 lone parent employment has risen by 6 percentage points more than would have been predicted from a population of singles without children with the same characteristics as lone parents.

If we believe that the relative employment gains made by lone parents between 1992 and 1998 were due entirely to policy reforms then this simple difference-in-difference model provides an estimate of the policy reforms before 1998. We might consider this an upper bound estimate. The employment gain attributable to policy change over and above the rate of gain made prior to 1998 is then estimated by taking account of changes in relative employment rates between 1992 and 1998. This suggests that policy changes led to a 5 percentage point gain in employment. Any impact from improvements in incentives to work prior to 1998 have now been deducted from our estimates, meaning that our estimates of the impact from 1998 onwards of the policy reforms on employment are if anything biased downwards. These estimates seem to offer a reasonably tight plausible range of the likely impact of the policy reforms from 1998 onward on the

Table 7.3 Estimated impact of welfare reform on lone parent employment rates

	1992	1995	1998	2002	1998–1992	2002–1998	Difference in difference
Lone parents	42.1	43.9	46.6	53.2	4.5 (0.76)	6.6 (1.65)	3.6 (0.89)
					1.6 (0.27)	5.7 (1.43)	4.6 (1.15)
All non-lone parents aged 16–59	73.3	74.1	76.2	77.1	2.9 (0.48)	0.9 (0.23)	−1.0 (−0.26)
Lone parents	42.1	43.9	46.6	53.2	4.5 (0.76)	6.6 (1.65)	3.6 (0.89)
					−1.5 (−0.25)	5.2 (1.29)	6.2 (1.54)
Women in couples with children	60.4	63.5	66.4	67.8	6.0 (1.01)	1.5 (0.36)	−2.6 (−0.64)
Lone parents	42.1	43.9	46.6	53.2	4.5 (0.76)	6.6 (1.65)	3.6 (0.89)
					1.1 (0.18)	5.1 (1.26)	4.3 (1.08)
Single women without children	65.2	66.0	68.6	70.2	3.5 (0.58)	1.6 (0.39)	−0.8 (−0.19)

Note: Figures in brackets are average annual changes over respective periods.

Source: Authors' calculations, LFS.

110

Table 7.4 Estimated impact of welfare reform on lone parent employment rates – matched samples

	1992	1995	1998	2002	1998–1992	2002–1998	Difference in difference
Lone parents	42.1	43.9	46.6	53.2	4.5 (0.76)	6.6 (1.65)	3.6 (0.89)
					1.7 (0.28)	6.0 (1.49)	4.9 (1.21)
Single without children Matched on lone parents	63.3	64	66.1	66.8	2.9 (0.48)	0.6 (0.16)	–1.3 (–0.32)
Lone parents 16 hours+	34.1	37.1	38.9	48.5	4.8 (0.80)	9.6 (2.40)	6.4 (1.60)
					1.7 (0.28)	8.4 (2.09)	7.2 (1.81)
Single women without children 16 hours+ matched sample	60.2	60.8	63.3	64.6	3.1 (0.52)	1.3 (0.31)	–0.8 (–0.20)

Note: Brackets denote annualised figures.

Source: Authors' calculations.

employment of lone parents, suggesting policy reform led to at least a 5 percentage point increase in employment. This means an increase of around 80,000 more lone parents in work.

This pattern of results was perhaps surprisingly similar across lone parents irrespective of education levels and only slightly larger for those with young children (see Gregg and Harkness, 2003, for details). The Childcare Credit in the WFTC meets up to 70 per cent of childcare costs up to a limit of £100 a week. So as these payments were only available for formal childcare arrangements this is likely to be of most value to parents with pre-school children. On the other hand, IS payments for those not working have increased most for those with younger children. From 1998–2002 the payment for a child under 11 rose by £16.15 (£17.35 to £33.50) whilst for children aged 11–15 the rate rose by just £8.15 (£25.35 to £33.50) as the pre-existing age differences in support rates were removed. While these changes were also mimicked in WFTC there may still be a wealth effect from increased financial support while out of work.

Hours of work

The WFTC and its predecessor have a relatively unusual feature for tax and welfare systems in that they are conditional on working a minimum number of hours.[5] Lone parents must work a minimum of 16 hours in order to claim the tax credit, and there is a supplementary tax credit if they work in excess of 30 hours. These thresholds are designed to reduce the likely effect of high marginal effective tax rates leading people to choose shorter hours of work. As a result the move to the WFTC is likely to have had a mixed impact on hours of work. The increased generosity of the scheme would be expected to encourage those previously working less than 16 hours to increase their hours of work so as to become eligible for the increased tax credits, while those working more than 16 hours may decide to reduce their hours of work as a result of the 'windfall effect' of increased benefits. However, the reduction in the rate at which credits are withdrawn from 70 per cent of after-tax earnings to 55 per cent would be expected to have the opposite effect on those currently receiving tax credits. Finally, the extension of coverage to lone parents who would have previously been ineligible because they had relatively high earnings would introduce an incentive to reduce hours of work.

Table 7.5 shows that average hours of work among all lone parents (including those who are not in work) rose by 2.5 or just over 20 per cent. Obviously this includes the impact of the increase in employment described above. Average weekly hours of work amongst working lone parents increased from 27.3 to 28.5 hours (or nearly 5 per cent). There are three issues we may wish to consider in the context of hours choices made by lone parents and the welfare reform process. First, did the reforms induce people working less than 16 hours to enter into WFTC by increasing their hours of work? Second, did the large numbers entering employment after the reforms do so at different hours than those already there? And third, what was the net effect on hours among those working already above 16 hours? The first question is relatively easy to assess. We simply repeat the earlier analysis to look at changes in the proportion employed for more than 16 hours a week. Difference-in-difference estimates of 16 hours+ employment are reported in Table 7.4 (lower panel). The difference-in-difference estimate suggests that policy has raised 16 hours+ employment by 7.2 percentage points, which equates to 120,000 more lone parents working 16 hours or above a week.

Table 7.5 Average hours of work among lone parents, 1998–2002

| | Average hours of work | | |
	1998	2002	Change
All lone parents	11.7	14.2	2.5
Working lone parents	27.3	28.5	1.2
Working lone parents 16+ hours	32.1	30.9	–1.2
Incumbents –			
paired lone parents			
1998–2002	32.0	31.5	–0.5
Entrants –			
unpaired lone parents 2002	–	29.5	–

The question of whether those entering employment did so at different hours to the incumbents, and whether those already in employment reduced their hours of work, is addressed by pairing the 1998 and 2002 samples of lone parents. The increase in employment means that there are many more lone parents working 16 hours+ in 2002 in our data. We identify those who would have worked 16 hours+ in the absence of the reforms by matching pairs of lone parents in the 1998 and the 2002 LFS samples. We match on personal characteristics such as age, number of children, education and region, and job characteristics, such as industry type and occupation. In 2002 employed lone parents who do not have a match in the 1998 dataset are considered to be those that have entered into employment as a result of policy reform. It is notable that since 1998 employment of lone parents has risen by most in two sectors: 'retail and catering' and 'other private services'.

As to the third issue, Table 7.5 shows that average hours of work among all those working at least 16 hours fell by just over an hour between 1998 and 2002. The pairing suggests that those who were additionally employed as a result of policy reforms, labelled 'entrants', worked fewer hours than those who had a match (the incumbents) in 1998. We predict that incumbents have had a small response to the windfall effect of increased benefits, reducing their average hours of work by half an hour. This fall is not statistically significant, and any failure in the pairing would tend to bias down this estimate. This conclusion is in line with US evidence as we do not find any significant hours effect among lone parents who would have worked in the absence of policy reform. As would be expected, those who have entered work in response to policy reforms work on average two hours less than those who would have worked anyway in the absence of reform.

Conclusion

Lone parent households contain one in four of all children in the UK. Until very recently many of these families have faced extremely high rates of poverty and worklessness by international standards. From 1998 the Labour government introduced a series of reforms aimed at reducing both worklessness and poverty by raising welfare payments to families both in and out of work, improving financial incentives to work and introducing a more proactive welfare system. The results presented here suggest that these policies have raised the employment rates of lone parents by around 5 percentage points, or 80,000. We estimate that 7 per cent more lone parents are now working at least 16 hours a week in order to claim tax credits. So the proportion of lone parents working at least 16 hours is estimated to have risen by 7 percentage points, or 120,000, as a result of the policy changes. Hours of work among those already working over 16 hours appear to be broadly constant and these employment gains appear not to have come at the expense of lower earnings. The remaining non-working lone parents are increasingly less skilled and concentrated in rented housing, a group for whom work incentives remain weak. This suggests it will be hard to achieve further gains of the same magnitude.

These employment gains have come from a welfare reform package that does not require lone parents to search for jobs, or uses time limits in welfare programmes. In addition these gains have been achieved despite generous increases in welfare payments for lone parents who do not work. These earnings gains combined with the more generous welfare are making rapid progress in reducing child poverty (see Chapter 19). Increased welfare generosity and attempts to improve work incentives have continued beyond the time period of this analysis. New welfare reforms are still being introduced, and a revised system of tax credits came into force in April 2003. However, the progress being made on employment is not yet sufficient to realise the government's target of getting 70 per cent of lone parents into work by 2010.

Notes

1. Data from the GHS is pooled to overcome problems of small sample sizes.
2. Family Credit replaced Family Income Supplement, which was a relatively minor benefit paid to low-waged working families.
3. Source: LFS.

4. This counterfactual population includes men, as around 8 per cent of lone parents are men.
5. The Canadian SSP required full-time working for lone parents to be eligible and had the effect of reducing numbers working part-time.

References

Blank, R., Card, D. and Robins, P. (1999), 'Financial Incentives for Increasing Work and Income among Low-Income Families', NBER Working Paper No. 6998, NBER: Harvard.
Brewer, M. and Gregg, P. (2003), 'Eradicating Child Poverty in Britain: Welfare Reform and Children Since 1997', in R. L. Walker and M. Wiseman (eds), *The Welfare We Want*, The Policy Press: Bristol, forthcoming.
Eissa, N. and Liebman, J. (1996), 'Labour Supply Response to the Earned Income Tax Credit', *Quarterly Journal of Economics*, May, pp. 605–37.
Gregg, P. and Harkness, S. (2003), 'Welfare Reform and Lone Parents Employment in the UK', CMPO, University of Bristol mimeo.
OECD (2001), *OECD Employment Outlook 2001*, OECD: Paris.

Further reading

Blank, R. (2002), 'Evaluating Welfare Reform in the US', NBER Working Paper No. 8983, NBER: Harvard.
Eissa, N. and Hoynes, H. (1998), 'The Earned Income Tax Credit and Labor Supply of Married Couples', NBER Working Paper No. 6856, NBER: Harvard.
Millar, J. and Rowlingson, K. (2001), *Lone Parents Employment and Social Policy: Cross-National Comparisons*, The Policy Press: Bristol.

8
The Labour Market Performance of Ethnic Minorities in the Recovery

Jonathan Wadsworth

Key findings

- Employment rates for British born minorities and immigrants are much lower than those of British born whites with the same age and level of educational attainment.
- Over the recovery, employment and unemployment differentials narrowed for some, but not all, minority groups relative to British born whites.
- Employment differentials narrowed more for British born ethnic minority individuals than for immigrants.
- For Afro-Caribbean and Bangladeshi men, however, no such improvement in employment prospects can be observed.
- Both employment *and* unemployment rates are generally higher for most British born minorities relative to immigrants of the same ethnic group. This apparent anomaly can be explained by the much higher and worrisome rates of economic inactivity among immigrants.
- Relative pay differentials tend to be smaller among women. Despite there being little difference in pay between British born ethnic minority women and British born white women once age, region and education are accounted for, wages among men and immigrant ethnic minority women remain relatively low and these relative positions have changed little over the recovery.

Introduction

Some 4.5 million individuals in Britain, 9 per cent of the population, were born outside Britain. The children of immigrants now form a small, but growing, share of the labour force, currently around 2.5 per cent or 1 million individuals.[1] We know (see *State of Working Britain* update, 2002), that the relative labour market performance of minorities depends on the economic cycle. In recessions, minorities tend to do relatively badly, but do relatively well in better times. In what follows we assess whether this pattern has been followed over the latest economic recovery. If ethnicity and country of origin matter when describing labour market performance, then there is a need to dissaggregate as much as possible whenever data sources allow. Of course, disaggregation still disguises much heterogeneity within minority groups and all of the averages presented below should be interpreted with this in mind.[2]

Demographics

We begin, in Table 8.1, by highlighting some simple facts about various ethnic minority groups in Britain. The numbers are taken from the 2001/02 Labour Force Surveys (LFS), pooled across these years in order to provide us with adequate sample sizes. We focus on the population of working age (men aged 16–64 and women aged 16–59). The largest immigrant groups currently comprise those born in the European Union outside Britain and Ireland. The largest ethnic minority, immigrant and British born, are of Indian origin, comprising some 1.8 per cent of the potential workforce, around 1 million individuals, of whom around one-third were born in Britain.[3] Next come members of the Pakistani, Black African and West Indian communities each comprising around 1 per cent of the population, around 350,000 people. The average immigrant has already spent around 17 years in Britain. This average conceals some large differences across the various ethnic groupings, reflecting the history and geographic pattern of immigration into Britain over the past 50 years. As much Irish and West Indian immigration took place in the 1950s, so the average age of these immigrants is higher than among more recent arrivals, such as those from elsewhere in the European Union. Most new arrivals are from Europe or countries that have not been traditional suppliers of population in the past.

The historical pattern of immigration also shapes the relative numbers of British born members of the various ethnic minorities that can be identified in the data. Since the West Indian community have been in Britain the longest, the average age of the British born generation is correspondingly highest, at around 33.[4] Table 8.1 also shows that many immigrants and ethnic minority individuals live in the capital. London contains around 9 per cent of the total population, but around half of all immigrants and ethnic minority individuals. The Pakistani, Chinese and white immigrant communities are less concentrated in the capital than other groups, but still live predominantly in London. As employment prospects and, particularly, wages vary between London and elsewhere, this regional concentration means that it is important

Table 8.1 Immigrants and British born whites in Britain 2002 (population of working age)

	GB born white	GB born non-white	All immigrants	West Indian	Black African	Indian	Pakistani	Bangladeshi	Other non-white	Irish	Other EU	Non-EU European	Other white born elsewhere
% share of pop.	**88.1**												
Immigrant			9.4	0.4	0.7	1.2	0.7	0.3	1.0	0.7	1.3	0.5	2.0
GB born		2.6		0.6	0.2	0.5	0.3	0.1	0.5				
% share of new arrivals				1.3	8.0	5.5	4.4	1.5	20.0	1.7	16.6	11.5	29.5
Average age													
Immigrant	39		37	47	37	43	39	32	37	48	36	34	39
GB born		27		35	33	28	26	22	31	33	13	5	20
Average years here	–	–	18	34	9	26	19	15	9	33	13	5	20
% immigrants who enter <16	–	–	32	48	19	34	34	41	17	35	35	16	46
% in London													
Immigrant	9		45	61	78	49	18	65	50	34	36	57	33
GB born		43		57	70	42	14	69	38				
% with degree													
Immigrant	16		19	8	15	19	8	7	23	15	22	13	28
GB born		19		11	25	29	16	14	19				
% with no quals.													
Immigrant	16		19	28	14	21	41	50	20	25	11	18	7
GB born		11		8	7	10	16	10	14				

Notes: All figures population weighted. New arrivals refers to origin area of immigrants arriving in 2001 and 2002 LFS.

Source: LFS.

to try and control for regional dispersion in any analysis of wage and employment differentials.

Educational attainment

The final rows of Table 8.1 outline the differential levels of educational attainment across ethnic minority groups. Around one-third of all immigrants arrive before the age of 16 and so have some experience of the British schooling system. It is apparent that educational attainment among immigrant and ethnic minority groups as a whole is more disperse on average than British born whites. There are more graduates and more people with no formal qualifications among immigrants compared with British born whites. Again, there are substantial variations around these averages. The Black African, Indian and Chinese groups contain many more graduates than British born whites and a correspondingly lower share of those with no qualifications. Around one-quarter of the Chinese population living in Britain have a degree, compared to 15 per cent of British born whites. In contrast, the West Indian, and particularly the Pakistani and Bangladeshi communities contain fewer graduates than the national average and more with no qualifications. Around 40 per cent of all Bangladeshis have no formal qualifications, compared to 16 per cent of British born whites and 13 per cent of those in the Black African group. In general it also seems that the offspring of relatively more educated immigrant groups do relatively better in terms of educational attainment. There are nearly three times as many graduates among British born Indians than among British born West Indians.

Employment over the recovery

We know (see *State of Working Britain* update, 2002), that the immigrant and ethnic minority community as a whole have lower employment rates than British born whites, and that this average conceals large differences across different groups. As Table 8.2 and Figures 8.1a and 8.1b show, the Indian community contains almost as many individuals in work as British born whites, but employment rates among other groups, particularly Bangladeshis are much lower. These employment differentials are much larger amongst women. Nearly three-quarters of British born white females are currently in work, but only one-quarter of Pakistani women and around 15 per cent of women from the Bangladeshi community. The unemployment rates show a similar pattern.

British born ethnic minority individuals generally have higher employment rates than those born outside Britain. Relative to their British born white peers (90 per cent of the second generation are under the age of 40), employment and unemployment rates for the second generation are generally worse. Employment rates for young black men seem particularly low. Among

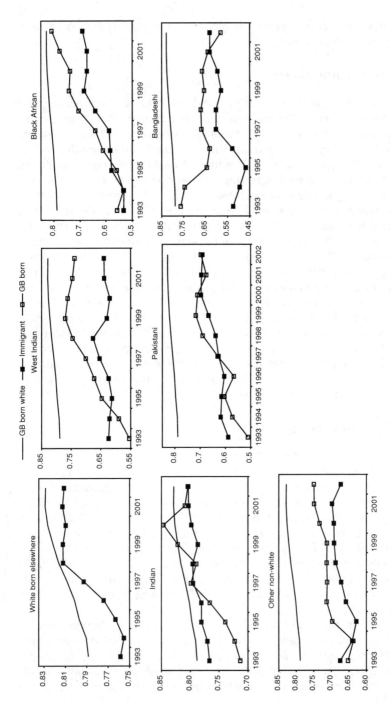

Figure 8.1a Male employment rates by ethnic origin and immigrant status relative to GB born white, 1993–2002

Source: LFS.

120

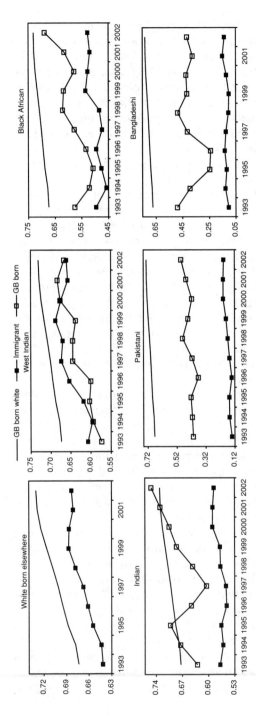

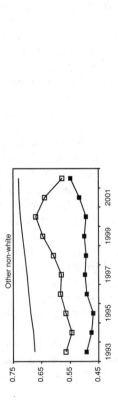

Figure 8.1b Female employment rates by ethnic origin and immigrant status relative to GB born white, 1993–2002

Source: LFS.

121

British born women the lowest employment rates are found in the Pakistani and Bangladeshi communities. Note that both employment *and* unemployment rates are generally higher for most British born minorities relative to immigrants of the same ethnic group. This can be explained by the much higher rates of economic inactivity among immigrants. Whilst worthy of concern in themselves, higher inactivity rates make lower employment and higher unemployment rates more likely. Employment rates for ethnic minorities and immigrants are much lower than those of British born whites *with the same level of educational attainment.*

Figures 8.1a and 8.1b track the evolution of employment rates, disaggregated by gender, for these immigrant and ethnic groups over the recovery since 1993. We exclude students to net out any trends in enrolment in tertiary education. It is apparent that employment rates among most immigrant ethnic minority men have not converged toward that of British born whites over the last ten years. Only among whites born outside Britain has the employment gap relative to white British born narrowed. Neither does the employment rate among Afro-Caribbean immigrant men show any absolute improvement over the recovery. Things are a little better for ethnic minority men born in Britain where employment rates can be seen to draw closer to that of British born white men. There are two notable exceptions to this general pattern. First, the initial recovery in employment rates among British born Afro-Caribbean men stops and goes into reverse at the end of the 1990s. Second, the employment rate among British born Bangladeshi men hardly rose at all at any stage of the recovery.

Recovery did not, in general, bring any improvement in the employment position of female immigrants relative to white British women, but did bring the average employment rates of ethnic minority women born in Britain closer to that of British born white women. The employment rate for Afro-Caribbean British born women, unlike for men, has risen and become closer to the British born white women. Employment rates for Indian women seem to have already reached parity with that of British born white women for some time now. Among Bangladeshi women there is little sign of any relative or even absolute improvement in employment.

If certain groups were younger or had fewer qualifications or were resident in areas where labour demand was weak then this could help explain the differences observed in Figures 8.1a and 8.1b. Table 8.3 therefore examines whether differences in age, location or educational attainment across individuals can account for any of these employment gaps. The results suggest not. Differences in the level of educational attainment across groups are not the main causes of these differentials. The inclusion of age, region and education controls has little impact on the employment gaps at the start and end years of the recovery (or indeed in any intervening year). For some groups (Black African, and Indian), employment differentials widen despite the higher educational attainment of these groups. Net of age, education and region,

Table 8.2 Employment and unemployment rates by ethnic origin and immigrant status, 2002

	British born white	All immigrants	British born non-white	West Indian	Black African	Indian	Pakistani	Bangladeshi	Other non-white	Other white
Men										
% in work	83	76	75	64 (74)	69 (80)	80 (80)	69 (70)	63 (58)	67 (75)	81
% unemployed	5	8	14	15 (16)	13 (14)	5 (10)	12 (17)	21 (30)	10 (14)	5
% inactive	13	17	13	25 (14)	21 (7)	16 (11)	22 (16)	20 (17)	25 (13)	15
Women										
% in work	73	58	64	66 (67)	53 (69)	59 (75)	20 (49)	14 (42)	55 (58)	67
% unemployed	4	6	10	8 (10)	12 (16)	6 (6)	14 (11)	14 (26)	9 (13)	5
% inactive	24	38	29	28 (25)	40 (18)	37 (20)	76 (45)	84 (43)	40 (33)	29

Notes: Numbers outside brackets are for immigrants. Numbers in brackets refer to British born. All numbers population weighted based on eight-quarter average. Estimates relate to the population of working age. Rates exclude students.

Source: LFS.

Table 8.3 Accounting for differences in employment rates 1993–2002

	GB born white rate	White born elsewhere	West Indian Immig	West Indian GB born	Black African Immig	Black African GB born	Indian Immig	Indian GB born	Pakistani Immig	Pakistani GB born	Bangladeshi Immig	Bangladeshi GB born	Other non-white Immig	Other non-white GB born
			Percentage point difference relative to British born white											
Men														
1993														
Differential	79	-3	-14	-19	-20	-19	-2	-7	-17	-23	-21	-1	-9	-12
–with controls		-3	-7	-18	-23	-19	-4	-7	-14	-16	-13	-1	-13	-11
2002														
Differential	82	-1	-15	-7	-11	-1	-3	-2	-12	-11	-17	-19	-13	-6
–with controls		-3	-9	-13	-15	-10	-4	-7	-10	-11	-10	-13	-14	-8
Women														
1993														
Differential	68	-3	-6	-10	-17	-10	-10	-5	-57	-26	-62	-18	-17	-11
–with controls		-5	-4	-11	-16	-11	-9	-6	-51	-19	-53	-16	-18	-11
2002														
Differential	73	-4	-7	-6	-19	-2	-13	+2	-50	-22	-59	-29	-16	-13
–with controls		-6	-4	-9	-17	-8	-11	-4	-42	-22	-48	-20	-17	-14

Note: Controls net out effect of differences in age, education and region.

Source: LFS, author's calculations.

Black African men, immigrant or British born, have higher employment rates than Afro-Caribbean men. Indian men, immigrant or British born, have higher employment rates than Pakistani or Bangladeshi men.

Segregation

One way of assessing the extent of divergence between ethnic minority groups and whites is to compare the industrial or occupational spread of employment across groups. If work were distributed randomly, there should be little difference between the share of whites employed in, say, manufacturing, and the share of non-whites employed in manufacturing. In contrast, if certain groups specialise or concentrate in particular jobs then there should be a big difference in the jobs mix across groups. One way of summarising any differences is the Duncan segregation index which takes the value 0 if there is no difference between any two groups and 100 if there is complete segregation.[5] The value of the index gives the percentage of each group that

Table 8.4 Industrial and occupational segregation by ethnic origin, 1994–2002

	West Indian	Black African	Indian	Pakistani	Bangladeshi	Other non-white
Men						
Industry						
1994/5	13.7	23.5	21.4	24.0	62.9	27.4
1997/8	12.4	24.2	16.8	26.4	61.3	25.4
1999/2000	9.1	24.3	19.0	25.5	48.5	24.3
2001/2	11.8	23.8	18.2	25.8	50.7	23.7
Occupation						
1994/5	18.6	21.8	14.5	21.0	41.5	22.1
1997/8	12.5	23.9	15.7	24.1	41.0	19.3
1999/2000	13.4	23.6	14.7	19.7	33.9	19.5
Women						
Industry						
1994/5	9.9	12.8	15.3	11.3	13.3	14.1
1997/8	10.9	9.8	9.8	9.9	17.3	9.6
1999/2000	9.1	8.2	12.8	7.6	13.8	8.5
2001/2	6.7	7.6	10.4	7.2	12.8	8.9
Occupation						
1994/5	12.8	14.3	20.6	18.3	30.0	10.5
1997/8	13.1	18.6	13.9	15.0	19.7	6.3
1999/2000	8.6	12.3	15.9	17.5	15.2	10.8

Notes: Data pooled over eight quarters. Figures are Duncan segregation indices based on 13 industries and 9 occupation groupings. Occupation data not available on a consistent basis after 2000.

Source: LFS.

would have to be in a different occupation or industry to achieve the same distribution as British born whites. The results in Table 8.4, comparing whites with six non-white minority groups, are quite sensitive to the number of industries/occupations used, take no account of differences in characteristics like age, region of residence that could influence the type of job taken or reveal anything about pay differences between jobs. Small sample sizes oblige us to combine immigrants and British born. Given these reservations, Table 8.4 does suggest that segregation by job type is higher among men than women, highest for Bangladeshis, lowest for Indian men and West Indian women. It also seems that segregation by industry has fallen among all ethnic minority groups since 1994. Occupational segregation, however, appears to have fallen less over time.

Wages

Has recovery improved relative pay for ethnic minorities and immigrants? The small sample sizes of ethnic minority individuals in work makes it harder to assemble accurate information on pay.[6] Also when comparing pay levels it is important to net out any differences in pay that may be attributable to area of residence. Since around half of all ethnic minorities live in London and wages in London are typically 20 per cent higher than elsewhere, failure to net out a 'London effect' could give the wrong signals about relative pay rates. Figures 8.2a and 8.2b therefore track average (mean) inflation adjusted hourly wages of minority groups relative to British born whites net of any regional differences. While employment differentials may have narrowed for some over recovery, there is less evidence to suggest that pay differentials have narrowed.

Again the trends in relative pay vary by minority group. Average rates of pay are lower for all non-white ethnic minority groups, but much more so among the Pakistani and Bangladeshi communities. Average pay gaps among women are smaller than those for men. Indeed among British born ethnic minority women there is little evidence of any significant pay gap between these women and British born whites. The contrast in the economic fortunes of West Indian men and women is again apparent. Average rates of pay among West Indian women have achieved near parity with that of British born white women, whilst average pay among West Indian men is some 20 per cent below the average of British born white men. Relative pay for immigrant workers has fallen behind over recovery. Only among men of Black African or Bangladeshi origin or women of Pakistani origin, is there any sign that relative pay has converged among British born minority workers.

Controlling additionally for differences in age, education and region (Table 8.5) increases the pay gaps for West Indian, African and Indian workers, but reduces it marginally for Pakistani and Bangladeshi workers. This reflects the much younger average age of the Pakistani and Bangladeshi workforce relative

Table 8.5 Accounting for real hourly wage differences, 1994–2001

	British born white hourly pay	White born elsewhere	Percentage difference relative to British born white						
			All non-white	West Indian	African	Indian	Pakistani	Bangladeshi	Other non-white
Men									
1994	9.70								
Net of region	+9		−19	−21 (−25)	−20 (−29)	−22 (−22)	−26 (*)	−75 (*)	−2 (−29)
+ age, education	+6			−22 (−9)	−31 (−13)	−15 (−1)	−24 (−17)	−53 (*)	−12 (−5)
+ job controls	+8			−21 (−7)	−24 (−11)	−14 (1)	−21 (−18)	−37 (*)	−7 (−3)
2001	10.70								
Net of region	+9		−18	−26 (−19)	−22 (−17)	− 8 (−9)	−34 (−20)	−75 (*)	−9 (−20)
+ age, education	+9			−17 (−12)	−28 (−21)	−16 (1)	−26 (− 9)	−53 (*)	−12 (−8)
+ job controls	+10			−16 (−10)	−23 (−18)	−14 (1)	−20 (−5)	−33 (*)	−6 (−5)
Women									
1994	7.10								
Net of region	+8		−9	−3 (1)	−17 (−18)	−15 (−9)	−17 (*)	−24 (*)	−9 (−5)
+ age, education	+6			−3 (1)	−16 (−14)	−14 (−1)	− 8 (*)	−19 (*)	−12 (−4)
+ job controls	+5			−5 (−1)	−18 (−13)	−14 (1)	− 8 (*)	−20 (*)	−11 (−3)
2001	7.90								
Net of region	+9		−6	−11 (−1)	−19 (−2)	−7 (−4)	−22 (−7)	−30 (*)	−7 (−5)
+ age, education	+6			− 9 (−1)	−19 (−6)	−9 (−2)	−17 (−1)	−22 (*)	−8 (1)
+ job controls	+6			−11 (−2)	−18 (−6)	−11 (−1)	−15 (−1)	−21 (*)	−8 (2)

Notes: All figures are based on LFS data pooled over ten quarters centred on year indicated. Figures in brackets are estimates for British born. * indicates small sample – estimates not shown. Figure in italics indicates estimate insignificantly different from zero. All estimates shown are net of differences highlighted in column 1. Job controls include industry, part-time, temporary working and public sector.

Source: LFS.

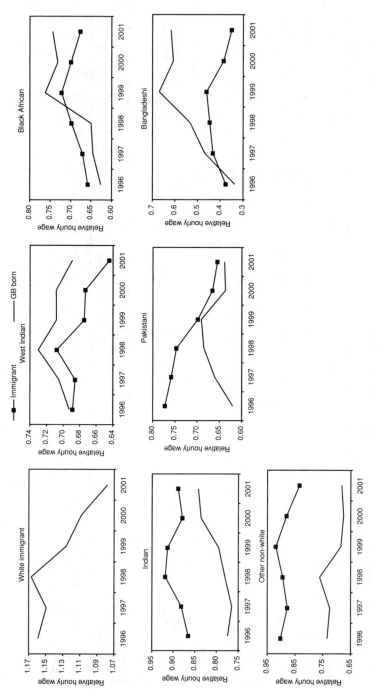

Figure 8.2a Real hourly wages relative to GB born whites, 1994–2001 (men)

Source: LFS.

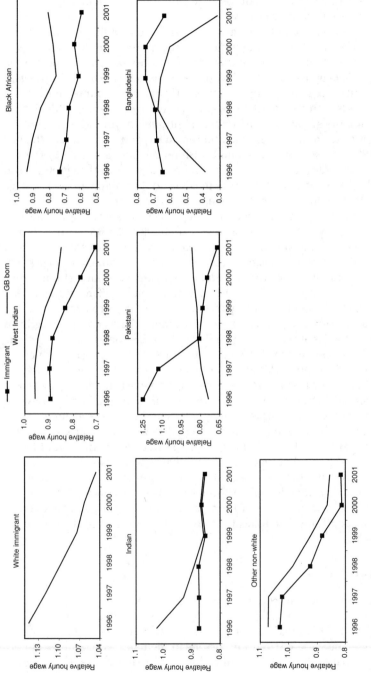

Figure 8.2b Real hourly wages relative to GB born whites, 1994–2001 (women)

Source: LFS.

to others. None of the percentage wage gaps for men are in single figures, despite these education controls.

Pay and working conditions also vary widely depending on the characteristics of the workplace and ethnic minority groups in different sectors of the economy often differs from that of the majority population (see *State of Working Britain* update, 2002). Allowing for these factors reduces the pay gaps further, but there remain large differences that are unaccounted for.

There is also some evidence to suggest that average pay among British born ethnic minority groups is closer to that of British born whites. Netting out the effects of differential educational attainment explains around half the pay gap between West Indian men and British born whites and reduces the pay gap for Bangladeshi men by around 20 per cent. For other groups, and particularly women, any differences in educational attainment are not large enough to explain much of the average pay gap.

It is often suggested that labour market prospects of some new immigrants are influenced by lack of language skills or familiarity with British institutions. Over time these disadvantages wane as immigrants gain experience. It is also suggested that there may be differences across cohorts of immigrants, depending on which countries and which individuals dominate the inflow of immigrants. The two factors are related. Failure to account for cohort differences could lead to a wrong assessment of the pace of any convergence process among immigrants. However, given the heterogeneity between ethnic groups highlighted so far, it seems essential that inflows be disaggregated by ethnic groups. Unfortunately the LFS data are too small to disaggregate each group by year of arrival and so this important issue must be left for future work.[7]

Another feature that needs more investigation when analysing pay gaps is that differential rates of labour force withdrawal across minority groups and this may affect estimates of wage differentials. If the employment rate varies across different groups and, as in Chapter 6, shows labour force withdrawal is concentrated on the less skilled, then any wage differentials that fail to account for the fact that there may be relatively more less-skilled workers in some groups than others would tend to under-estimate the true effect of any wage gap. Unfortunately, there is little consensus on how to deal with the problem[8] and the estimates of the wage gap can be quite sensitive to the various assumptions used to deal with the issue. As such this issue is left for future work.

Pay distributions

Analysis of average pay rates does not indicate the extent of pay dispersion within ethnic minority groups. One way to examine this issue is to see how closely pay distributions overlap with that for British born whites.[9] Table 8.6 shows that the wage distribution for Indian men and women most closely resembles that of their British born white counterparts. Net of differences in age, education and region of residence, the pay of more than 40 per cent of Indian men and women is above the median and the pay of around 20 per cent is greater than the top quartile level of pay of British born whites. Despite there being relatively few Pakistani women in the workforce, it does seem that the earnings distribution of those who do work closely mirrors that of British born whites. Less than a third of West Indian, Pakistani and Bangladeshi men earn more than the median hourly pay of British born white men.

Table 8.6 Distribution of minority pay relative to British born whites, 2001–02

Origin	% of minority with pay in GB born white wage quantile indicated		
	< Bottom 25%	> Median	> Top 25%
Men			
West Indies			
Immigrant	36	35	13
GB born	35	41	15
Africa			
Immigrant	49	27	14
GB born	40	33	15
India			
Immigrant	39	37	20
GB born	20	48	22
Pakistan			
Immigrant	49	29	11
GB born	27	41	15
Bangladesh	70	12	07
Other non-white			
Immigrant	39	40	22
GB born	30	44	21
Women			
West Indies			
Immigrant	22	42	15
GB born	23	50	27
Africa			
Immigrant	42	32	13
GB born	31	40	25
India			
Immigrant	35	38	19
GB born	23	49	24
Pakistan			
Immigrant	41	34	12
GB born	26	47	21
Bangladesh	37	39	15
Other non-white			
Immigrant	34	43	23
GB born	20	53	26

Notes: Data for Bangladesh for immigrants only due to small sample size. Controls include region, age and education.

Conclusion

It seems that the longest, most sustained economic recovery experienced for many years has not been sufficient to erase the substantial employment and wage differentials experienced by immigrant and ethnic minority workers. Relative employment prospects have improved for some groups, mostly among ethnic minority groups born in Britain. There are notable exceptions to this however, as employment rates among British born Afro-Caribbean and Bangladeshi men appear to have declined despite the recovery. Wage differentials remain largely unmoved by recovery. The notable differences in regional concentration or differences in educational attainment relative to British born whites do not appear to be behind these trends. As ever, more information on experiences *within* each minority group would be welcome, but lack of data is a major restriction to progress in this area.

So what is to be done? If we cannot rely on economic recovery to bring good prospects for all then it seems that more targeted policies are needed. Perhaps it is time to look at affirmative action policies, as pursued for example in the US, to see whether something similar could be of use in Britain.

Notes

1. According to the LFS, British born ethnic minorities comprise more than 11 per cent of children under 1, compared with 6 per cent of all current 20 year olds.
2. For a summary of the issues that have dominated the literature on ethnicity and immigration in the labour market see Smith and Welch (1989) and Borjas (1994).
3. The LFS asks only ethnicity of non-white individuals born in Britain, so the children of white immigrants cannot be identified in the data.
4. These numbers will also be influenced by differential fertility rates across the groups, though this information is not contained in the data analysed here.
5. The index is calculated as $^1/_2 \sum_{j=1}^{j} |Group1_j - Group2_j|$ where j is the jth occupation/industry and $Group1_j$ is the share of group 1 working in job type j.
6. The data is taken from the LFS, pooled over eight successive quarters beginning in 1993, so as to produce a workable sample size. The *General Household Survey* contains information on ethnic minority pay over a longer time interval, but the sample sizes are too small to disaggregate the ethnic minority group.
7. As must a decomposition of any observed wage gap into differences in characteristics and differences in returns to characteristics, until sample sizes allow.
8. For an introduction to these issues, see Heckman, Lyons and Todd (2000).
9. The distributions on which Table 8.6 is based are the residuals from a regression of hourly pay on age and region controls.

References

Borjas, G. (1994), 'The Economics of Immigration', *Journal of Economic Literature*, Vol. 32, December, pp. 1667–717.

Heckman, J., Lyons, T. and Todd, P. (2000), 'Understanding Black–White Differentials, 1960–1990', *American Economic Review*, Vol. 90, May, pp. 344–9.

Smith, J. and Welch, F. (1989), 'Black Economic Progress After Myrdal', *Journal of Economic Literature*, Vol. 32, June, pp. 519–64.

State of Working Britain 2002 (Update), Centre for Economic Performance, London School of Economics.

Part II:

Hours, Effort and Representation at Work

9
The Demands of Work

Francis Green

Key findings

- With relatively low unemployment, the quality of work is increasingly under the spotlight. Job satisfaction declined among workers in Britain during the 1990s.
- However, the picture of change for some important aspects of job quality is a little more optimistic in recent years. There has been a reduction in the proportion of workers working long hours from a peak of 36 per cent in 1995 to 30 per cent in 2002. This reduction signals a possible resumption of the historical trend to hours reduction.
- The notion that 'Britons work the longest hours in Europe' has always been a myth. Even though British *men* have till recently worked the longest hours, *women* in Britain have worked hours below the European average. Now, men working full-time still work long hours in Britain, but no longer are their weekly hours the longest in Europe. As of 2001, that accolade falls to Greek men, closely followed by Irish men.
- Government has had a significant impact on workers' paid holidays: the proportions of women workers deprived of any entitlements to paid holidays fell from 15 per cent in 1996 to just 6 per cent in 2001, and this was almost certainly due to the European Directive on Working Time.
- Up to the late 1990s, the pace of work was being intensified in British workplaces, with the greatest intensification being in the public sector. High workloads are associated with stress and lower job satisfaction. But since 1997 there has been no significant change on average in the perceived intensity of work.
- Rising skill requirements signal that jobs continue to become more challenging and rewarding. By 2001, computers had become essential in four out of every ten jobs, up from less than one in three in 1997. Over

the same period, the proportion of jobs requiring a degree or equivalent vocational or professional qualification rose from 24 per cent to 29 per cent, while the proportion requiring no qualifications at all fell from 32 per cent to 27 per cent.

Introduction

For many years up until the middle to late 1990s, despite rising real earnings workers in Britain were accustomed to their jobs becoming ever more demanding. Employers, recruiting for increasingly complex jobs, were requiring higher qualifications for their new hires. A rising proportion of jobs appeared to need workers to attend for inordinately long hours, and for most people the pace or intensity of effort during work hours was increasing. The 1990s saw the growth of a stress industry, a small army of occupational psychologists and human resource specialists devoted to alleviating and resolving workplace stress. These changes made for an ambivalent impact on the quality of work life in Britain. As work becomes more skilled it potentially becomes more rewarding, but increasingly stretched workloads are a sign of things getting worse.

With steadily declining unemployment rates the quality of work has also grown as an issue for public concern. The Labour government now sets itself three goals for its labour market policy: 'full employment, high levels of productivity, and higher standards – including greater diversity and choice – in the workplace. More jobs, better jobs, and high performance workplaces' (Patricia Hewitt, speech to the Work Foundation, 29 May 2002). In part, this aim to achieve 'better' jobs is a response to the problems of the increasingly demanding jobs. Recent policies in Britain have been directed at raising skill levels, while legislating basic employment rights, implementing the European Directive on Working Time, and carrying out a promotional campaign on the 'work–life balance'. The quality of work is also now the focus of attention from the European Commission, following the Lisbon summit of European leaders in March 2000. Perhaps unsurprisingly, there is as yet no coherent and comprehensive framework for depicting exactly what is meant by 'better' jobs, or high quality work (beyond agreement that high paid jobs are desirable).

One indication that job quality may be declining rather than improving is shown in Figure 9.1: the expressed level of job satisfaction declined between 1992 and 2001, especially in the public sector. Overall, the proportion of workers who expressed themselves as very or completely satisfied with their job fell from 52 per cent to 43 per cent of the workforce.

This chapter focuses on what has been happening to two key dimensions of work quality in recent years. First, it examines what has been happening to the average workload which workers experience, as captured both by the extensive load (hours and holidays) and by the intensive load – that is, the pace of work during work hours. Second, the chapter looks at the average skill level of jobs. Higher skilled jobs are typically thought of as better jobs, as well as signalling higher levels of economic performance. On these aspects, is there evidence of improvement in the quality of jobs?

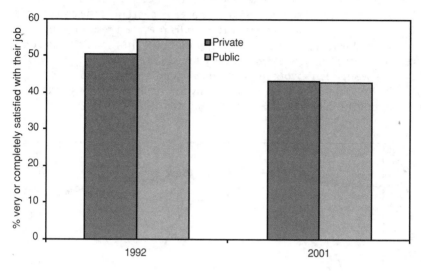

Figure 9.1   Job satisfaction, 1992 and 2001

Source: 1992 Employment in Britain survey (Gallie et al., 1998) and 2001 Skills Survey (Felstead et al., 2002).

The long-hours culture: a bit of relief

The long-hours culture in many jobs in Britain has meant increasing pressures on the non-work parts of people's lives. The new Labour government declared itself in favour of a better 'work–life balance', arguing in effect that this was a win–win solution: improved well-being for workers, and greater productivity and performance for companies. It dropped the previous administration's outright opposition to the European Working Time Directive. The Directive, whose stated aim was to 'protect the health and safety of workers', limited the average working week to a maximum of 48 hours, and mandated paid holiday entitlements for all workers. Albeit with some concessions to employers, the new regulation became effective in October 1998. From 2000 the government followed this up with a campaign to promote changes in company policies which would improve employees' work–life balance. What has been happening, in practice, therefore, to the long-hours culture in British workplaces in recent years?

In the period since 1997, the length of the working week for men has fallen but only modestly, while for women it remains stable. Figure 9.2 shows the trend in actual weekly hours of full-time workers for males and females. The average for men fell from a peak of 40.9 hours in the second quarter of 1996 to 39.1 hours in the same quarter of 2002. There has also been a significant fall in the proportions of workers working long hours, from a peak of nearly 36 per cent of all workers in 1995 to just over 30 per cent at the end of 2002. It is too early to be sure whether these falls presage a resumption of the historical downward trend in weekly work hours. In the mid-nineteenth century British male workers typically toiled for an average of at least 55 hours a week. Men's work hours dropped significantly around the time of the First World War, and again fell steadily throughout the 1950s, 1960s and 1970s, but this fall came to an abrupt end after 1981 (Green, 2001).

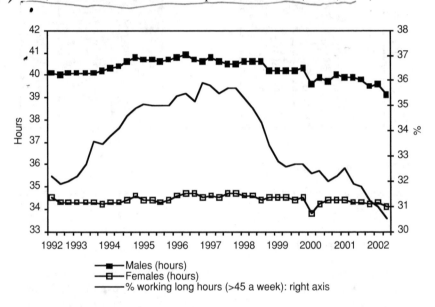

Figure 9.2   Weekly hours, Q1 1992 – Q2 2002

Source: National Statistics at http://www.statistics.gov.uk/statbase/TSDtimezone.asp

The long-hours culture is very much a gendered phenomenon. Four out of five people doing over 48 hours paid work per week are men. When commentators have stated, as they often have done, that 'Britons work the longest hours in Europe', they have been unconsciously sexist, because the statement was only true if, by 'Britons', one means only the males in the workforce who worked full-time. The average number of weekly work hours for all workers in the United Kingdom was 36.2 hours in 2001, the third lowest in the European Union.[1] This average conceals the fact that, among women, both part-time and full-time workers put in less hours than the

European Union average; while men working full-time do 43.5 hours, which is above the European Union average. Nevertheless, the latter figure is exceeded by male full-time workers in Germany (43.7), Greece (44.2) and Ireland (44.1). So the myth that 'Britons worked the longest hours in Europe' is now no longer true even for British male full-timers.

Looking at Figure 9.2, one might at first sight conclude that the fall in long-hours working is attributable to the European Directive on Working Time. However, a closer investigation casts doubt on that conclusion. To begin with, the downward trend began before the autumn of 1998 when the Directive came into force. Perhaps firms began cutting hours in anticipation of the Directive? This is a possibility. Nevertheless, further doubt is suggested by Table 9.1, which compares proportions working 48 hours or more in some sectors that were excluded by the Directive with those in other sectors. Not all sectors excluded in law can be identified easily with the data,[2] but the table compares the self-employed and transport workers (who were excluded) with the rest of the workforce. It can be seen that working hours decreased for those not covered by the Directive, just as it did for those that were covered.

Table 9.1   Proportion of male workers usually working 48 hours a week or more

	1997, 3rd quarter	2002, 3rd quarter
All workers	35.0	30.7
Employees	32.1	28.2
Self-employed and transport workers	49.3	43.9

Source: LFS.

People work long hours for both voluntary and involuntary reasons. Voluntary reasons include the desire for promotion and career progression, and sometimes because the work is found to be satisfying. Involuntary reasons derive sometimes from the nature of the job, or from unreasonable employer pressure, or more pervasively from a long-hours culture that infers poor work from anyone who does not stay late at the workplace. Since the European Directive allowed voluntary exemption from the 48 hour limit requirements, one might predict that only those suffering long hours against their choice would be affected. The distinction between voluntary and involuntary reasons is, however, liable to be blurred in practice, as some employees may prefer not to go against their employer. For whatever reason, large numbers of employees signed exemption statements. In many cases working beyond 48 hours has been balanced by working less in other weeks, so that the limit was not breached over the legislated 17-week period. The extent of employer resistance and non-compliance with the 48-hour rule has thus been limited, because compliance has been quite easy to effect without major change.

The above evidence suggests only a moderate relief for British men from the long-hours culture, and in any case the hours reduction has been due as much to economic growth as to the government's intervention. Taking the long-term view, over the past century or more we have seen several periods of sustained falls in the length of the paid working day for men, interspersed with periods of stability such as in the inter-war years. The long-term fall is generally interpreted as a consequence of affluence: we take part of our new-found wealth as leisure time away from paid work. The last few years could be interpreted as a resumption of this long-term declining trend. However, other countries in the European Union have also been reducing hours, notably France through its restrictions to a 35-hour week for those working in larger companies. Unless the long-hours culture continues to be eroded as rapidly in the next five years, British males will still be well represented among Europe's workaholics, and the work–life balance for families still elusive.

Though workers and employers might agree to opt out of the Directive's provisions for limiting weekly hours, the impact of the Directive on holiday entitlements was predicted to be substantive, if only because in this case there was to be no possibility of opting out (Green, 1997). No payments were to be made in lieu of holidays, nor were there to be any excluded sectors. Following the abandonment in 1986 of legal minimum rights to holidays in the Wages Council industries, there were many workers in low paid industries, with little protection from collective bargaining, who received no holiday rights. Since records became available in 1992, about one in ten workers came into this category, the majority of these women. From October 1998, however, workers became eligible for mandated rights to at least three weeks' holiday (pro rata for part-time workers), rising to four weeks in November 1999. Figure 9.3 shows that the Directive did have the desired effect: the proportions of people who are deprived of holiday entitlements has been substantially reduced. As with many such provisions for low paid workers, it is women who have benefited the most, but men have benefited too. The prime gainers have been in the Hotel and Restaurant industry, where the proportions without holiday entitlements fell from 37.3 per cent in 1996 to 12.5 per cent by 2001.[3] It is possible that some of these worker gains may have been compensated by falls in pay or entitlements, reductions in bank holiday entitlements, or increases in weekly hours. However, the reductions in pay are unlikely for workers on or near the new legal minimum anyway, and there have been no compensatory increases in average weekly hours in the Hotel and Restaurant industry. Though other off-setting changes might have taken place, it is in this area that the Directive can be counted as successful, in delivering significant benefits for certain sectors of the workforce. Whether it will thereby achieve its ultimate objective of raising the health and safety of the workforce, and at what cost, remains to be evaluated.

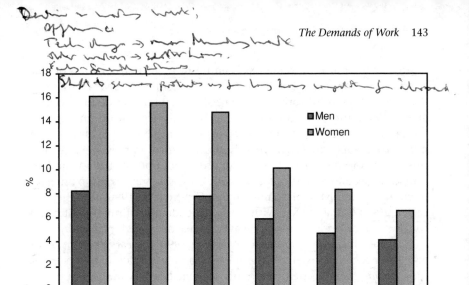

Figure 9.3 Proportions of workers with no paid holiday rights

Source: LFS.

The intensification of work effort: enough is enough

For the majority of people in Britain, the quality of work has been threatened not so much by the length of time spent at work as by the intensity or pace of work effort. Though crucial, the level of work effort is impossible to quantify objectively, except in rare experimental circumstances. But differences over time in subjective estimates of work effort allow us to gauge the direction, if any, of change (Green, 2001). A range of qualitative and quantitative evidence points to a sustained intensification of work effort through much of the 1980s and 1990s. Gallie et al. (1998) show that work intensification was often associated with the extra skills and responsibilities that jobs were demanding over this period. Table 9.2 shows some of the evidence, and brings the picture up to 2001.

Comparing 2001 with 1992, an increasing proportion of workers are experiencing work at high speeds, report that they are 'working under a great deal of tension', and agree strongly that 'my job requires me to work very hard'. Though this evidence is subjective, as long as the responses use the same points of reference at successive time periods, the changes between the replies are meaningful. The responses are taken from surveys that are representative samples of British workers aged 20–60. The questions are asked with identical wording and scales. Similar evidence from another data source points to the same conclusion, that work in Britain was intensified in the first part of the 1990s.

Since 1997, however, there has been no further intensification of work effort. According to the first indicator (the percent who reported that their job required them to work very hard), all the rise in work effort occurred before 1997, and since then there has been no significant change. The indicator showing the proportions reporting that they often or always 'come home from work exhausted' actually shows a small improvement, though this indicator combines the experienced effect both of the job and the commuting to and from the place of work. Two other surveys, again using representative data, paint the same picture for the later 1990s (Burchell and Fagan, 2002; Gallie, 2002). With this independent confirmation, it can be concluded that work effort had on average reached a high plateau by 1997.

The intensification of work until the late 1990s appears likely to be the consequence of the sustained technological and organisational changes that the economy was experiencing in this era. One has only to think of the call

Table 9.2   The intensification of labour and job satisfaction, 1992–2001

	1992	1997	2001
% who strongly agree that 'my job requires me to work very hard'			
Private sector	31.7	38.3	36.7
Public sector	31.9	44.4	43.2
All	31.6	39.9	38.3
% whose job involves working at high speed all or almost all of the time			
Private sector	18.7		25.2
Public sector	13.8		26.3
All	17.3		25.6
% who agree or strongly agree that they 'work under a great deal of tension'			
Private sector	45.8		56.9
Public sector	54.0		62.7
All	47.7		57.4
% who often or always 'come home from work exhausted'			
Private sector		20.1	16.1
Public sector		18.6	17.6
All		19.8	16.5

Sources: 1992 Employment in Britain survey, the 1997 Skills Survey and the 2001 Skills Survey. See, respectively, Gallie et al. (1998), Ashton et al. (1999) and Felstead et al. (2002).

centre, which became a paradigm for the new workplace: the
allowed almost perfect monitoring of workers' effort, and,
importantly, allowed work to be allocated to workers seamlessly. The 'po..
of the working day' (to use Marx's phrase) could now be virtually eradicated.
In other workplaces, new forms of work organisation, including team working
and quality management systems, had similar effects on the flow of work to
workers.[4] These changes came about in the context of an increasingly
competitive environment, and concomitant market pressures to raise the
performance of establishments. The public sector was by no means immune
from these changes, and indeed the squeeze on public resources meant that,
overall, intensification was even greater in the public than in the private
sector (see Table 9.2), at the same time as the public/private pay differential
was falling. But there are inherent limits, physical and mental, to the extent
to which workers can be induced to work harder. So, intensification of effort
is hardly viable as a long-term strategy for sustainable growth. The limits may
have been reached in Britain by the late 1990s.

It might be argued, somewhat optimistically, that some workers prefer
harder work to a more relaxed job other things equal. Many people find their
work fulfilling and like to be kept busy, rather than hanging around waiting
for the next task. Nevertheless, there is abundant evidence that on average
work overload is associated with mental strain at work and lower levels of
satisfaction. The decline in worker satisfaction indicated in Figure 9.1, which
took place despite rising pay and, eventually, slightly shorter weekly hours
and longer holidays, was associated with the intensification of effort in many
jobs and greater stress levels.

The demand for skills: still rising

Just as technological and organisational changes at work have brought on
rises in effort levels, so also these changes have tended to require higher skill
levels from workers. For at least two decades, the average skill level of jobs in
Britain has been rising (though see Chapter 5 for evidence that this average
rise may disguise changes at each end of the skill distribution). In this trend,
Britain is by no means unusual: it is found all over the industrialised world,
and in many third world countries. Figure 9.4 is one piece of evidence that
the trend has continued in recent years. From 1997 to 2001, the proportion
of jobs that required no qualifications fell from 32 per cent to 27 per cent,
having been as high as 38 per cent in 1986. At the other end of the scale, the
number of jobs requiring a degree or some equivalent vocational or
professional qualification rose from 24 per cent in 1997 to 29 per cent in
2001, having been only 20 per cent in 1986.

Other indicators of the broad skill levels required in jobs have also shown
an increase over the years since 1986. For example, the proportion of jobs
requiring more than a year to learn to do competently rose from 34 per cent

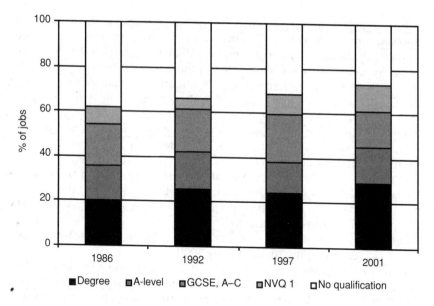

Figure 9.4 Highest qualification requirements, 1986–2001

Source: 2001 Skills Survey. See Felstead et al. (2002).

in 1986 to 38 per cent in 2001 – a rather slower increase than the qualification requirements, but pointing in the same direction. Similarly, the proportion of jobs requiring a period of prior training (as opposed to qualifications) of at least one year rose from 27 per cent in 1986 to 30 per cent in 2001, though in this case the rise has been erratic, and the proportion of long-training jobs has fallen in recent years.

On the face of it, more skilled jobs might be regarded as of higher quality – more challenging and more satisfying. Nevertheless, more highly educated people do not always express greater levels of job satisfaction. One reason can be that the jobs do not come up to their expectations. While the jobs are more skilled than in an earlier era, the workers that fill them have qualifications whose levels have risen somewhat faster. Workers who are 'over-qualified' for the jobs they do express lower levels of job satisfaction. Since there has been a small increase in the proportion of the workforce who are over-qualified (Felstead et al., 2002), this helps to explain why the increase in skill levels has not brought about higher levels of job satisfaction.

Apart from the above broad indicators of job skills, employers have for a number of years reported their need for a range of generic skills, such as problem-solving, communication, team-working, IT, and basic literary and numeracy skills.[5] Some of these skills, like IT, are related quite strongly to educational outputs, but other skills are acquired in the workplace or elsewhere. With the exception of physical skills, the demand for all other generic skills increased between 1997 and 2001. The increase over this relatively short period was modest in most cases, but the demand for IT skills in particular rose rapidly. As Figure 9.5 shows, the proportion of jobs where computer usage was deemed essential rose from 31 per cent in 1997 to 40 per cent in 2001: a substantial rise in so short a time. In 2001, seven in every ten employees were reporting that computers or PCs were fairly important, very important or essential in their own jobs. There is no doubt a limit beyond which computerisation cannot penetrate more broadly across the workforce, but these figures show that this limit was not reached in recent years. Moreover, the spread of computer use in jobs has not been merely for lower types of usage, such as e-mailing and word processing: the demand for more sophisticated usages, such as for programming, also rose between 1997 and 2001.

Jobs in Britain are becoming more skilled, on average, because Britain is part of a global economy in which modern technology and forms of work organisation require, on average, a more skilled workforce. Although old skills, often difficult to acquire, may also be disappearing, being replaced owing to

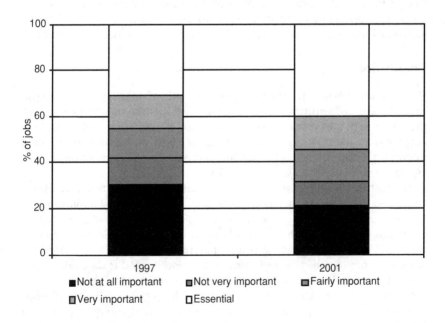

Figure 9.5   The importance of the use of PCs or other types of computerised equipment to jobs, 1997 and 2001

Source: 2001 Skills Survey. See Felstead et al. (2002).

automation and the continued presence of Tayloristic forms of dividing up labour, on balance economic evidence tells us that where the new technologies of the current era are being introduced and diffused through the economy there is a corresponding rise in the level of demand for skilled labour. This connection is most direct in the case of computer skills which, 30 years ago, would have been largely unknown to most workers. The industries where skill demands are rising fastest tend to be the same in different countries.

Skill demands may also be increasing because of the increased part played in the global economy by third world countries such as China, where wage costs are very much lower than in Britain. According to one economic theory, competition with firms in such countries will induce employers in a developed country such as the UK to specialise in products and services that require higher skill levels, leaving the relatively low-skilled manufacturing jobs to firms located in the low-cost countries. *Prima facie* evidence for this is that the rising inequality of wages in industrialised countries over recent decades has taken place while the third world countries in 'the South' have rapidly increased their share of manufacturing markets. Nevertheless, expert opinion is divided over how important this development has been so far, both as a cause of changing inequality, and as a source of accelerating skill demands. In coming years the integration of Eastern European nations into the global economy, accelerated by their accession to the European Union, will afford a further source of pressure on the labour markets of the richer countries.

Conclusion

Unlike in the 1980s, when the most pressing issue for millions was to find the route back to something like full employment, it is the quality rather than the quantity of jobs that has been the concern of many in recent years. This emphasis is likely to remain, as long as there is no return to mass unemployment. This chapter has focused on two of the most important aspects of work quality: skills and workload.

The picture on skills is mixed: workers' skill and qualification levels have continued to rise, but these do not necessarily lead to perceived improvements in work quality, especially if the available jobs do not keep up with the supply of qualifications. The picture on workload is a little optimistic. Compared to what had been happening for some time up till the mid-1990s, there has emerged what may be the beginning of a renewed trend towards declining work-hours, and a reduction of long-hours working. Though, in my judgement, little of the decline is attributable to the maximum 48 hour regulation, the state can take credit for inaugurating significant changes in holiday entitlements, giving for many the right to paid holidays for the first time. The intensity of work remains an issue of considerable concern, but at least it has not deteriorated any further in recent years. This may be because many workers have reached their limit, and are resisting further increases in the pace of work, or it may be because the forces of organisational and technological change are no longer generating such a strong demand for increasingly intense work as occurred in the 1980s and early part of the 1990s.

Notes

1. *Labour Market Trends*, January 2003: 15–16.
2. The Directive also excluded 'managing executives or other persons with autonomous decision-making powers'.
3. Remaining non-entitled workers will be made up of non-eligible casual workers with less than 13 weeks in the job, and cases of non-compliance.
4. I have elsewhere described this as a process of 'effort-biased technological change' (Green, 2001).
5. Mention is also frequently made of attitudes and behavioural characteristics, such as punctuality and honesty, but these are even harder to measure.

References

Ashton, D., Davies, B., Felstead, A. and Green, F. (1999), *Work Skills In Britain*, Oxford and Warwick Universities: Oxford SKOPE.

Burchell, B. and Fagan, C. (2002), *Gender and the Intensification of Work: Evidence from the 2000 European Working Conditions Survey*, Conference on Work Intensification, Centre D'Etudes De L'Emploi, Paris, 22–23 November.

Felstead, A., Gallie, D. and Green, F. (2002), *Work Skills In Britain 1986–2001*, DfES Publications: Nottingham.

Gallie, D. (2002), *Work Intensification in Europe 1996–2001?*, Conference on Work Intensification, Centre D'Etudes De L'Emploi, Paris, 22–23 November.

Gallie, D., White, M., Cheng, Y. and Tomlinson, M. (1998), *Restructuring the Employment Relationship*, Clarendon Press: Oxford.

Green, F. (1997), 'Union Recognition and Paid Holiday Entitlement', *British Journal of Industrial Relations*, 35(2), pp. 243–56.

Green, F. (2001), 'It's Been a Hard Day's Night: The Concentration and Intensification of Work in Late 20th Century Britain', *British Journal of Industrial Relations*, 39(1), pp. 53–80.

10
The Household Division of Labour: Changes in Families' Allocation of Paid and Unpaid Work, 1992–2002

Susan Harkness

Key findings

- Female employment grew rapidly in the 1990s, and this has accelerated the demise in the numbers of families headed by a male breadwinner. In 2002, three-quarters of married or cohabiting couples, and 56 per cent of those with children under school age, were supported by two-earners.
- Women in couples where both partners work full-time have always worked long hours, an average 40-hour week in 2002. What has changed over the decade is that there are significantly more of these families.
- The problem of long family hours of work is most predominant among the highly educated. In 2002 couples where women had some higher education supplied an average of 73 labour market hours a week. In contrast, those with O-levels or less supplied just 60 labour market hours. This difference is even starker among those with pre-school children.
- In one-half of families with children at least one parent usually works during the evening, while in one in ten families with pre-school children parents work shifts, with men working during the day and women during the evening or night.
- In spite of women's increasing labour market attachment, women still take responsibility for the vast majority of household chores even when they work full-time.
- The burden of housework is more evenly split where women earn an amount equal to or greater than their partners. These families are also particularly likely to 'buy back' time through the purchase of hired help, such as cleaners, and labour saving devices, such as dishwashers.

Introduction

One of the most striking labour market trends to have emerged over recent decades is the rapid rise in women's employment, particularly among those with young children (see also Robinson, Chapter 15). In this chapter the impact of this change on household patterns of employment and hours of work are examined over the last decade. I then go on to assess what impact the improved relative labour market position of women has had on the sexual division of labour within the household. In spite of the fact that I examine change over a relatively short time period, from 1992 to 2002, the economic boom of the late 1990s meant that this was a period of rapid change. By 2002, the rate of female employment among 25–49 year olds had risen by 6 percentage points to 73 per cent, while for those with pre-school children employment grew by 11 percentage points over the decade, reaching 55 per cent in 2002. This change clearly has important implications for ways in which families organise their labour, both in and outside the home.

Historically much of economic policy has been based on the premise that households, and in particular those with children, choose to specialise in their division of labour with men concentrating their efforts on market work and women in household production. Recent decades have however seen a rapid decline in the male breadwinner model of employment as the numbers of dual earner and single adult households have grown.[1] Yet in spite of increasing female employment, male employment patterns underwent little change in the 1990s, and in particular there was little evidence of a significant reduction in the number of hours being worked by men.[2] In 2002, the OECD reported that full-time men in Britain worked some of the longest-hours in Europe, while press reports suggest that the 'macho' long hours culture in Britain is leading to an increasingly stressed workforce, having an adverse effect on family relationships, and contributing towards the relatively poor status of women in the labour market.[3] The net effect of the rising female employment has been a large rise in the number of hours of market work within families. There is evidence too that workers would increasingly be happy to forgo pay for a reduced working week. In spring 2002, data from the Labour Force Survey (LFS) shows that around one-third of workers would be happy to work fewer hours even if it meant forgoing pay, and this figure rises to over 40 per cent for full-time workers. While a substantial number of men would be willing to sacrifice pay for shorter working hours, the demand for a shorter working week is particularly large among full-time working women with children, with 52 per cent desiring shorter working hours.

Increasing feelings of time pressure may also be a response to changes in working hours. The move towards a '24 hour' economy means that relatively few people now work a '9 to 5' five-day week, with no evening, night or weekend work. Research in the US has shown that evening and night-time work among parents is associated with poor child educational outcomes. Heymann (2000) has shown that children where at least one parent works during the evenings are substantially more likely to be in the bottom quartile in maths tests, and are more likely to get into trouble or be suspended from school. Other studies have emphasised the stress that evening and night work puts on relationships, and Presser (2000) has shown that those who work atypical hours are at increased risk of divorce. In this chapter I also look at how families schedule the times at which they work, looking particularly at how work times are influenced by the presence of children.

The increase in the number of market hours that families are working clearly has implications for the time available for other activities, including work within the home and leisure. As gender roles change, an important question then is whether, in response to increasing gender equality in the labour market, the division of labour within the household has also become more egalitarian. Or is it the case that as women enter into the labour market they increasingly face a 'double burden' of household and market work, or alternatively have the number of hours spent on household production fallen with households substituting away from home production, either by investing in labour saving devices (such as dishwashers and ready made meals) or purchasing services (such as cleaning) previously provided at home?

Throughout this chapter data from the LFS and the British Household Panel Survey (BHPS) are used to chart these changes. The sample is restricted to those aged 25–49 in order to concentrate on the prime-age workforce. The majority of those who have taken early retirement or who are still in education are therefore omitted. This also allows for a better comparison between families with and without children, as many of those aged 50 and above may have children who have now left home. Throughout I report *usual* hours of work. This differs from actual hours of work largely because respondents have reported being ill or having taken holiday (annual leave or bank holidays) over the last week, so actual hours are not a good reflection of the typical working week. Full-time workers are defined as those working more than 30 hours a week.

Changes in household patterns of work

Throughout the 1990s the rapid expansion of female employment seen in the 1970s and 1980s continued, with particularly large rises amongst those with young children. This change has led to dramatic shifts in families' employment structures. Harkness, Machin and Waldfogel (1997) have documented some of the shifts in family employment that occurred between 1979 and 1992. The last decade has seen an increased pace of change, which is illustrated in Figure 10.1 and Table 10.1. Figure 10.1 shows that since 1992 there has been a continued steady increase in the number of married couple households supported by two earners: in 2002 almost three-quarters of married/cohabiting families were supported by two earners compared with 65 per cent a decade earlier. Much of this growth in employment has been in the number of households where both partners work full-time, accounting for 38 per cent of couples in 2002. The number of women working part-time also grew considerably. This growth in the number of two-earner households has largely been at the expense of a decline in the number of male breadwinner families, although the number of households with no earners also fell back after 1996 (see Chapter 2).

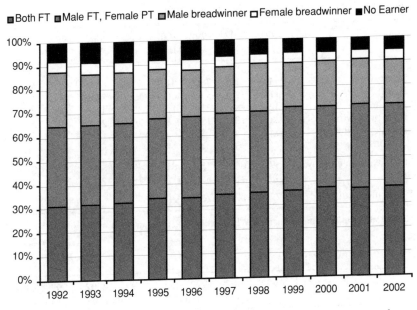

■Both FT ▣Male FT, Female PT ▣Male breadwinner ▢Female breadwinner ■No Earner

Figure 10.1 Family employment patterns: married and cohabiting couples aged 25–49, 1992–2002

Source: LFS.

The specialisation model of household production is particularly relevant to families with children. In Table 10.2 household work patterns are reported for those with and without children, and for those with children aged less than five. In 2002, two-thirds of households with children had two earners, and 56 per cent of those with children under five. This is a vast increase over the decade, representing a 9 percentage point increase in the number of two-earner households among those with children and 12 per cent rise for families with children under five. However, much of this increase was in part-time employment, with only 17 per cent of families with young children (and 24 per cent of those with children) containing two full-time workers. On the other hand part-time work grew by 8 per cent among couples with pre-school children, and by 11 per cent for single parents with young children. Alongside the rise in two-earner households has been an increase in the number of single person households. In these families too, and in particular among single parent families, employment has grown rapidly over the decade (see also Gregg and Harkness, Chapter 7). However, while rates of full-time employment among single parents have risen, they remain stubbornly low at just 22 per cent in 2002, limiting career development and long-term income prospects.

Table 10.1   Household work patterns, all aged 25–49

	1992	2002	1992	2002	1992	2002	1992	2002
	All		No kids		Kids <16		Kids <5	
Couples								
Two earners	64.5	71.9	76.2	81.4	57.6	66.2	44.6	56.4
Both FT	31.6	37.6	54.5	66.4	19.2	23.5	13.0	17.2
Female PT	32.9	34.3	21.7	17.0	38.4	42.7	31.6	39.2
Male breadwinner	23.6	19.5	13.4	8.9	29.5	25.0	41.7	35.3
Female breadwinner	4.2	3.5	5.6	4.0	3.4	3.1	2.6	2.3
No earner	7.7	5.0	4.8	3.7	9.4	5.6	11.1	6.0
Single women employed	59.8	66.0	77.3	81.6	40.6	53.0	23.8	39.0
FT	43.1	45.7	66.6	72.7	18.0	22.3	8.8	13.3
Single men employed	72.1	79.4	75.1	79.9	–	–	–	–

Notes: Data from LFS, Spring Quarters. Where cells are blank, data is too small.

Table 10.2   Usual hours of work

	1992	2002	1992	2002	1992	2002	1992	2002
	All		No kids		Kids <16		Kids <5	
Women								
All	20.4	23.3	28.6	32.5	15.1	18.0	10.7	14.4
Married/cohabiting	20.1	23.2	28.2	32.4	15.7	18.9	11.3	15.0
Two earners	29.2	30.7	34.6	37.2	25.5	26.9	23.6	25.3
Both FT	41.2	40.6	41.4	41.7	40.9	40.1	40.6	40.1
Female PT	18.7	20.9	20.8	23.6	18.1	20.3	16.6	19.3
Female breadwinner	29.8	30.7	33.8	35.2	26.6	28.1	27.1	26.6
Single women employed	34.7	34.7	38.9	40.2	26.8	28.0	23.1	27.8
FT	41.9	42.1	42.3	43.0	40.6	39.7	39.5	39.3
PT	16.5	18.3	19.4	20.1	15.3	17.9	13.5	17.0
Men								
All	39.9	40.1	38.7	39.2	40.7	40.9	40.2	40.7
Married/cohabiting	41.4	41.6	41.8	42.2	41.1	41.4	40.7	41.4
Two earners	46.6	45.2	46.1	44.8	46.9	46.3	47.5	45.4
Both FT	47.5	45.2	46.9	45.1	48.3	46.2	47.5	44.8
Female PT	46.7	45.8	46.0	43.8	46.9	46.2	46.8	45.8
Male breadwinner	46.9	44.7	46.3	46.2	47.1	44.4	46.7	44.2
Single men employed	44.4	43.8	44.6	44.1	–	–	–	–

Notes: Data is from the LFS, Spring Quarters. Where cells are blank data is not available as sample sizes are too small.

There is also evidence of large differences in household employment status across education groupings. This is illustrated in Figure 10.2. The male breadwinner model of employment is most frequently seen among the least well educated, while 'dual career' couples, where both partners work full-time, are substantially more common among those with some higher education. Differences, and changes over the decade, are particularly notable among those with young children (panel B) with almost 40 per cent of women with pre-school children and low educational qualifications supported by a male breadwinner, compared to 30 per cent of those with higher educational qualifications. In these families almost twice as many women with higher educational qualifications were 'dual career', and part-time work was also much more prevalent. The change over the decade is also striking, with the male breadwinner model of the family being rapidly replaced by the dual earner household among families with young children, and with part-time work growing particularly fast.

Hours of work

In 2002, the average woman aged 25–49 worked 23 hours a week, three hours longer than a decade previously. Men on the other hand saw no change on average in their hours of work, which remained constant at 40 a week (see Chapter 9 for more details on hours among all workers). This change reflects both increased rates of employment and changes in the number of hours worked by those in work. Table 10.2 reports changes in average working hours for men and women, by family employment status and the presence of children in the household.

Looking first at women's hours of work, in the upper panel of Table 10.2, rising average hours of work can be seen to have resulted from both an increase in employment and a rise in the number of hours worked among those in employment. However even among married and cohabiting women in dual earner households, average hours of work rose by 1.5 hours to 31 hours a week. This rise was however predominantly among those working part-time with part-time working women with children employed for an average of 20 hours a week in 2002. Women in 'dual career' couples, on the other hand, saw a marginal reduction in their working hours with full-time working mothers in 'dual career' couples working for an average of 40 hours a week. Where women do combine maintaining a full-time career with having children they work very similar hours to childless women in dual career households. This suggests that for women with full-time careers there is little accommodation in their working schedule when they have children. Instead any adjustments to the presence of children in the family rely on women shifting either into part-time work with significantly lower hours (and correspondingly worse pay and career prospects) or out of the labour market. For single mothers too,

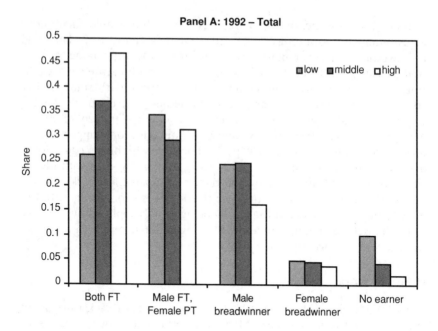

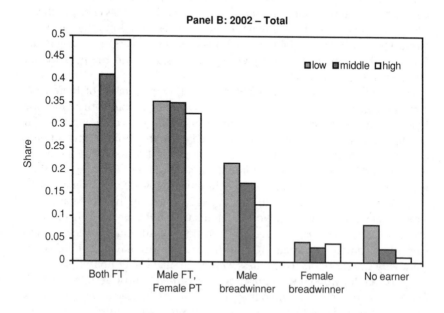

Figure 10.2 Household work patterns by level of education: married and cohabiting families aged 25–49, 1992 and 2002

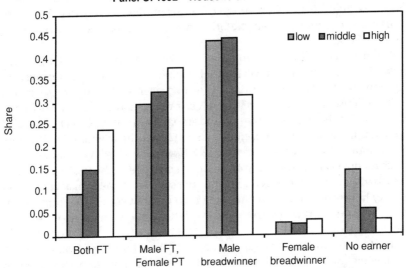

Panel C: 1992 – Households with children under 5

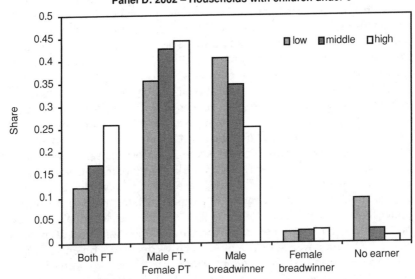

Panel D: 2002 – Households with children under 5

Notes: 'High' includes all those with higher educational qualifications, 'middle' includes those with A-level or equivalent, and 'low' includes all those below O-level.

Source: LFS.

average hours of work have increased, although again this is primarily a result of increasing hours of work amongst those employed part-time. Full-time working single mothers, on the other hand, are employed on average 40 hours a week.

For men, the trend in working hours has been the reverse. Looking first at men's hours of work, in the lower panel of Table 10.2, the small rise in average hours worked appears to be primarily a consequence of rising employment. Within household types however it is clear that average hours of work have fallen, with this fall being most marked among fathers of young children and for those in 'dual career' households. In 2002 'male breadwinner' fathers saw their hours of work decline by over 2.5 hours a week to 44.4 hours, while dads in 'dual career' couples worked an average of 46.2 hours, or two hours less than a decade earlier. Yet it remains the case that fathers on average work longer hours than married/cohabiting men without children or single men, and, even where their partners also work full-time, men carry on working relatively long hours.

In 2002 the average 'dual career' couple supplied 86 hours of labour a week and, while there has been little change in the number of hours these families supply over the decade, the dual career couple is becoming increasingly common and it may be this change that is leading to feelings of increased time pressure. Is the problem of lengthy family working hours one that is confined largely to a relatively well-paid and highly qualified middle class? It has already been noted that dual career couples are most frequently found among the more highly educated. Table 10.3 looks in more depth at differences in hours of work by education. The upper panel reports hours of work for those with higher education qualifications, while the lower panel shows hours of work for those with O-levels or below. For married and cohabiting women with higher educational qualifications, average hours of work were 29.5 hours a week in 2002, an increase of 2.5 hours over the decade. For those with children aged less than five, hours of work have increased particularly dramatically, by an average of 3.2 hours a week to a total of 21.3 hours. However most of this increase has resulted from increased labour force participation and increasing hours of work among part-time workers. For those working full-time, hours of work have stayed relatively constant at an average of 43 hours a week, and at 42 hours a week for those with children under five. In comparison, for those with low level educational qualifications (O-level and below) working hours in 2002 averaged just 20 hours a week, 10 hours fewer than the more highly educated women's average. Moreover, even among those employed full time the average workweek was almost 4 hours shorter. Nor do the partners of highly educated women reduce their working hours in order to compensate for this difference. For men average hours of work are similar across educational groups once account has been taken for differences in employment rates. As a result there are large differences in hours of family labour supply across educational groupings. In 2002, the families of women with higher education supply an average of 73 labour market hours a week, while for those with O-level or below hours of family labour supply average just 60 hours a week. Among those with young children the difference is even starker, with the families of more educated women with children under five supplying on average 65 hours a week compared to an average 50-hour week for the families of less well educated women.

Table 10.3   Hours of work by education, aged 25–49, 1992 and 2002

	1992	2002	1992	2002	1992	2002	1992	2002
	All		No kids		Kids <16		Kids <5	
A) HIGHER								
Women								
All	29.1	31.4	37.4	39.4	23.2	24.8	18.1	21.3
Married/cohabiting	27.0	29.5	36.3	38.6	22.1	24.3	17.9	21.1
Two earners	33.1	34.2	39.3	40.8	29.2	29.8	27.3	28.8
Both FT	42.6	43.2	42.9	43.7	42.0	42.4	41.8	42.1
Female breadwinner	36.1	37.9	38.0	41.6	34.2	35.8	33.7	31.7
Single women in work	40.4	40.0	42.1	42.4	34.2	33.8	29.7	34.9
Men								
All	44.2	43.0	42.5	42.0	45.5	43.7	45.3	43.2
Married/cohabiting	45.2	43.7	44.2	42.9	45.7	44.0	45.5	43.6
Two earners	46.4	44.9	45.6	44.4	46.9	45.1	46.7	45.1
Both FT	46.5	45.7	45.7	45.4	47.8	46.1	47.9	45.3
Male breadwinner	47.3	45.4	46.7	43.6	47.4	45.6	47.4	45.6
Single men in work	44.7	43.9	46.7	44.0	–	–	–	–
B) LOW								
Women	17.9	19.3	25.0	27.0	13.2	15.2	8.5	10.7
Married/cohabiting	18.2	20.2	25.1	27.8	14.1	16.5	9.3	11.6
Two earners	27.8	28.8	32.3	34.2	24.2	25.6	21.9	23.1
Both FT	40.7	39.6	40.9	40.3	40.7	38.8	40.3	38.4
Female breadwinner	28.0	27.4	31.2	31.4	25.3	24.8	24.9	23.0
Single women in work	31.8	31.0	36.3	37.2	24.5	25.5	21.1	24.4
Men	37.5	37.1	36.8	35.9	38.0	38.0	37.1	37.8
Married/cohabiting	39.3	39.4	40.7	41.0	38.5	38.7	37.8	38.8
Two earners	46.5	45.2	46.3	45.1	46.6	45.3	46.5	46.6
Both FT	47.9	46.2	47.5	45.8	48.5	46.5	47.1	45.8
Male breadwinner	46.8	43.7	46.4	46.8	46.9	43.2	46.7	46.9
Single men employed	44.0	42.9	44.2	43.3	–	–	–	–

Notes: Data from the LFS, Spring Quarters. 'High' includes all those with higher educational qualifications and 'low' includes all those below O-level.

The timing of work

The 2002 LFS respondents were asked whether it is usual for them to work during the day, evening or night, and on what days they work. As there is a change from the way in which the question was asked in 1999, it is not possible to compare responses to the 2002 survey with earlier survey years. Table 10.4 reports responses for men and women with and without children. In 2002, one-third of men and one-quarter of women usually worked during the evenings, and patterns of work were not strongly influenced by the presence of children in the family. Night working was much more prevalent among men (and slightly more common among parents), with almost one-fifth of fathers reporting night working as being usual compared to fewer than one in ten mothers. Weekend working is also commonplace, and again there are some gender differences, although the presence of children does not appear to have a large effect on weekend working. Table 10.5 shows how dual earning couples schedule their working time, both for those without children and for those with children under 12. Among those with children under 12, one in ten couples report that they *both* regularly work during the evening while in an additional 40 per cent of families at least one parent regularly works during the evening. Working during the evening is particularly common for part-time working mothers, with one-third of part-time working mums regularly working at this time (compared to one-quarter of mothers who are full-time employed). Indeed there is evidence that many mothers who work part-time perform a difficult juggling act. In almost 10 per cent of families with a child under five, and 7 per cent of families with a child under 12, men usually work during the day while the women usually work only in the evenings or nights. This suggests a pattern of shift working among families with women taking responsibility for childcare during the day and going out to work after fathers come home in the evening. The high costs and limited availability of daytime childcare are likely to have contributed towards families adopting such patterns of work.

Table 10.4 Proportion usually working during the day, evening, night and at the weekend by family type, age 25–49

| | Men | | | Women | | | |
| | Married & cohabiting | | Single | Married & cohabiting | | Single | |
	Kids	No kids	No kids	Kids	No kids	Kids	No kids
Day	.961	.974	.963	.934	.978	.947	.975
Evening	.363	.336	.346	.248	.240	.233	.320
Night	.184	.164	.165	.089	.079	.100	.118
Saturday	.318	.299	.314	.216	.209	.234	.240
Sunday	.188	.171	.187	.143	.136	.154	.156

Source: LFS.

Table 10.5   Percentage of husbands and wives working during the day, evening and night by family type

	Neither work during ...	Man works during ...	Woman works during ...	Both work during ...
No children				
Day	0.3	1.5	2.2	96.0
Evening	55.2	20.8	12.3	11.7
Night	79.4	12.8	5.3	2.4
Children <12				
Day	0.3	7.4	3.3	89.1
Evening	48.9	25.9	14.9	10.3
Night	74.4	16.3	6.9	2.4
Couples, both FT, children <12				
Day	0.3	2.9	4.1	92.7
Evening	48.2	24.8	13.6	13.3
Night	72.9	17.0	7.3	3.7
Couples, woman works PT, children <12				
Day	0.3	9.6	2.5	87.7
Evening	49.5	26.5	25.3	8.8
Night	75.7	15.8	6.7	1.8

Source: LFS.

Household division of labour

What impact have these recent changes in household employment had on the division of unpaid work within the home? In this section I assess whether rising female employment has led to a 'double burden' for women, with their increasing working hours in addition to the hours of unpaid work done within the home. Alternatively it may be that men have taken on some of the burden of domestic work in response to their partners' increasing labour supply, or it may be that there has been a reduction in time spent on unpaid work, either because of increased use of labour saving household technology (e.g. dishwashers) or because services previously provided in the home are now being purchased (e.g. cleaners).

In this section data from the BHPS are used to examine how the division of household tasks varies with employment status. In the BHPS married and cohabiting respondents are asked who carries out a range of household chores. From 1992 to 2001 respondents were asked who undertook the grocery shopping, cooking, cleaning, washing and ironing, and who had responsibility for childcare. Possible responses were 'mostly self', 'mostly partner', 'shared between self and partner', or 'paid help' and 'others'. In Table 10.6 the responses in 2001 are reported for married and cohabiting women aged 25–49 by family employment status. Responses from all married and cohabiting women suggest that women take responsibility for the majority of household tasks: grocery shopping, cooking, cleaning and washing and ironing are done 'mostly' by women in between 65 and 80 per cent of families, and mostly shared between partners in other families. The tasks most likely to be undertaken by men are grocery shopping and cooking, with men doing most of, or sharing, these tasks in over one-third of families. Cleaning is the only task where a significant number of families rely on paid help, with 6 per cent of families paying for help with cleaning, and it is more common for families to rely on hired help than for men to be mainly responsible.

How do variations in family employment status effect the division of family labour? The second panel in Table 10.6 reports the division of household work for 'dual career' families, where both partners work full-time. Even among these families, the cooking, cleaning and washing/ironing is done mostly by the woman in over one-half of families. Grocery shopping and cooking are the tasks that men are most likely to take responsibility for, with these tasks being undertaken mostly by men or shared equally in almost one-half of families. In the third and fourth panels the division of tasks among families where the man works full-time and the woman part-time or is out of the labour force are reported. The division of tasks in these families is almost identical: in 80 per cent of these families the cooking, cleaning and the washing/ironing is undertaken mainly by women.

Models of household specialisation, such as that of Becker (1991), predict a reallocation of household tasks as labour market specialisation declines. This appears to be the case where women have moved into the labour market and work full-time. Part-time work on the other hand has little impact on the division of household tasks. An alternative theory might be that as women's earnings rise relative to their partner's, their bargaining position within the family increases, leading to a reallocation of household tasks (Lundberg and Pollak, 1996). The bottom panel of Table 10.6 reports how the distribution of household tasks changes when women earn a weekly wage that is similar to or greater than that of their partner. Here women earning 90 per cent or more of their partner's weekly wage are assumed to have earnings roughly equal to or greater than their partner. Clearly we would predict that, as women's pay rises relative to their partner's, household tasks are more likely to be shared, with men particularly likely to undertake grocery shopping and cooking. Moreover, where women earn a larger share of the household income they are particularly likely to hire paid help for cleaning (10 per cent of families) and are more likely to own labour saving devices such as dishwashers and tumble-dryers.

For those with children, questions are also asked about who is responsible for arranging childcare, who pays for childcare and who nurses children when they are sick (see Table 10.7). The responsibility for childcare is undertaken mostly by women in around 80 per cent of families in which the woman does not work or who works part-time. However in families where both partners work full-time, and in female breadwinner families, men take shared responsibility for childcare in around 60 per cent of families. Looking at who pays for childcare is also revealing. This shows that the costs of childcare are borne entirely by women in 60 per cent of families where they work part-time. Even where women work full-time, 44 per cent pay the entire costs of childcare from their salaries. It is only when women's earnings are similar to or greater than those of their partners that the costs of childcare are likely to be shared.

Table 10.6   Division of household tasks, women 2001

Who does the ...	Mostly self	Mostly partner	Shared	Paid help/other
Grocery shopping?	59.8	8.6	31.3	0.4
Cooking?	65.6	9.8	24.0	0.7
Cleaning?	69.3	4.0	21.2	5.6
Washing/ironing?	79.2	2.7	16.2	1.9
Both FT				
Grocery shopping?	47.7	11.1	40.3	0.9
Cooking?	51.5	13.7	33.7	1.0
Cleaning?	58.9	4.0	29.9	5.9
Washing/ironing?	70.4	3.5	24.9	1.1
Man FT, woman PT				
Grocery shopping?	71.8	6.1	22.2	0.0
Cooking?	77.1	5.7	16.9	0.3
Cleaning?	79.9	2.9	12.4	4.8
Washing/ironing?	88.3	0.5	9.0	2.2
Male breadwinner				
Grocery shopping?	65.5	5.3	28.4	0.9
Cooking?	78.0	4.6	16.4	0.5
Cleaning?	80.5	3.1	12.2	4.3
Washing/ironing?	87.0	1.6	9.7	1.8
Female breadwinner				
Grocery shopping?	41.9	26.7	31.4	0
Cooking?	42.4	25.1	31.1	1.4
Cleaning?	43.7	16.7	35.0	4.6
Washing/ironing?	62.5	9.7	27.8	0
Woman earns >.9 of male *weekly earnings*				
Grocery shopping?	47.2	8.6	43.7	0.5
Cooking?	50.3	16.0	33.0	0.8
Cleaning?	50.3	4.3	35.8	9.7
Washing/ironing?	69.9	3.2	25.3	1.6

Source: 2001 BHPS.

Respondents were also asked who nurses sick children. In three-quarters of cases working women report that this is undertaken by them and, even where the earnings of women are similar to or greater than those of their partners', it is still the case that in 60 per cent of families it is women who take time off to nurse sick children, while only 14 per cent of men take on this task (with nannies and other paid carers being more likely to nurse sick children than fathers, even when women's earnings are on a par with or greater than their partners').

Table 10.7   Sharing household tasks

Who is responsible for childcare?	Mostly self	Mostly partner	Shared	Paid help/other
All	66.1	2.3	30.6	1.0
Both FT	38.2	2.9	57.3	1.7
Woman PT	77.4	1.1	21.4	0
Male Breadwinner	85.5	0.6	13.0	1.0
Female Breadwinner	24.8	8.6	63.7	2.9
No earner	48.5	8.9	40.2	2.4
Woman earns >.9 male weekly wage	37.8	2.0	60.2	0

Who pays for childcare?			Women in work only			
	All from respondent's wages	Most from respondent's wages	Share costs with partner	Most by spouse/ partner	All by spouse/ partner	Other
All in work	57.8	1.4	34.6	2.3	3.1	0.8
Both FT	40.7	2.7	50.2	1.1	2.8	2.5
Woman PT	57.1	0.7	33.1	4.4	4.9	0
Woman earns >.9 partner's weekly wage	32.4	0	63.8	3.8	0	0

Who nurses sick children?	Respondent	Spouse/ partner	Mothers help/nanny	Relative	Friends/ neighbour	Other/ varies
All	73.4	9.0	1.0	11.2	0.3	18.0
Both FT	67.0	10.5	1.1	11.1	0.5	9.7
Woman PT	77.5	7.4	1.1	8.9	0	5.0
Woman earns >.9 partner's weekly wage	60.9	14.0	0	9.9	0	15.3

Source: 2001 BHPS.

All respondents to the BHPS were also asked, 'About how long do you spend on housework in an average week, such as time spent cooking, cleaning and doing the laundry?' This allows the question of the division of household labour to be analysed in more depth, although it should be noted that time spent on childcare is not included. These results are reported in Table 10.8. Over the decade average hours that women spend on housework have fallen by three hours, to 17 hours a week in 2001. For men, on the other hand, hours spent on housework remain unchanged at an average of 5.5 hours a week. Some of this decline for women has resulted from changes in employment patterns, as women in male breadwinner families for example do more hours of housework than those in 'dual career' households. However, even within dual career households time spent on housework has declined by almost two hours over the decade to 12 hours a week in 2001. Women in male breadwinner families on the other hand spent an average of 23 hours on housework. While men in dual career households did on average 2 hours more housework than those who were breadwinners, they still spend substantially less time doing unpaid work than their partners, and total hours of home production are considerably lower in dual career couples (at 19.5 hours a week) than in families where women work part-time (at 24 hours a week) or in male breadwinner families (at 32 hours a week).

Table 10.8   Hours of non-market work

| | 1992 | 2001 | 1992 | 2001 | 1992 | 2001 | 1992 | 2001 |
	All		No kids		Kids		Kids <5	
Women	19.9	16.6	14.1	11.5	24.4	20.2	25.5	21.5
Married/cohabiting	21.4	17.7	16.3	13.1	24.7	20.3	25.8	20.8
Two earners	18.8	15.7	15.2	12.2	21.8	18.2	21.2	16.9
Both FT	13.9	12.1	12.4	10.3	17.1	14.6	14.1	11.8
Woman PT	23.3	20.0	21.7	19.0	23.8	20.2	23.2	18.9
Male breadwinner	28.2	23.4	24.2	18.1	29.2	24.5	29.1	24.7
Female breadwinner	16.9	15.3	12.7	12.1	22.9	17.3	22.2	23.8
No earners	27.7	25.7	21.0	20.6	30.2	29.2	31.8	34.0
Single women	10.8	10.4	13.4	12.3	22.5	19.7	26.1	31.9
FT	8.5	8.7	7.4	7.9	14.2	12.5	–	–
PT	18.6	16.1	–	–	27.1	23.7	–	–
Not employed	22.3	20.1	13.4	12.3	17.2	15.8	16.0	12.6
Men	5.5	5.5	5.7	5.5	5.4	5.5	5.4	5.4
Married/cohabiting	5.2	5.3	5.3	5.4	5.2	5.3	5.4	5.3
Two earners	5.1	5.3	5.0	5.3	5.1	5.3	5.6	5.6
Both FT	5.6	5.8	5.4	5.5	6.1	6.2	5.8	6.1
Male breadwinner	3.7	4.0	4.8	3.8	3.5	4.1	3.8	3.6
Female breadwinner	10.3	10.3	9.1	9.1	11.3	11.1	10.8	10.2
No earners	8.5	9.2	7.8	10.4	8.6	8.9	9.2	9.9
Single men employed	5.4	5.6	9.1	6.9	–	–	–	–
Not employed	10.1	7.7	5.4	5.4	–	–	–	–

Note: Where cells are blank data is not available as sample sizes are too small.

Source: BHPS.

Clearly the presence of children influences the amount of housework to be done: in 2001 married and cohabiting women spent 7 hours longer a week on housework compared to their childless counterparts. However, working full-time does considerably shorten the time spent by mothers on housework; in 2001 hours of housework for full-time working mothers averaged 15 hours a week, 2.5 hours fewer than a decade earlier and 10 hours fewer than undertaken by women in male breadwinner households. So who is doing the housework? Looking at men's hours of unpaid work, those with full-time working wives spent an average of 6 hours a week on housework, 2 hours longer than 'breadwinning' men, although this difference clearly does not nearly compensate for the difference in time spent by wives. Again the reduction in time spent on unpaid work in two-earner households implies that either dual career households are making greater use of labour saving technologies, buying in home help, or because less housework is being done.

Bargaining models of household decision-making would suggest that gender roles within households are linked to relative earnings as well as employment status. Over the decade the ratio of wives' to husbands' (or partners') earnings increased from 60 to 65 per cent, and the proportion with weekly earnings on a par with or greater than their husbands' (defined as 90 per cent of the weekly wage or above) rose from 19 to 23 per cent (while over one-third had hourly wages greater than their partners'). In dual career couples, this share was even larger with 42 per cent of those without children and 28 per cent of those with children earning a weekly wage equal to or greater than 90 per cent of their partners' wage. How does this translate into time spent on unpaid household work? Table 10.9 reports hours spent on market and household work by husbands and wives who earn more than their partners (over 110 per cent of the husband's weekly wage), earn a similar amount to their husbands (between 90 and 110 per cent of his weekly wage) and earn less than their partners (under 90 per cent of his wage). Notable here is that as women's relative earnings rise, the number of hours spent on housework declines. However even wives who earn more than their partners put in significantly more hours at home, although this has been changing. Between 1992 and 2002 wives who earned more than their partners had a reduction in their housework hours by 1 hour to an average of 11 hours a week, while their partners' hours increased by 2 hours over the decade to 7 hours a week. In families where women earn less than their partners however there has been no such convergence as men's housework hours remain low and are if anything declining. There are also notable differences between families with and without children: in households without children the distribution of household tasks has become relatively equitable where wives earned more than their partners, but where children are present this is much less true with women spending twice as long as their partners on household chores in spite of 'role reversal' in earnings.

Table 10.9   Hours of market and unpaid work and relative earnings

| | 1992 | | 2001 | |
	Market	House	Market	House
All				
Weekly ratio >1.1				
Men	44.3	5.0	41.2	7.2
Women	41.8	12.4	41.4	10.8
Ratio 0.9 to 1.1				
Men	46.8	5.6	45.9	4.9
Women	40.5	11.7	42.1	10.9
Ratio <0.9				
Men	45.9	5.3	46.8	4.9
Women	28.5	19.2	29.8	16.8
Kids				
Weekly ratio >1.1				
Men	38.0	5.6	40.8	6.7
Women	46.7	14.8	40.1	13.1
Ratio 0.9 to 1.1				
Men	39.8	5.3	41.5	5.5
Women	43.2	13.8	47.5	13.3
Ratio <0.9				
Men	46.4	5.3	46.5	5.1
Women	24.1	21.5	26.6	19.0
No kids				
Weekly ratio >1.1				
Men	42.6	4.6	41.7	7.4
Women	44.5	10.7	41.7	9.6
Ratio 0.9 to 1.1				
Men	46.4	5.6	45.0	4.5
Women	40.7	10.3	42.4	9.5
Ratio <0.9				
Men	45.0	5.3	47.3	4.7
Women	34.9	16.0	36.4	12.2

Source: BHPS.

Conclusion

The rapid growth in employment over the last decade has seen a radical restructuring of family employment structures. However, the organisation of time within the home and in the workplace has been slow to respond to this change. This has led to increasing time pressure, particularly for full-time working mothers in 'dual career' and single parent families. The problem of long family working hours is however most predominant among a relatively well-paid and highly educated middle class: in 2002 couples where women had some higher education supplied an average of 73 labour market hours a week. In contrast, those with O-levels or less supplied just 60 labour market hours. This difference is even greater among those with pre-school children, with more educated families supplying 65 labour market hours a week compared to a 50-hour average for the less educated.

The assumption that children affect only women's time use remains largely true. Fathers' hours of work are if anything greater than those of single or married men without children, while men in 'dual career' couples work the longest hours of all. There is no evidence that dads reduce their working hours in order to accommodate their partners' increasing labour supply. Moreover, while 'dual career' dads do marginally more hours of unpaid work than men who are breadwinners (putting in an average of 6 hours' housework a week), they spend far less time on unpaid work than their partners. For mothers who work full-time, there is also little difference in hours worked between those with and without children in spite of large differences in time spent on unpaid work. Instead, any adjustment in hours to the presence of children in the family relies on mothers moving into part-time work (with significantly worse pay and career prospects) or out of the labour market.

While women still take responsibility for the vast majority of household chores even where they work full-time, the burden of housework is slightly more evenly split where women earn an amount equal to or greater than their partners. Women who earn more than their partners are particularly likely to use their bargaining power to 'buy back' time through the purchase of hired help such as cleaners, and labour saving devices such as dish washers. Yet even in these households 60 per cent of women take time off to nurse the children when they are sick, and nannies and other paid help are more likely to undertake this role than fathers.

Long hours of market work among full-time working parents, and of unpaid work for mothers, have led to increasing time pressure for many. Full-time working mothers in dual career couples and single parents are particularly burdened by long hours of paid and unpaid work, and this is true even before account is taken of time spent on childcare. The constraints placed on full-time working women, and in particular mothers, by household responsibilities hold back mothers' earnings power. While some of the newly introduced policies aimed at improving work–life balance, such as the introduction of paternity leave, may help redress some of the current imbalances seen in the household, other policies, such as new rights of full-time carers (mostly women) to request flexible working conditions, may reinforce the current gendered division of household labour.

Notes

1. See also Gregg and Wadsworth Chapter 2 for more on the polarisation of work across households.

Labour*

2. Since the 1970s however male employment rates have fallen significantly, although in the 1990s they did see some recovery.
3. See Green (Chapter 9) for more on trends in actual hours of work and work pressure.

References

Becker, G. (1991), *A Treatise on the Family*, Harvard University Press: Cambridge: MA.

Harkness, S., Machin, S. and Waldfogel, J. (1997), 'Evaluating the Pin Money Hypothesis', *Journal of Population Economics*, 2, pp. 137–58.

Heymann, S. J. (2000), *The Widening Gap: Why American Working Families are in Jeopardy and What Can Be Done About It*, Basic Books: New York.

Lundberg, S. and Pollak, R. (1996), 'Bargaining and Distribution in Marriage', *Journal of Economic Perspectives*, 10(4), pp. 139–58.

Presser, H. (2000), 'Non-standard Work Schedules and Marital Instability', *Journal of Marriage and the Family*, 62, pp. 93–110.

Trade Unions

David Metcalf

Key findings

- At its peak UK membership stood at 13 million in 1979 but haemorrhaged 5.5 million in the subsequent two decades. Presently 29 per cent of employees belong to a union, three in five in the public sector but under one in five in the private sector; 36 per cent of workers are covered by a collective agreement. Union members are now disproportionately well educated and in professional, often public sector, occupations.
- The sustained decline in membership in the 1980s and 1990s was a consequence of interactions among the composition of the workforce and jobs; the roles of the state, employers and individual workers; and of unions' own structures and policies.
- Unions now impact only modestly on pay, productivity, financial performance and investment. The negative association between recognition and employment growth, even assuming it is not causal, will depress future membership if it continues. Unions are a force for fairness in the workplace: they narrow the pay distribution, boost family-friendly policy and cut accidents.
- Legislative changes since 1997 have had a minimal impact on membership and recognition of trade unions. There are around 3 million free-riders who are covered by a collective agreement but not themselves union members, and another 3 million employees who would be very likely to join a union if one existed at their place of work. The challenge for the union movement is to organise these workers (a twentieth a year is 300,000 extra members) while still servicing their existing 7 million members.

Introduction

This chapter analyses the decline of trade unions over the last 20 years or so and asks whether a resurgence is possible. British unions presently cover three employees in ten. Membership declined by over 5 million in the two decades after the 1979 zenith of 13 million. The future of British unions turns in large part on what they do – to economic efficiency, fairness and to industrial relations – and any resurgence of unions depends on where the new jobs are, support from the state, interactions with employers and unions' own servicing and organising policies.

Membership and decay 1980s, 1990s

Membership figures

Union membership rose by 4 million between 1950 and 1979. At its peak in 1979 it stood at 13.2 million but haemorrhaged 5.5 million in the subsequent two decades (see Table 11.1). Presently union membership is 7.34 million,

Table 11.1   Trade union membership and density, UK

Certification officer data	Membership (000s)	Density (%) Among civilian workforce
1950	9,289	40.6
1960	9,835	40.9
1970	11,178	45.9
1980	12,947	49.0
1990	9,947	35.3
2000	7,779	26.2

Labour Force Survey		Among employees
1990	9,100	38.1
1993	8,001	35.1
1998	7,396	29.9
1999	7,498	29.6
2000	7,580	29.5
2001	7,330	29.1
2002	7,340	29.0

Notes and sources:
Top panel – Membership data are from successive *Annual Reports* of Certification Officer. They are self-reported by trade unions and include some retired, self-employed, unemployed and non-UK residents. Therefore it is not possible to precisely match the numerator and denominator when calculating density. The civilian workforce consists of employees, self-employed and unemployed from British Labour Statistics *Historical Abstract*, HMSO 1971 and successive issues of DE *Gazette* and *Labour Market Trends*.
Bottom panel – From LFS, autumn of each year. Membership data refer to total membership and include some 300,000 members who are self-employed. Density refers to the proportion of employees who are members. From 1995 to 2001 UK membership (which includes Northern Ireland) was 3 per cent above GB membership. Data for 1989, the first time the union membership question was asked in the LFS, through 1994 are only available for GB. Those figures have therefore been multiplied by 1.03 to give the corresponding UK figure. Density data 1995–2001 are virtually identical for UK and GB, so the GB figure is used for density for earlier years. See Brook (2002).

consisting of 7.1 million employees and 0.3 million self-employed people. Since the Blair government came to power in 1997 the number of employees who are members has been roughly constant at a little over 7 million. This is equivalent to a density figure (i.e. percent unionised) of 29 per cent.

Density alters by demographic, job and workplace characteristics (see Table 11.2). It varies little by gender or ethnic origin but rises with age, falling off slightly past age 50. Those with higher education have density levels sub-

Table 11.2   Characteristics of union density UK, employees in employment, autumn 2001

Characteristic	Density (%)	Characteristic	Density (%)
All	29	*Workplace*	
Demographics		**Sector**	
Gender		Private	19
Male	30	Public	59
Female	28		
		Size	
Age		<25 employees	15
<20	5	25+ employees	36
20–29	19		
30–39	30	**Selected industries**	
40–49	38	Manufacturing	27
50+	35	Energy & water	53
		Hotels & restaurants	5
Ethnic origin		Business services	11
White	29	Public administration	59
Non-white	26	Education	53
		Health	45
Highest qualification			
Degree	37	**Country**	
Other Higher	44	England	28
A-level	28	Scotland	35
GCSE	23	Wales	39
None	24	Northern Ireland	40
Job-related		**Regions of England**	
Length of service		North East	39
<2 years	14	North West	34
2–10 years	27	Yorks & Humberside	31
10+ years	53	East Midlands	28
		West Midlands	30
Selected occupations		East	23
Professional	48	London	26
Skilled trades	30	South East	22
Sales	13	South West	26

Source: Brook (2002), Tables 2, 3, 4. Data from Labour Force Survey, autumn 2001.

stantially above those with fewer qualifications. Teachers, nurses and other professional workers have the highest density of any occupation (48 per cent) and sales occupations the lowest (11 per cent). Density rises sharply by tenure, a mirror image of the well-known finding that labour turnover is lower in workplaces which recognise a union.

Public sector aggregate membership is larger than that in the private sector. People who work in public administration, education and health are far more likely to be members than those employed in business services or hotels and restaurants: in the public sector, three employees in five are members but the corresponding figure for the private sector is fewer than one in five. Manufacturing now has a union density (27 per cent) below that for the whole economy (29 per cent). Small workplaces (under 25 employees) have density levels less than half those of larger establishments. And an individual is more likely to belong to a union if she or he lives in the northern part of the UK than in southern regions.

The number and structure of unions has altered dramatically too. A century ago there were 1,300 unions and at the end of the Second World War there were still nearly 800. Mergers, takeovers and the decline of unions for specific craft groups, like the Jewish Bakers and Sheffield Wool Sheep Shearers, has reduced this figure to 226. Indeed, the 11 unions each with over 250,000 members now account for almost three-quarters of total membership (see Table 11.3). But some small unions do survive – including the Association of Somerset Inseminators and the Church and Oswaldwistle Power Loom Overlookers Society.

Table 11.3   Trade unions: distribution by size, 2000

Number of members	Number of unions	Membership	% of all unions	% of all members
Under 100	50	1,744	22.1	0.0
100–999	62	26,253	27.4	0.4
1,000–9,999	61	206,347	27.0	2.7
10,000–99,999	37	1,147,134	16.4	14.7
100,000–249,999	5	764,881	2.2	9.8
250,000+	11	5,633,034	4.9	72.4
Total	226	7,779,393	100	100

Source: Calculated from Certification Office for Trade Unions and Employers' Associations, *Annual Report*, 2001–2002.

Going hand in hand with the decline in union penetration has been a profound change in the type of mechanisms that provide employees with a voice – a big switch away from representative voice to direct voice (see Table 11.4). Representative voice occurs via a recognised trade union or works council. Direct voice bypasses these intermediate institutions. Instead, management and employees communicate directly with one another through, for example, team briefings, regular meetings between senior management and the workforce and problem solving groups, such as quality circles. Between 1984 and 1998, the proportion of workplaces with only representative voice arrangements halved, while those relying just on a direct voice nearly trebled. What happened was that unionised workplaces added complementary direct communication systems, while nearly all new workplaces opted for direct communication methods without recognising unions.

Table 11.4   Changes in worker voice arrangements, 1984–98 (%)

Type of voice arrangement	1984	1990	1998
Union only	24	14	9
Union and non-union	43	39	33
Non-union only	17	28	40
No voice	16	19	17
Representative voice only	29	18	14
Representative and direct voice	45	43	39
Direct voice only	11	20	30
No voice	16	19	17

Notes: Base – all workplaces with 25 or more employees, approximately 2,000 workplaces in each year. Union voice defined as one or more trade unions recognised by employers for pay bargaining or a joint consultative committee meeting at least once a month with representatives chosen through union channels. Non-union voice defined as a joint consultative committee meeting at least once a month with representatives not chosen through union channels, regular meetings between senior management and the workforce, briefing groups, problem-solving groups, or non-union employee representatives.

Source: Adapted from Millward, Bryson and Forth (2000), Tables 4.13 and 4.15.

The decline in membership

How can the relentless, sustained decline of membership in the last two decades of the twentieth century be explained? There is no single factor. Rather it was the consequence of interactions among the composition of the workforce and jobs; the roles of the state, employers, and individual workers; and of unions' own structures and policies.

It used to be thought that the business cycle also helped explain membership such that persistent unemployment led to declining density. But since 1993 unemployment has fallen continuously and so has density – the reverse of predictions from business cycle models – so this explanation can be ruled out.

Shifts in the composition of the workforce and jobs are one ingredient. More highly unionised sectors like cars and ships or the public sector, and individuals with a greater likelihood of being a member – males or full-timers for example – now account for a smaller proportion of total employment. So, as a matter of arithmetic, union membership also falls. But it turns out that such composition effects are less important than commonly realised, accounting for around a quarter of the fall in membership. Rather, the bulk of any explanation turns on convergence of membership within groups: unionisation of men has fallen to a similar rate to women and some convergence has also occurred for unionisation rates between full-timers and part-timers, large and small workplaces, and manufacturing and non-manufacturing.

Activities and policies of the state affect union membership both directly, for example by legislation promoting or undermining union security, and indirectly via its influence on the environment in which employers and unions operate. In the 1980s and 1990s the environment in which employers and unions conducted their activities was profoundly affected by the onslaught on public sector activities and greater emphasis than previously on product market competition. Public sector unions faced privatisation, compulsory competitive tendering and contracting-out. Collectivism was damaged by taking a million nurses and teachers out of collective bargaining. And in the private sector by promoting company-based payment systems like profit sharing and employee share ownership schemes through tax breaks (although there was surely no market failure to justify this) while disabling public protection for the lower paid by abandoning both Fair Wage Resolutions and wages councils. Product markets were altered for ever by abandoning state subsidies to sectors like coal, steel and shipbuilding, axing exchange controls and, less obviously, by policies such as selling rather than allocating commercial TV franchises and building the channel tunnel which undermined the monopoly power of the ferry companies. Each of these policies had the side effect of rupturing the previous, sometimes cosy, relationships between capital and labour.

Industrial relations legislation plays a more direct role in the ebb and flow of membership. In the 1980s, legislation impaired union security by weakening and then outlawing the closed shop and interfering in check-off arrangements. The strike threat, a fundamental source of union power, was weakened by a succession of laws which permitted a union to be sued, introduced ballots prior to a strike, and outlawed both secondary and unofficial action. This legislation simultaneously raised the cost to unions of organising and reduced the costs to employers of opposing them.

Did employers become more hostile to unions in the 1980s and 1990s? There is no evidence that union activity – the wage premium causing higher labour costs for example – resulted in a higher rate of closures among union plants compared with their non-union counterparts. Nor did management embark on wholesale derecognition of trade unions: the derecognition rate was around 1 per cent a year between 1984 and 1998. Although derecognition in some national newspapers, TV and docks generated bitter industrial disputes and considerable media interest, such management action in other sectors was quite rare.

Rather, union decline turns mainly on the inability of unions to achieve recognition in young workplaces reflecting, for example, Thatcherite views among some managers, the growth of individualism and breakdown of class solidarity, and more investment from overseas. In 1980 three-fifths of establishments under ten years old recognised unions, similar to the fraction of workplaces ten or more years old. But over the next two decades unions found it progressively harder to organise new workplaces (see Table 11.5). By 1998 just over a quarter of workplaces under ten years of age recognised a trade union, only half the corresponding figure for older workplaces. This inability to get much of a foothold in new workplaces was not confined to private services. More stunning was the virtual collapse of recognition in newer manufacturing plants. Only 14 per cent of manufacturing workplaces set up after 1980 recognise a union compared to 50 per cent of those established in 1980 or before.

Table 11.5   Union recognition by age of establishment (%)

Proportion of establishments with any union recognised for collective bargaining	1980	1984	1990	1998
A. Aggregate	64	66	53	42
B. By age of establishment				
Under 10 years	59	58	34	27
10+ years	65	68	59	50
C. By set-up date				
1980 or before	64	66	61	56
After 1980	–	54	35	30
D. Union recognition in	All	Private sector	Private sector	Public
1998 by set-up date	establishments	manufacturing	services	sector
1980 or before	54	50	28	88
After 1980	29	14	18	85
Gap	–26	–36	–10	–02

Notes: 1) Aggregate (i.e. all establishments with 25 or more workers) percentages taken from the sourcebooks for the 1980, 1984 and 1990 WIRS and the 1998 WERS. 2) 1998 recognition data recodes recognition to zero for 15 workplaces which recognised teacher unions but who in fact had pay set by the Pay Review Bodies (this follows the same procedure as in Chapter 10 of Cully et al., 1999).

Sources: Machin (2000) Table 3 (panel D); Machin (2003) Table 1 (panels A, B, C).

One key advantage to the individual employee of belonging to a union is the wage premium compared with equivalent non-members. This premium was approximately constant at around 10 per cent in the 1980s but at least halved in the 1990s – indeed some studies report there is no longer any

See p178—9

premium to joining a union. Partly as a consequence of such lower benefits to membership there has been a large rise in the fraction of the workforce that has never been a union member, up from 28 per cent in 1983 to 48 per cent in 2001. It is not that extant members are quitting but more that unions cannot get individuals to join in the first place. Another facet of declining overall membership is the ebbing of density where unions are recognised. Younger employees are much less likely to belong to a union than older workers and this gap in membership rates by age has grown dramatically recently. This is a worrying trend from the unions' viewpoint because such non-membership is prone to persist across generations. Therefore union membership in future turns on getting recognised in newer workplaces and attracting younger employees into membership – a difficult task if they (or their parents) have never experienced membership and if the benefits of membership are demonstrably, or perceived to be, below those two decades ago.

Unions' own structures and policies matter too. Consider a couple of examples concerning structure. Some unions, like TGWU and ASLEF, did not find it easy to align the shop steward role in a decentralised system with the need for a national voice. And many union mergers were simply market share unionism – shuffling around existing members – rather than designed to achieve scale economies in order to release resources for organising.

Policy was often not clear either. The balance between servicing existing members and organising new ones was not always thought through. And, till recently, concerns of female members – work–life balance, parental leave etc. – have had low priority. In dealing with employers the union movement took an age to come to terms with the break-up of national bargaining in the private sector and single union deals. Recent emphasis on cooperative industrial relations ('partnership') hints that these lessons have now been learnt.

So it is not surprising that union membership plummeted in the 1980s and 1990s. The conjunction of hostile forces played a major part. How could unions resist the altered structure of jobs, rising unemployment (in the 1980s and early 1990s), a belligerent state, more intense employer opposition and the growth of individualism? Unions do not thrive in adversity. In the 1950s and 1960s, under the post-war settlement and the growth of the welfare state, unions flourished. Then, in the 1970s, when that settlement disintegrated the union movement was well dug in – the fifth estate of the realm which many joined even if they disliked it. But in the last two decades of higher unemployment, altered industrial structure and intense product market competition, unions needed the support of workers and employers. By and large they did not get it. What had previously been conforming behaviour – to recognise and to belong to a union – became deviant. Whether or not this trend continues turns, in large part, on what unions do – to which we now turn.

What do unions do?

Forty years ago Alan Flanders, the most perceptive contemporary observer, suggested that unions have both a 'vested interest' and 'sword of justice' effect. The vested interest impact, similar to the monopoly face of unions set out by Richard Freeman, turns on unions' influence on pay, productivity, profits, investment and employment. The question is, essentially, what effect do unions have on workplace and firm performance? The sword of justice – vividly described by Flanders as unions' 'stirring music' – is more about fairness and due process. In addition unions also impact on employee relations through their bearing on the industrial relations climate and job satisfaction. These will be considered in turn.

Workplace performance

If the presence of a union in a workplace or firm raises the pay level, unless productivity rises correspondingly, financial performance is likely to be worse. If the product market is uncompetitive this might imply a simple transfer from capital to labour with no efficiency effects, but it is more likely to lead to lower investment rates and economic senescence. In the 1970s and 1980s the evidence indicated that union members received a pay premium, but without the corresponding rise in productivity. If anything demarcations, unofficial industrial action and multi-unionism lowered productivity. Hence profitability in workplaces with union recognition was below that in non-union workplaces. But, as we saw above, the world has moved on: what effect have those changes had on workplace performance?

One major reason for belonging to a union is that, historically, union members have received a pay premium ('wage gap') over similar non-union members. A recent exhaustive survey concluded that for the 1980s 'the consensus in the literature was that the mean hourly wage gap was approximately 10 per cent'. The outlawing of the closed shop in 1990, falling density where unions are recognised, more intense product market competition and the loss of nearly 6 million members was bound eventually to result in a lower wage premium. And so it has – evidenced in a number of recent studies.

Machin's (2001) study is particularly informative and is summarised in Table 11.6. For men, the wage premium fell from 9 per cent in 1991 to zero in 1999, while for women it fell from 16 per cent to 10 per cent over the eight years. More importantly, there is now no (wage) benefit to joining a union and no cost to leaving. Machin summarises his work: 'For men it used to pay to be in a union (in the early 1990s) and it used to pay to join a union, but by the end of the 1990s it does not. For women the answer is: it does still pay to be in a union, but not by as much as it used to, and it does not pay to newly join.'

By the end of the 1990s the average union–non-union differences in labour productivity were also negligible (Pencavel, 2003). Card and Freeman (2003) suggest that the elimination of the previous negative union productivity gap in the 1980s and 1990s contributed a 4.3 percentage point gain in aggregate productivity over this 20-year span. This is about one-sixth of the difference in the growth rates between what they call 'pre-reform 1960–79' and 'post-reform 1979–99'.

Table 11.6 Union wage effects 1991, 1995, 1999 (%)

	Cross section	Joiners	Leavers
Males			
1991	+9	+9	–13
1995	+6	0	0
1999	0	0	0
Females			
1991	+16	+15	–14
1995	+16	+6	–8
1999	+10	0	0

Notes: 1) Data from BHPS waves 1, 5–9 (1991, 1995–99) between 1,288 and 1,943 men and 1,300 and 1,939 women. 2) Definition of union: (i) cross section, union recognition in workplace; (ii) joiners and leavers, union membership. 3) Data refer to average union/non-union wage gap (%) controlling for age, age squared, education qualifications, industry, pt/ft, public/private sector.

Source: Machin (2001).

There remain two sets of circumstances when union recognition continues to be associated with lower labour productivity. First, productivity is lower in workplaces with multi-unionism and fragmented bargaining (Pencavel, 2003). But such multi-unionism is now rather unusual – only 7 per cent of workplaces are characterised by fragmented bargaining. Second, when the product market is monopolistic, with just one to five competitors, productivity is also lower (Metcalf, 2003b).

In the past, the impact of union recognition on wages and productivity fed through into an adverse effect on profitability or financial performance. Now there are no significant overall links, on average, between union presence and financial performance – reflecting the weaker union impact on both pay and productivity levels that unions now have compared with one or two decades ago. But, again, this 'average' result conceals some interesting findings. Multi-unionism still results in worse financial performance where the bargaining remains fragmented. Where the firm recognises a union it will have a less good financial performance if the union organises under half the workforce: encompassing unions yield superior performance to weaker ones. Finally, the product market remains crucial. Any union effect turns on there being few competitors in the product market – permitting unions to switch some of the surplus from owners of capital to labour.

Thus, on average, the impact of unions on firms' pay, productivity and profitability is now small and probably confined to monopolistic and/or multi-union workplaces. In these circumstances it is not surprising that there is also no strong evidence that union recognition hinders investment in plant and machinery. Anyway there has never been much such evidence. Despite the decline in unionisation rates and the apparent shift to more cooperative relations with employers, the rate of growth of capital per worker (or per hour) did not accelerate in the 1980s and 1990s relative to that in West Germany or France (Card and Freeman, 2003). This implies unions probably did not dampen investment in the earlier period. Further, the evidence on investment in human capital is that unionised workplaces invest more in their workforce than their non-union counterparts (Metcalf, 2003b).

But one profoundly worrying trend remains for unions. Other things equal, employment in a unionised workplace grows some 3 per cent a year more slowly (or falls 3 per cent a year more quickly) than in a non-union workplace (see Table 11.7). Even though it is unlikely that union activity is itself the cause of this differential change in employment – which has now been in evidence for 20 years – if it persists the implications for future membership levels are very serious.

Table 11.7   Employment change, % yearly, private sector workplaces, 1990–98

	Change in employment % per year		
	All workplaces	Manufacturing	Services
Raw change			
Union recognition	–1.8	–0.7	–2.4
Non-union	1.4	1.5	1.4
Net union	–3.2	–2.2	–3.8
After including controls	–3.9	–3.4	–4.7

Notes: from WIRS panel 1990–98, 558 workplaces, employing 25+ employees in 1990 and 1998. Controls are: workplace size; % non-manual; single independent workplace; region; sector; uses short-term contracts; no good/service accounts for 25 per cent+ sales; number of competitors; financial performance better than average; operating considerably below capacity.

Source: Calculated from Bryson (2001).

Sword of justice

Any impact of trade unions on economic performance is more muted than it was 20 years ago. But unions still wield the sword of justice in the workplace. Unions narrow the distribution of pay, promote equal opportunity and family friendly policies, and lower the rate of industrial injuries (Metcalf, 2003a).

The spread of pay among unionised workers is smaller than the spread among their non-union counterparts. This is because unions protect the pay of those on low earnings and because unionised workplaces make more use of objective criteria – seniority for example – in setting pay rather than subjective factors – like merit – preferred in non-union establishments. Unions also compress the pay structure between different groups in the labour market: women and men, blacks and whites, and those with health problems and the healthy. If there were no unions the gender pay gap would be 2.6 per cent wider and the race pay gap 1.4 per cent bigger. These are very substantial effects. When it was introduced in 1999, the National Minimum Wage particularly impacted on female pay – two-thirds of those affected were women – but it only narrowed the gender pay gap by a little under 1 per cent. The impact of unions on narrowing the gender pay gap is three times as strong as that of the National Minimum Wage.

Union recognition is associated with a much greater likelihood of the workplace having some form of equal opportunity policy and an array of family friendly policies designed to encourage female employment. These practices include parental leave, working from home, term only contracts, the possibility of switching from full- to part-time employment and job shares. Women in unionised workplaces are much better off in terms of career opportunities, flexible work arrangements and general support for family responsibilities than their counterparts in non-union workplaces.

Such family friendly policies go hand-in-hand with better performing workplaces. An establishment with an array of family friendly policies has a greater likelihood of above average financial performance, labour productivity, product or service quality, and lower quit and absentee rates than a workplace without such practices. Even if the causal mechanism behind such associations is unclear this evidence is surely something for unions to build on in their attempts to appeal simultaneously to management and workers.

Unions also cut industrial accidents. An accident in this context is where an employee has sustained any one of eight injuries during working hours over the last 12 months, including bone fractures, burns, amputations and any injury that results in immediate hospitalisation for more than 24 hours. Unions tend to organise in workplaces where an accident is more likely to occur, but their presence lowers the rate by a quarter, compared with non-union plants. This favourable effect of lowering accidents occurs because unions lobby for safety legislation and take industrial action locally to make the workplace safer. Many trade unions also provide health and safety courses. Further, a union presence will tend to promote 'voice' over 'exit': where a union is recognised, employees with concerns about accidents are more likely to be listened to rather than labelled as a nuisance.

Effect on industrial relations

A union presence also influences workers' perceptions about the governance of their organisation. This includes the climate of relations between management and employees, the trust employees have in their managers, and managerial performance. On average, workplace governance is perceived as poorer among employees in workplaces with recognised unions, relative to their counterparts in non-union establishments. Better perceptions about governance in non-union workplaces may flow from the use of direct voice – briefing groups, team meetings and the like – rather than representative voice via the union, discussed above.

This 'average' finding is only part of the story. Once the decision is taken to recognise a union, governance is profoundly affected by the way the parties go about their business. First, governance is perceived to be better by workers when there is a balance of power between management and union in the workplace. Very strong or very weak unions detract from a good climate or high trust. Second, when the union is recognised it is better for management to support membership: recognition coupled with hostility to individual membership produces worse outcomes. Third, unions are perceived to be more effective when workplace governance is good. Managers' perceptions of the climate of employee relations have also been analysed and confirm the thrust of these findings concerning individual employees. Unions with on-site representatives, which have the capacity to operate as a strong voice for workers, or a strong agent for the employer, are held by managers to generate a good climate. The implications are clear cut. Once the decision is taken to recognise a union it makes sense to encourage membership and ensure that the union is effective in representing employees. This suggests, for example, that partnership arrangements promoting cooperative employee relations are likely to yield superior governance to adversarial, fragmented relations.

Membership or non-membership of a union may also influence job satisfaction. The standard finding is that union members are less satisfied in their jobs than otherwise similar non-members. This is normally attributed to union voice politicising workers, but our research suggests otherwise. Rather, lower job satisfaction among union members flows from the demographic characteristics of employees who become union members and the characteristics of workplaces (size, region, etc.) that employ them – unions themselves do not lower satisfaction in the job.

The future: dissolution or resurgence?

What can unions do to reverse declining density and achieve a sustained rise in membership? Broadly there are two routes to revival. Either employment in unionised sectors of the economy has to grow relative to non-union employment or unions must engage in more intense organising activity and enhance their appeal to both employers and potential members.

In the 1950s and 1960s employment in manufacturing was approximately stable at around 9 million. Unionisation rose by some 2 million then partly reflecting the spread of membership from male and/or craft workers in a plant – drivers and engineers for example – to female assembly line workers. Later, in the 1970s, the number of jobs in the highly unionised public sector grew by 1.6 million and the closed shop extended rapidly in both manufacturing and the public sector. The closed shop stretched into manufacturing sectors it had not previously reached including food, drink and tobacco; clothing and footwear; and chemicals. But more important was the increased penetration of the closed shop into the nationalised industries where three-quarters of employees, including white collar workers, were covered. By the end of the 1970s 5.2 million employees, a quarter of the total, were in a closed shop. In the 1980s and 1990s manufacturing employment plunged by 5 million, the public sector lost 2 million jobs and the closed shop was outlawed. If differential employment growth is to be one mechanism to hike membership the question is whether alterations in the structure of jobs in the next decade or so will follow the 1960s and 1970s or, from the unions' viewpoint, the barren 1980s and 1990s.

It is unlikely that any boost in the aggregate number of jobs will occur disproportionately in the unionised sector. In the public sector, while the number of teachers, nurses and police is rising, overall there will not be much growth in employment in the next decade. In manufacturing, employment now is only a little over a third of its 1966 peak and jobs continue to go. In the last year, for example, many jobs were axed in ailing high-tech companies like Ericsson, Marconi and Motorola, and proud British brands like Dyson vacuum cleaners, Raleigh cycles and Jensen Motors moved production abroad. Anyway unions find it just as difficult to get recognised in new manufacturing plants as in private services. Similarly there is no suggestion of strong growth in jobs in utilities or transport. It is likely, instead, that the major share of any growth in employment will occur in private services with a present union density of 15 per cent. So disproportionate growth in employment in the union sector is not the route to the restoration of unions' fortunes.

Alternatively, unions can invest more in organising and servicing activity, which may yield a larger return presently than in the last two decades because the climate of opinion fostered by the state is no longer hostile to collective labour institutions. But the allocation of such servicing and organising investment requires considerable thought. Consider Table 11.8: 36 per cent of employees are covered by a collective agreement on pay but over one-third of these (14 per cent) are free-riders, not members of a union. Looking at the evidence the other way round, a quarter (7 per cent) of total union members (29 per cent) are not covered by collective agreements for their pay. This includes teachers and nurses whose pay is settled by arbitration rather than collective agreements. And in the last decade many (particularly smaller) workplaces have abandoned collective bargaining over pay without actually derecognising the union. By far the majority of employees (57 per cent) are neither covered by a collective agreement nor are a union member.

In the 1990s one in three private sector workplaces abandoned collective bargaining, but only a quarter of these formally derecognised the union (Charlwood, 2002). This reinforces Brown et al.'s (1998) point that recognition and derecognition are not all-or-nothing decisions: 'The depth of recognition is important. This is most clearly defined by the scope of bargaining permitted. An employer can refuse to bargain over some issues, such as manning, or machine speeds, or pay, and unless the union can force to the contrary, that set of issues remains under (or returns to) management unilateral control.'

Table 11.8   Coverage of collective agreements on pay and conditions and union membership: UK employees in employment, autumn 2001

| | Pay and Conditions covered by collective agreement? | | |
	Yes	No	Total
Union member	5.5m	1.7m	7.2m
	22%	7%	29%
Not union member	3.4m	14.1m	17.5m
	14%	57%	71%
Total	8.9m	15.8m	24.7m
	36%	64%	100%

Source: Calculated from Brook (2002). Example: 8.9 million employees (36 per cent) are covered by collective bargaining. Of these, 5.5 million (22 per cent) are union members and 3.4 million (14 per cent) are not union members.

The evidence in Table 11.8 provides remarkable food for thought for unions. Consider each cell in turn. First, unions must continue to service the 5.5 million workers (22 per cent) who have their pay set by collective bargaining and belong to a union. The majority are in the public sector. Negotiating collective agreements is a vital element of the service provided by the union but activities on behalf of individual members also form a major component of the tasks performed by union officers and shop stewards. These include advice on employment matters, representing members in employers' procedures and before courts and tribunals, and providing members with information about their company or organisation. Some unions have adopted partnerships with management to improve services. In water supply, for example, one supplier was in the process of shedding 1,000 jobs at a rate of 200 a year for five years. A partnership agreement emphasising retraining and redeployment was signed in the middle of this process and over half the potential redundant group were retrained and employed elsewhere in the utility. Other gains for members from the partnership agreement, as reported by the union, include a shorter work week and improvement in the work–life balance via a choice of either 12- or 8-hour shifts.

Second, absorbing the 3.4 million free-riders (14 per cent of employees) – so called 'in-fill' recruitment – is a potentially attractive (cheap) method of boosting membership. The growth in free-riding runs parallel with the rise in the number of 'never members'. So union intervention at the recruitment stage is important. For example a recent partnership agreement in the insurance sector permits the union to make a presentation at induction meetings where the management also encourage employees to join the union. UNISON – whose membership density has probably dropped to around 60 per cent (from 85 per cent 20 years ago) – has set up a training course – Winning the Organised Workplace – to motivate officials, shop stewards, members and staff to revitalise workplace membership. It provides organising skills including dealing with face-to-face recruitment and team building; it also trains lay representatives to talent spot potential new shop stewards from among new members. A particular problem for UNISON and other unions pursuing in-fill recruitment is the dispersion of workers across geographic locations. School meal workers, for example, are located across several schools within a Local Education Authority and in the voluntary sector many workplaces of an individual charity are scattered across Britain, often with only a few workers.

In many ways the 1.7 million employees (7 per cent) who are union members but not covered by a collective agreement on pay are the most interesting group. It includes members of staff associations, some teachers and nurses whose pay is set by arbitration, some members signed up in organising campaigns which have not yet reached fruition, and workers in firms who have derecognised the union for pay bargaining but perhaps continue to recognise for dealing with individual grievances – as Brown et al. (1998) point out, recognition is not all or nothing and its scope varies greatly. HSBC provides a nice cameo of this group. It withdrew recognition for managerial grades in the mid-1990s but a mishandled introduction of performance-related pay, an imposed inferior pay deal and growing redundancies gave a boost to membership. In 2001 recognition was restored for this grade – but without an agreement to negotiate on pay. Unions face a hard task convincing such members that membership remains worthwhile.

Last but not least are the 14.1 million (57 per cent) of employees who are neither members nor have their pay and conditions set by collective bargaining. Unions must perform a delicate balancing act here: organising expenditure on this group represents a 'tax' on existing members. If sub-scriptions rise to finance the necessary organising so will the number of free-riders if new recruits to the organisation choose to remain non-union.

Around a fifth of these 14 million workers either desire union representa-tion or would be very likely to join a union if one were available. This suggests a 'representation gap' of some 2.8 million employees, a potentially rich pool of employees for unions to organise. However, in order to achieve recognition these employees need to be concentrated by firm or workplace or there will never be a union available to join. There are some interesting occupations involved here. MSF-Amicus now has some 2000 members from the Church of England clergy who have no employment rights – their employer is held to be divine not earthly. And the GMB has had some success in recruiting lap dancers – almost precipitating an inter-union dispute. The steel union,

ISTC, argued that as the dancers worked with metal poles it should have jurisdiction over this occupation!

Recognition occurs voluntarily or, since 2000, via the law. Voluntary recognition stems either from true love (cooperation between capital and labour) or a marriage of convenience (a pragmatic second best). The legal route, inevitably associated with adversarial industrial relations, is a shotgun marriage, imposed on a reluctant employer by an arm of the state. Under the legal route, if a union can prove a majority of membership in the bargaining unit, then it gains recognition. If not, a ballot is held in which the union must win 50 per cent+ of the votes cast in the ballot and must have at least 40 per cent of the workforce in the bargaining unit voting 'yes'.

The direct effect of this law has been tiny. The law came into effect in June 2000. Between then and December 2002 there were 52 cases of statutory recognition covering fewer than 20,000 workers. However, its indirect or shadow effect is larger. Over 1,000 voluntary agreements – partnerships or marriages of convenience – have been signed in the last three years bringing around a quarter of a million new workers under recognition (DTI 2003). But the union focus remains traditional: (ex-) public services, manufacturing, finance and transport and communication. Only one in six newly covered workers is in the rest of the private sector.

It is plausible that, in the longer run, the passage of the EU Directive on Information and Consultation will influence unions' futures rather more than the recognition law. It establishes, for the first time, permanent and general arrangements for information and consultation for all workers in the UK in organisations employing more than 50 employees. It will cover three-quarters of the British labour force. Some employers may see this as an opportunity to create weak voice mechanisms; for others it may constitute a chance to institute stronger arrangements complementing other aspects of human resource management. The tough job for unions is to build on these schemes and to maintain and expand their role within them. The evidence seems to be that a union presence complements these arrangements and makes them more effective. This legislation might also be the catalyst for greater emphasis on pan-European unions.

In broad terms there are just over 3 million free-riders and just under 3 million employees who would be very likely to join the union if one existed at their place of work. If unions could organise annually a twentieth of this pool of 6 million potential members their fortunes would be transformed. The challenge for the union movement is to organise these extra 0.3 million members a year while still servicing their existing 7 million members.

References

Brook, K. (2002), 'Trade Union Membership: an Analysis of Data from the Autumn 2001 LFS', *Labour Market Trends*, July, pp. 343–54.

Brown, W., Deakin, S., Hudson, M., Pratten, C. and Ryan, P. (1998), *The Individualisation of Employment Contracts in Britain*, DTI Research Paper, June.

Bryson, A. (2001), 'Employee Voice, Workplace Closure and Employment Growth', PSI Discussion Paper 6.

Card, D. and Freeman, R. (2003), 'What Have Two Decades of British Economic Reform Delivered?', in R. Blundell, D. Card and R. Freeman (eds), *Seeking a Premier League Economy*, University of Chicago Press for NBER: Chicago.

Charlwood, A. (2002), 'Why Do Non-Union Employees Want to Unionize?', *British Journal of Industrial Relations*, 40 (3), pp. 463–92.

Cully, M., Woodland, S., O'Reilly, A., Dix, G. (1999), *Britain at Work: As Depicted by the 1998 Workplace Employee Relations Survey*, Routledge: London.

Department of Trade and Industry (2003), *Review of the Employment Act 1999: Consultation Document*, February.

Gospel, H. and Wood, S. (eds) (2003), *Representing Workers: Trade Union Representation and Membership in Britain*, Routledge: London.

Machin, S. (2000), 'Union Decline in Britain', *British Journal of Industrial Relations*, Vol. 38(4).

Machin, S. (2001), 'Does It Still Pay to Be in or to Join a Union?', mimeo, Centre for Economic Performance, London School of Economics.

Machin, S. (2003), 'Trade Union Decline, New Workplace And New Workers', in H. Gospel and S. Wood (eds), *Representing Workers: Trade Union Representation and Membership in Britain*, Routledge: London.

Metcalf, D. (ed.) (2003a), *Future of Unions in Modern Britain*, Mid-Term Report on Leverhulme Trust-Funded Research Programme 2000–2002: http://cep.lse.ac.uk/future_of_unions

Metcalf, D. (2003b), 'Unions and Productivity, Financial Performance and Investment: International Evidence', in J. Addison and C. Schnabel (eds) *International Handbook of Trade Unions*, Edward Elgar.

Millward, N., Bryson, A. and Forth, J. (2000), *All Change at Work?*, Routledge: London.

Pencavel, J. (2003), 'The Surprising Retreat of Union Britain', in R. Blundell, D. Card and R. Freeman (eds), *Seeking a Premier League Economy*, University of Chicago Press for NBER: Chicago.

Part III:
Wages

12
Wage Inequality Since 1975

Stephen Machin

Key findings

- Wage inequality has risen significantly in the UK since the late 1970s.
- The most rapid widening of the gap between well paid and low paid workers occurred in the 1980s, but wage inequality probably continued to rise (at least for men), albeit at a much slower pace, through the 1990s.
- An important feature of rising wage inequality in the last quarter century was increased wage gaps between workers with high levels of education as compared to those with low education levels.
- Educational wage differentials rose at the same time as the education levels of the workforce rose suggesting that the relative demand for more educated workers increased.
- There is some preliminary evidence that wage differentials by education may have stopped rising at the end of the 1990s and start of the 2000s, which is consistent with the very rapid supply increases that occurred with the expansion of the higher education system.

Introduction

A striking feature of the UK labour market of the recent past has been rapidly increasing wage gaps between higher paid and lower paid workers. In fact levels of wage inequality are higher than at any point since the Second World War and probably since representative statistics were first collected at the end of the nineteenth century (Machin, 1996). Rising wage inequality has received wide attention from academics and policy commentators, for example with various aspects of recent labour market policy (like the National Minimum Wage, or the Working Families Tax Credit) being geared towards having some impact on the widening distribution of labour market rewards.

This chapter updates numbers on wage inequality to consider the most recent moves in the structure of wages. It first reports overall indices measuring the inequality of wages from a variety of different microdata sources, before considering wage changes at different points of the wage distribution. The focus then shifts to consider how wage differences by education level are related to increased inequality of wages. This is important since education levels have increased very dramatically over the period of rising wage inequality, yet so have wage differences between higher and lower education groups. Studying shifts by education enables one to have some insight into one of the more important factors underpinning increased wage inequality.

Changes in wage inequality

There are many ways to measure wage inequality, but a common statistic used in many official publications on the distribution of income and wealth is the Gini coefficient. The Gini coefficient is calculated from looking at shares of people at particular points in the distribution of interest and ranges from zero (complete equality if shares are equally distributed) to one (complete inequality). I have used Gini coefficients in previous descriptive pieces on wage inequality (e.g. Machin, 1999) and its advantage is that it gives a clear and simple depiction of the changes in inequality through time.

Data sources

There are a number of data sources that one can use to track trends in wage inequality in the UK. Each has its own advantages and disadvantages so I use a combination of them here. The longest time series are available from the household-level Family Expenditure Survey (FES) and the employer reported New Earnings Survey (NES). The potential drawbacks with the FES are its relatively small sample size, as it covers only around 10,000 people in work each year, and the fact that it does not contain any data on educational qualifications (containing information on years of schooling only since 1978). Sample size is not a problem for the NES which, in principle, covers 1 per cent of the working population (those whose National Insurance numbers end in 14), thereby generating large sample sizes (in what follows in the order of over 100,000 a year). But it should be noted that the NES has its own problems if one wishes to consider inequality trends: (i) it under-samples low wage part-time workers and (ii) there is no data on education.

The other data sources I draw upon are the General Household Survey (GHS) and the Labour Force Survey (LFS). A concern with the GHS is that it does not report hourly wages on a consistent basis through time. However, like the FES and NES it also spans a long time period, but unlike them it also has the big advantage of reporting data on the highest educational qualification of individuals. So, when I turn to shifts in wages across education groups I mainly use the GHS. The LFS only has wage data since 1992 (when it became a quarterly survey) and so is of less use to look at longer run changes. However, it is made available to researchers more rapidly than the other data sources and can therefore be used to look at more contemporary aspects of the wage structure.

Trends in Gini coefficients

Tables 12.1a and 12.1b report Gini coefficients between 1975 and 2001 for men and women respectively, from the three data sources that have wage data going back to 1975, together with the LFS since 1994. The temporal pattern of the Gini coefficients is clear in the 1970s and 1980s, irrespective of whether one looks at weekly or hourly earnings, and is rather similar by

Table 12.1a   Changes in overall male wage inequality, Gini coefficients, 1975–2001

	Weekly wages				Hourly wages		
	FES	NES	LFS	GHS	FES	NES	LFS
1975	.244	.236	–	.249	.239	.223	–
1976	.240	.239	–	.242	.235	.229	–
1977	.238	.233	–	.240	.236	.221	–
1978	.244	.239	–	.237	.244	.227	–
1979	.246	.245	–	.231	.240	.228	–
1980	.262	.245	–	.244	.256	.233	–
1981	.266	.251	–	.250	.264	.246	–
1982	.260	.254	–	.277	.258	.248	–
1983	.279	.260	–	.256	.276	.253	–
1984	.276	.274	–	.281	.273	.261	–
1985	.292	.275	–	.283	.285	.261	–
1986	.298	.279	–	.294	.287	.266	–
1987	.319	.289	–	.301	.305	.277	–
1988	.311	.295	–	.298	.299	.284	–
1989	.302	.298	–	.302	.291	.288	–
1990	.324	.299	–	.301	.312	.289	–
1991	.321	.303	–	.313	.301	.294	–
1992	.330	.306	–	.316	.309	.296	–
1993	.338	.311	–	.314	.319	.301	–
1994	.338	.316	.311	.324	.320	.308	.317
1995	.326	.322	.310	.325	.358	.317	.317
1996	.329	.325	.328	.312	.335	.318	.331
1997	.337	.320	.320	–	.327	.319	.321
1998	.350	.328	.322	.326	.340	.325	.322
1999	.356	.328	.321	–	.348	.325	.319
2000	.346	.331	.321	–	.341	.326	.323
2001	.361	.338	.324	–	.357	.333	.325
Change 1975–80	.018	.009	–	−.005	.017	.010	–
Change 1980–90	.062	.054	–	.057	.056	.056	–
Change 1990–2001	.037	.039	.013[*]	.025[**]	.045	.044	.008[*]

Notes: [*] denotes change from 1994 to 2001; [**] denotes change from 1990 to 1998.

gender. There was a slight fall in inequality in the mid to late 1970s, after which inequality rises. From the late 1970s and through the 1980s the inequality of earnings rose massively for both sexes. For example, the average increase in the five reported Gini coefficients for male earnings in Table 12.1a over the 1980–90 period was .057. This corresponds to over a 20 per cent increase relative to the 1980 level. For females, the averaged Gini also rises sharply, by .054 between 1980 and 1990.

Table 12.1b   Changes in overall female wage inequality, Gini coefficients, 1975–2001

	Weekly wages				Hourly wages		
	FES	NES	LFS	GHS	FES	NES	LFS
1975	.356	.281	–	.349	.256	.215	–
1976	.360	.294	–	.350	.261	.225	–
1977	.353	.288	–	.349	.244	.206	–
1978	.353	.290	–	.347	.258	.205	–
1979	.355	.295	–	.342	.252	.203	–
1980	.359	.300	–	.350	.253	.210	–
1981	.377	.313	–	.365	.279	.231	–
1982	.381	.315	–	.371	.270	.227	–
1983	.388	.323	–	.364	.281	.230	–
1984	.381	.337	–	.375	.277	.236	–
1985	.387	.335	–	.390	.283	.236	–
1986	.386	.340	–	.390	.298	.237	–
1987	.397	.348	–	.400	.311	.240	–
1988	.394	.355	–	.392	.310	.250	–
1989	.393	.362	–	.394	.295	.260	–
1990	.401	.366	–	.395	.320	.260	–
1991	.396	.370	–	.401	.300	.268	–
1992	.409	.377	–	.402	.306	.270	–
1993	.403	.377	–	.414	.306	.277	–
1994	.403	.380	.386	.403	.307	.278	.307
1995	.407	.386	.382	.404	.300	.289	.307
1996	.400	.388	.403	.393	.312	.288	.320
1997	.403	.371	.387	–	.317	.288	.307
1998	.403	.373	.387	.404	.310	.288	.306
1999	.412	.373	.382	–	.317	.287	.300
2000	.404	.375	.382	–	.328	.288	.303
2001	.391	.379	.378	–	.314	.295	.301
Change 1975–80	.003	.019	–	.001	–.003	–.005	–
Change 1980–90	.042	.066	–	.045	.067	.050	–
Change 1990–2001	–.010	.013	–.008*	.009**	–.006	.035	–.006*

Notes: * denotes change from 1994 to 2001; ** denotes change from 1990 to 1998.

In the 1990s the pattern is rather less clear if one looks at all the data sources reported. Some show basically no change and others show some increase. For example, there are always seen to be increases in male wage inequality, but there is some difference by data source. The increases in the male Gini coefficients between 1990 and 2001 (or the nearest change possible), reported in the bottom row of Table 12.1a, ranged from .013 in the LFS to .039 in the NES for weekly earnings and from .008 in LFS to .045 in FES for hourly earnings. For women the last row in Table 12.1b shows a less clear pattern, again with differences across data sources, but with little evidence of much change in wage inequality over the 1990 to 2001 time period.

Changes at different percentiles of the distribution

The Gini coefficient is a single summary number describing the inequality of earnings at a point in time and is a good measure for considering aggregate inequality trends. It is less useful for identifying shifts that lie behind the overall change. Table 12.2 therefore looks in more detail and uses FES data to report on what has happened to male and female real hourly earnings at different points in the distribution. It reports the level of hourly earnings at each decile of the distribution from different FES years and reports 90–10, 50–10 and 90–50 ratios in the final three columns.[1]

Table 12.2 Hourly wages (£) at decile points of the wage distribution, 1975–2000

	Percentiles									Ratios		
	10th	20th	30th	40th	50th	60th	70th	80th	90th	90–10	50–10	90–50
Men												
1975	3.89	4.76	5.39	5.94	6.47	7.10	7.83	8.84	10.89	2.80	1.66	1.68
1980	3.92	4.94	5.66	6.32	7.03	7.82	8.67	9.84	12.10	3.08	1.79	1.72
1985	3.99	5.14	6.03	6.80	7.63	8.55	9.69	11.37	14.14	3.54	1.91	1.85
1990	4.14	5.54	6.55	7.46	8.44	9.61	11.07	13.15	16.43	3.97	2.04	1.95
1995	4.29	5.52	6.60	7.63	8.71	9.86	11.24	13.18	16.54	3.86	2.03	1.90
2000	4.35	5.56	6.57	7.69	8.90	10.33	12.07	14.22	18.09	4.16	2.05	2.03
Women												
1975	2.47	2.96	3.39	3.76	4.15	4.52	5.02	5.74	7.28	2.94	1.68	1.75
1980	2.66	3.24	3.56	3.87	4.25	4.68	5.23	6.09	7.87	2.96	1.60	1.85
1985	2.85	3.37	3.70	4.12	4.60	5.21	5.97	7.07	9.17	3.22	1.61	1.99
1990	3.15	3.76	4.21	4.76	5.41	6.10	7.19	8.68	11.41	3.62	1.72	2.11
1995	3.35	3.88	4.45	5.11	5.88	6.62	7.74	9.26	11.94	3.57	1.76	2.03
2000	3.66	4.20	4.83	5.57	6.51	7.62	9.06	10.89	13.86	3.79	1.78	2.13

Notes: Calculated from FES data. Hourly wages in 2001 prices.

First consider the 90–10 wage ratio. Reassuringly this shows much the same pattern as the Ginis in Tables 12.1a and 12.1b. Wage inequality for both men and women rises very sharply from the late 1970s to the late 1980s/early 1990s, but slows down in the 1990s. The ratios describing the evolution of the lower end of the distribution (the 50–10 ratio) and the upper end (the 90–50 ratio) demonstrate that the 1980s rise in wage inequality was characterised by an opening out at both ends of the distribution with the highest earners doing much better than those in the middle, but in turn the middle doing much better than the bottom. But in the 1990s wage inequality at the bottom was tempered as the 50–10 seemed to stop rising.

In terms of growth at particular deciles, Figure 12.1 shows the yearly percentage change in hourly wages of men at the 10th, 50th and 90th percentiles in the 1970s, 1980s and 1990s. The 1980s rise in wage inequality is illustrated very clearly as wage growth at the 90th percentile outstrips the 50th and 10th by some distance. But the period from the start of the 1990s to the middle of that decade is different, showing low real wage growth at all percentiles. Towards the latter half of the 1990s the top seems to grow quite rapidly again, with what rise there is in wage inequality coming from a widening out of the top relative to the middle. In fact data for the last couple of years show a little blip up at the 10th percentile reinforcing the pattern of no increase between the bottom and middle of the distribution in more recent years.

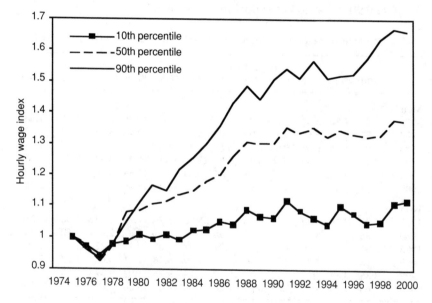

Figure 12.1   Men's real hourly wages (indexed to 1 in 1975)

Source: FES.

To summarise: the overall pattern over the last quarter century shows wage inequality falling a little in the 1970s, followed by the rapid rise of the 1980s, and then a slowdown, but with dispersion still increasing in the 1990s, though much less clearly in the latter part of the decade.

Wage differences by education

Education has long been recognised as an important determinant of earning power and there is a huge literature in economics on how to best estimate the wage gap between workers with more and less education (see Card, 1999). It is also true that rising wage gaps between workers with different education levels are closely linked to changes in the wage structure. Indeed, the recent period of rising wage inequality has also been characterised by rising wage differences between workers with high educational qualifications as compared to those with lower levels of education. This is despite the fact that the expansion of the higher education system now means there are more workers with higher qualifications working in the labour market.

Educational upgrading

Table 12.3 shows that there has been rapid upgrading of the educational status of the workforce since 1975. The table uses GHS data to report the percentage of workers in five bands according to their highest qualification: degree or higher; having a higher vocational qualification;[2] teaching/nursing; an intermediate group (comprising those with A-levels, or lower vocational qualifications); and no educational qualifications.

Table 12.3   Employment shares (%) by education, 1975–98

	1975	1980	1985	1990	1995	1998
Men						
Degree or higher	5.8	8.2	12.1	12.5	15.5	16.3
Higher vocational	4.7	6.8	10.5	11.4	11.7	12.1
Teaching and nursing	1.2	1.3	1.4	1.2	1.3	2.0
Intermediate	38.3	41.5	41.0	51.1	50.7	50.7
No qualifications	50.2	42.6	35.4	27.1	20.7	18.9
Women						
Degree or higher	2.2	3.6	6.2	7.5	10.8	12.5
Higher vocational	.7	1.3	2.0	2.9	3.8	2.7
Teaching and nursing	5.8	6.8	8.4	7.9	7.4	7.7
Intermediate	35.7	43.1	51.1	56.8	54.4	53.7
No qualifications	58.3	48.8	36.8	29.6	23.6	23.3

Notes: Calculated from GHS. For 1975 through 1995, statistics are based on three pooled years with the central year reported in the table.

The upper panel of Table 12.3 shows that the percentage of men with a degree rises from 5.8 per cent in 1975 to 16.3 per cent by 1998. Similarly the share of men with a higher vocational qualification goes up rapidly from 4.7 to 12.1 per cent. But most striking is the falling percentage of men with no qualifications which goes down from just over half (at 50.2 per cent) in 1975 to less than 20 per cent (18.9) by 1998.

The patterns for women, in the lower panel of the table, are even more marked. The share with a degree rises over fivefold from a very low initial level of 2.2 per cent in 1975 up to 12.5 per cent by 1998. Interestingly there is much less of a shift into higher vocational qualifications compared to men as only 2.7 per cent of working women possessed such qualifications in 1998. Again, there is a sharp fall in the percentage with no qualifications, which plummets from 58.3 per cent in 1975 to 23.3 per cent by 1998.

Wage differences by education

Other things being equal, one would expect this sharp increase in the supply of more educated workers to depress wage gaps between more highly qualified and less qualified workers. The logic here is simple, namely that because there are now more workers with higher education then employers have more of them to choose amongst and this increased competition for higher education jobs should lower their relative wages.

This, however, has not happened. Table 12.4 shows very clearly that wage gaps between more educated and less educated workers have widened out and that they are in fact an integral part of the widening wage structure. After a fall in the late 1970s the wage gaps between degree holders and those with no qualifications have persistently widened out. For example, men in 1980 earned a log (weekly wage) some 47.5 per cent higher than those with no qualifications. By 1998 this had risen to 71.7 per cent. The same pattern is true for women where the gap rises from 64.1 per cent in 1980 to 79.4 per cent by 1998.

Table 12.4   Weekly wage differences (full-time) by education, GHS, 1975–98

		Percent log (weekly wage) differences (base: no educational qualifications)				
	1975	1980	1985	1990	1995	1998
Men						
Degree or higher	54.2	47.5	54.9	62.8	67.1	71.7
Higher vocational	39.3	31.6	39.0	42.0	29.5	33.5
Teaching and nursing	30.8	25.2	26.4	36.2	41.4	38.4
Intermediate	14.1	14.2	19.9	23.1	23.6	23.8
Women						
Degree or higher	70.3	64.1	66.0	78.3	81.7	79.4
Higher vocational	59.1	45.4	52.3	61.3	67.1	61.5
Teaching and nursing	59.5	58.6	59.3	67.4	56.3	42.2
Intermediate	19.4	19.1	25.7	32.1	29.0	33.1

Notes: Calculated from GHS. For 1975 through 1995, statistics are based on three pooled years with the central year reported in the table. Derived from statistical regressions holding constant age and age squared.

The pattern is a little more mixed, and the changes over time less marked, for the other qualification groups. It is actually the case that the wage gaps for higher vocational qualifications did widen in the 1980s, but this pattern reversed itself in the 1990s. This conforms to the by now received wisdom that employers have, in the recent past, tended to confer less value on such vocational qualifications when compared to more traditional, academic qualifications. The wage gaps for female teaching/nursing qualifications also show an interesting pattern, falling away through the 1990s to much lower levels than before.

The Table 12.4 numbers end in 1998 as they are based on the last year of GHS data available at the time of writing. Table 12.5 therefore looks at more recent evidence from the LFS in three years, 1995, 2000 and 2002. The first, and very reassuring, point to note is that the 1995 weekly wage differentials are very similar to those in Table 12.4 for the same year. The pattern of change over the seven-year period in the table broadly shows wage differences rising between 1995 and 2000 and, in most cases, then falling back a little by 2002.

Table 12.5   Weekly and hourly wage differences (full-time) by education, LFS 1995–2002

| | Percent log (wage) differences (base: no educational qualifications) | | | | | |
| | Weekly wages | | | Hourly wages | | |
	1995	2000	2002	1995	2000	2002
Men						
Degree or higher	65.0	72.9	70.2	74.8	80.2	74.4
Higher vocational	40.7	38.8	33.3	44.6	41.3	34.0
Teaching and nursing	34.4	37.0	31.8	43.8	45.8	36.9
Intermediate	25.3	26.0	23.5	25.9	27.6	23.6
Women						
Degree or higher	78.8	79.6	83.4	83.0	81.0	74.2
Higher vocational	38.8	38.2	38.8	44.4	39.0	35.5
Teaching and nursing	61.8	59.5	59.5	66.7	61.3	51.1
Intermediate	30.6	28.0	30.6	30.3	29.8	28.3

Notes: Calculated from LFS. Derived from statistical regressions holding constant age and age squared.

Conclusions

It seems that, whilst the 1980s was the decade of rapidly rising wage inequality, the wage structure continued to widen out, at least for men, albeit at a slower rate in the 1990s. The same is true of wage differences by education and an important part of increased wage inequality has been rising relative wages for more educated, despite rapidly rising supply. If one thinks of a race between demand and supply for workers of different education levels then the fact that one has seen wage differences rise (and certainly not fall) at the same time as increased supply means that one has seen a relative demand shift in favour of the more educated. A body of research argues that this is inherently linked to technological changes that benefit more skilled and educated workers (Machin, 2002, 2003; Machin and Van Reenen, 1998).

Despite the clear evidence of relative demand shifts in favour of the more educated in the last quarter century or so, there is some preliminary evidence that wage differentials by education may have stopped rising at the end of the 1990s and start of the 2000s. This is perhaps not too surprising given the very rapid supply increases that occurred with the expansion of the higher education system in the recent past. This seems likely to have had a moderating influence on wage inequality as supply changes have bitten more to temper wage differentials by education. It will, however, prove interesting to see if this continues into the future, and to assess its impact on wage inequality, as the higher education system in the UK continues to expand (e.g. with government targets of having 50 per cent in higher education by 2010) and produce more graduates.

Notes

1. If we rank individuals by the level of pay, then the 10th percentile gives the pay of someone 10 percentage points from the bottom, the 90th percentile gives the pay of someone 10 percentage points from the top and the 50th percentile gives the pay of the person at the middle of the distribution.
2. The most important higher vocational qualifications include Higher National Certificates (HNC), Higher National Diplomas (HND) and full City and Guilds awards.

References

Card, D. (1999), 'The Causal Effect of Education on Earnings', in O. Ashenfelter and D. Card (eds), *The Handbook of Labor Economics*, Volume 3, North Holland: Amsterdam.

Machin, S. (1996), 'Wage Inequality in the UK', *Oxford Review of Economic Policy*, 12(1), pp. 47–64.

Machin, S. (1999), 'Wage Inequality in the 1970s, 1980s and 1990s', in P. Gregg and J. Wadsworth (eds), *The State of Working Britain*, Manchester University Press: Manchester.

Machin, S. (2002), 'The Changing Nature of Labour Demand in the New Economy and Skill-Biased Technology Change', *Oxford Bulletin of Economics and Statistics*, 63, pp. 753–66.

Machin, S. (2003), 'Skill-Biased Technical Change in the New Economy', in D. Jones (ed.), *Handbook of Economics in the Digital Age*, Academic Press, forthcoming.

Machin, S. and Van Reenen, J. (1998), 'Technology and Changes in Skill Structure: Evidence from Seven OECD Countries', *Quarterly Journal of Economics*, 113, pp. 1215–44.

13
Minimum Wage, Minimum Impact

Richard Dickens and Alan Manning

Key findings

- The Low Pay Commission (LPC), acting on advice from the Office for National Statistics, initially estimated that some 1.9 million workers (8.5 per cent of employees) would have their pay raised by the introduction of the National Minimum Wage (NMW). In the light of data problems this has been revised downwards a number of times and now stands at 1.2 million workers (5 per cent).
- This is still likely to be an over-estimate of the number of workers affected. We find, that at most, 3.7 per cent (815,000) of adult workers received a pay rise.
- The LPC have recommended future increases in the NMW to £4.50 in October 2003 and £4.85 in October 2004. They estimate that some 1.3 million workers will be affected by the first increase and 1.7 million by the second. While these are substantial real increases, we believe that these are over-estimates of the number of workers affected.
- Despite fears of wage rises further up the pay distribution if other workers attempt to restore pay differences, we find little evidence of spillover effects from the NMW.
- There is no discernable impact of introduction of the NMW on aggregate employment.
- However, in the care home sector, the lowest paying sector in Britain, the NMW had a huge effect on pay, raising the wages of 30 per cent of workers. This resulted in small falls in employment in this sector.
- The NMW has modest effects on household incomes and poverty. It should be seen in the context of a range of policies designed to make work pay.
- Despite the fact that three-quarters of the beneficiaries of the NMW are women the impact on the gender pay gap is small. The difference between average wages of men and women was closed by about 0.5 percentage points.

Introduction

In April 1999 the NMW was introduced into the UK. This was the first time a legally binding wage floor had been applied nationally. After wide consultation by the LPC the minimum wage set at £3.60 an hour for adult workers (aged over 22 years) and £3.00 an hour for youths (18–21 years). At these rates the government estimated that about 1.9 million workers (8.5 per cent of employees) would receive a pay rise of 30 per cent on average. Some welfare groups welcomed the minimum wage as a first step to reducing pay inequalities. But some commentators warned of job losses and the Bank of England predicted a temporary hike in inflation of about 0.4 per cent at introduction on the basis of these figures. However, when the NMW finally arrived it did so with more of a whimper than a bang. Nothing like the number of workers predicted received a pay hike and there was no discernable impact on inflation.

In this chapter we examine the reasons why the estimates of the number workers affected by the NMW were so far off the truth. We present the current estimates from the Office for National Statistics (ONS) but show why we think these may still be over-estimates. We then go on to examine any potential effects on employment, poverty and the gender pay gap from the introduction of the NMW.

How many workers affected?

Why were the first estimates of the proportion of workers affected by introduction of the minimum wage so far out? The short answer is bad data. None of the available national surveys in the UK provides an accurate measure of individual hourly wages. The survey commonly used for this type of analysis is the Labour Force Survey (LFS). This is a household based survey that samples around 60,000 households a quarter. Individuals are asked about their most recent earnings and the usual number of hours they work each week. Hourly wages are then derived from this information. However, there appears to be a large amount of measurement error in this data. Individuals may round both their earnings and hours of work; a large proportion of the responses are obtained from proxy respondents (often another household member); an individual's pay may well differ from usual even when working usual hours; pay may include overtime but the hourly wage that is relevant to the NMW is the basic hourly wage. The upshot of this is there appears to be a large amount of error in the measured hourly wages obtained from the LFS.

In most economic analysis, measurement error of this sort is not a big problem. For example, estimates of average wages are usually unaffected by measurement errors, since they tend to cancel each other out. However, since measurement error results in a wider distribution of observed earnings, when we look at the proportion of workers below a given threshold, say £3.60, we will over-estimate the extent of low pay. This is exactly what happened in predicting the numbers affected by the NMW; measurement error in earnings makes it look like there are more low paid workers than there really are.

The ONS did make some serious attempts to address this problem. Firstly, in spring 1999 it introduced a new question into the LFS whereby individuals are asked if they are paid by the hour and, if so, their hourly rate. This measure should give a much more accurate picture of true hourly rates of pay than that provided by the derived hourly pay. And the data suggests this is the case. When we look at the period just after the introduction of the minimum wage using this measure we find very few individuals still paid below the minimum, and a spike appearing in the pay distribution at £3.60. However, when we do the same with derived hourly pay, we find no increase in the numbers paid at £3.60 and many still below. This is what we would expect to see if the derived measure doesn't measure hourly rates well.

So why don't we just use actual hourly pay to measure the impact of the minimum wage? Problems arise because this is only reported by those who are paid by the hour: about half of all workers. Those who are hourly paid are more likely to be low paid so we cannot use this measure to infer wages for the whole population of workers. What is needed is an estimate of actual hourly pay for those workers for whom it is not observed. One way of doing this is to match individuals who don't have an observed actual hourly rate to those that do using other observed characteristics. For example, taking workers in similar jobs, of a similar age, sex, etc we can assign an actual hourly rate to those without one based on the observed actual rates of similar workers.[1] This is essentially the technique applied by the ONS to revise estimates of the proportion of workers affected by introduction of the NMW and also to examine the impact of subsequent increases in the minimum wage.[2] (See Dickens and Manning, 2002 for more details.)

ONS estimates of the numbers affected

As already discussed, initial statistics from the ONS estimated that about 1.9 million workers (or 8.5 per cent of employees) would have their wage increased by the NMW,[3] and these estimates are likely to be over-estimates since they were based on bad data. Since the publications of the first LPC report, the ONS has revised down these estimates a number of times; first to 1.5 million (6.4 per cent of workers) in February 2000, then to 1.3 million (5.5 per cent of workers) in March 2001 and lately to 1.2 million (5.0 per cent of workers)in October 2002. The top panel of Table 13.1 presents the current estimates of the number and percentage of workers affected by the adult and youth minimum rates at introduction. Some 4.8 per cent of adult workers and 6.1 per cent of youth workers are now estimated to have received a pay rise from the introduction of the NMW. These estimates are based on the matching technique described above. Note that these figures are the proportion paid below the threshold prior to introduction or up-rating. Since we observe about 1 per cent still paid below after the increase, these are likely to over-estimate the numbers receiving a pay rise.

Table 13.1   Low Pay Commission estimates of the number of workers affected by the NMW

	% of workers affected	Number of workers affected (000s)
April 1999		
18–21 years	6.1	96
22+ years	4.8	1,057
All 18+	5.0	1,153
October 2001		
18–21 years	5.3	90
22+ years	4.4	1,000
All 18+	4.5	1,100
October 2002		
18–21 years	4.9	90
22+ years	3.9	900
All 18+	4.0	1,000

Notes: (1) Figures are the proportion paid below prior to introduction or up-rating. (2) Based on data from LFS and NES surveys.

Sources: LPC reports and ONS website.

When the LPC were setting the rate at £3.60 an hour the Commission members thought that this would affect some 2 million workers. In fact, the first report from the LPC states that one of the criteria used in setting the rate was the proportion of workers affected. Clearly, the LPC (and the public) were badly informed. If the intention was to affect 8.5 per cent of workers then a much higher minimum wage was required. Using the most recent ONS estimates, a minimum rate close to £4 an hour would have been required to affect 9 per cent of workers. Of course it may well be the case that if the Commission had known this it would never have tried to affect so many workers.

The problems encountered in estimating the number of workers affected by the NMW at introduction were also faced in predicting the effects of subsequent up-rating of the minimum wage. Since introduction both the adult rate and the youth rate have been increased a number of times. The first increases were small, but then in October 2001 the adult rate was raised to £4.10 an hour and the youth rate to £3.50 an hour. The following October the two rates were again raised to £4.20 and £3.60 respectively. Prior to the October 2001 up-rating, the LPC estimated that some 1.4–1.7 million workers would be affected. The rest of Table 13.1 shows the current estimates of the number of workers affected (LPC, 2003). It is now thought that only 1.1 million workers were helped by the increase in 2001. The impact of the October 2002 up-rating is thought to be smaller since the increase was less than wage inflation at the time. The ONS do not count the number actually receiving a pay increase, rather the number paid below the NMW rate prior to up-rating. Because not all workers below are raised to the NMW, we find this over-estimates the actual number of gainers by about 1 per cent.

In their most recent report, the LPC recommend that the NMW be raised in October 2003 to £4.50 for adults and £3.80 for youths, and again in October 2004 to £4.85 and £4.10.[4] They estimate that overall this will affect 1.3 million workers in 2003 and 1.7 million in 2004. These are substantial increases in the real value of the minimum wage; the real increase from October 2002 to 2003 is about 3 per cent and around 7 per cent to 2004. If the estimates are correct there will be a substantial increase in the number of workers who benefit. But a question still remains as to whether these estimates are correct.

Are the revised government figures correct?

In our own work (Dickens and Manning, 2002) we show that there is evidence that the assumption underlying this methodology may be incorrect and that the technique is biased. Furthermore, the bias will lead to an over-estimate of the extent of low pay.[5] As such, it may be that the current set of revised ONS estimates, over-estimate the impact of the NMW.

Given this we make an alternative assumption to obtain estimates of the numbers low paid.[6] Intuitively, our approach is more realistic but it has proven harder to obtain precise estimates of low pay using this method. The best we can do using this assumption is to estimate upper and lower bounds on the number affected by the NMW.

Table 13.2 presents our estimates of these lower and upper bounds for adult workers just after the introduction of the NMW in May–July 1999 and after the up-rating to £4.10 in October–December 2001.[7] Our estimates suggest fewer workers were affected by the introduction of the NMW than the revised ONS figures. We find that (at most) 3.7 per cent or 815,000 adult workers had their pay increased by the NMW. This compares to the current ONS estimate of 4.8 per cent or 1.1 million workers. For the October 2001 up-rating, we find 3.6 per cent or 820,000 workers affected, which is not out of line with the ONS estimates of numbers actually receiving a pay rise. However, because they report *potential* beneficiaries, their estimates are higher, at 4.4 per cent (1 million) workers. The difference is that our figures examine the actual proportion at the NMW after the increase whereas the ONS figures examine the proportion paid below prior to the increase. This is likely to inflate their estimates because we still observe under-payment after the NMW increase.

Table 13.2   Lower and upper bounds on the number of workers affected by the NMW using an alternative methodology

	% of workers affected	Number of workers affected (000s)
May–July 1999		
22+ years	2.6 – 3.7	570 – 815
October–December 2001		
22 + years	2.7 – 3.6	610 – 820

Notes: (1) See Dickens and Manning (2002) for computations. (2) Based on LFS data. (3) Figures represent the estimated proportion paid at the NMW after introduction or up-rating.

It appears that our alternative assumption makes a difference when looking at the introduction of the NMW but not to subsequent up-ratings. This is in line with Beissel-Durrant and Skinner's (2003) evidence that the alternative assumptions make little difference to the estimates. But because the ONS insist on reporting *potential beneficiaries* their estimates are substantially higher. This is worrying since it also implies that the new recommendations just made by the LPC are also based on incorrect inference about how many workers will be affected because not all of these workers currently below the NMW will actually receive a pay increase.

Spillover effects

Prior to introduction of the NMW there were fears that workers paid above the minimum rate would ask for pay increases to restore pay differentials with the lower paid. This caused concern that the resulting increased wage pressure would put upward pressure on prices, and possibly interest rates. We can use our matching technique to examine what happened to wages across the whole pay distribution during the period of introduction. We find that there is little sign that workers paid above the NMW experienced any pay rises at the time of its introduction. Consequently the fears of large spillover effects on the wage distribution appear to have been largely unfounded. We also find no evidence of restoration of pay differentials following the subsequent increases in the NMW in October 2000 and 2001.

Did employment fall?

Most of the debate prior to the introduction of the NMW centred around the likely effect on employment. There were fears of job losses if extra burdens were placed on businesses that would harm the very people the NMW is intended to help. But some economists cited recent evidence that increases in the minimum wage might actually increase employment in some situations (e.g. Card and Krueger, 1995 or Dickens, Machin and Manning, 1999).

Consequently, what has happened to employment and unemployment since introduction is an important question from both a welfare point of view and as an indicator of how the labour market works. Of course, the fact that the NMW raised the pay of so few workers may mean that any effects are hard to uncover.

National studies

The NMW was introduced in a tight labour market, as employment had been growing strongly since the early 1990s. This growth continued after introduction so that employment reached a record level of 28.5 million by the end of 2002. Of course we don't know what would have happened to employment in the absence of the NMW, it may have grown even faster or perhaps slower. A simple way of attempting to evaluate this is to examine employment rates for different age groups. Since there is no minimum wage for 16–17 year olds and since the minimum wage for 18–21 year olds has a bigger impact on their wages, we may expect to see some substitution between these groups. In fact, estimates show that between spring 1999 and spring 2000 the employment share of 16–17 year olds actually fell, while that of 18–21 year olds increased. However, there have been other policy changes that will have affected these groups differently (e.g. New Deal and educational policies – see also Chapters 1, 7 and 17). Consequently it is very difficult to make judgements based on aggregate employment rates.

A more promising approach is to examine microeconomic evidence on employment change. The usual approach in micro studies is to examine differences in employment rates (or the rate at which individuals remain in work) for groups of individuals who are affected differently by the NMW. One way of doing this is to examine workers who have had their pay raised by the NMW and compare their employment probability with those who have not had their pay directly affected. The conventional labour market model would predict that employment rates for those directly affected would fall relative to those unaffected. Stewart (2003) presents evidence on this for the introduction of the NMW. He examines employment changes for two groups; those who would have to have their wages raised to comply with the legislation and those paid just above the NMW before the introduction. This second group is then considered to be similar enough to the first, but they are unaffected by the policy. His results show no significant difference in changes in employment rates of the two groups, implying that the minimum wage has had no discernable effect on aggregate employment.

Another way to analyse changes in aggregate employment due to the NMW is to exploit the regional variation in wages inherent in the UK. We would expect that those regions with a higher incidence of low pay, and hence more workers affected by the NMW, to exhibit differential changes in employment to those regions with fewer low paid workers. The standard labour market model would predict that those regions with the highest 'bite' from the NMW would experience relative employment declines. Stewart (2002) examines data from 140 regions of the UK. He finds that those regions with a higher incidence of low pay prior to the introduction of the NMW experienced a greater compression of wages when it was introduced. But he finds no evidence that employment in these regions suffered as a result.

Overall the empirical evidence on the impact of the NMW on employment cannot find any negative effects. This is contrary to the predictions of the standard competitive model of the labour market and in contrast to the fears of job losses put about by some commentators prior to introduction. However, it may be that since the NMW affected so few workers in aggregate it is not surprising that we find little evidence of job loss. If we were to look at a sector that had significant wage rises from the NMW we may well see some impact on jobs. For this we turn to evidence from one of the lowest paying sectors in the UK.

A sectoral study

The most detailed sectoral study of the impact of the NMW is by Machin, Manning and Rahman (2002). They conducted a survey of all residential care homes in Britain, collecting information on employment, wages and workers' characteristics. Each home was surveyed both before and after the introduction of the NMW to enable a study of wage and employment change over this period. The care home sector is possibly the lowest paying sector in the UK labour market. Prior to the introduction of the NMW, the average wage in this sector was about £4 an hour and over 32 per cent of workers were paid below the incoming minimum rate. The introduction of the NMW had a huge effect on the wage distribution. Virtually all of these workers below the NMW had their wages raised to the minimum, so that after April 1999 some 28 per cent of workers were paid exactly the NMW. The average pay increase for these workers was 40 pence an hour. This resulted in a sharp fall in wage dispersion. Prior to introduction the median hourly wage was 21 per cent above the 10th percentile hourly wage. This fell to 9 per cent by April 1999.

With such large changes in wages we may well expect to observe some changes in employment. A criticism levelled at many minimum wage studies is that they examine small changes in wages. In this sector the minimum wage really does 'bite'. Table 13.3 presents the results of Machin et al. (2002), using two different measures of employment (total employment and total hours worked) and two measures of the impact of the NMW (the initial proportion paid below the NMW and the Wage Gap – which is the wage increase required to bring everyone up to the NMW expressed as a percentage of the total wage bill in the firm).

Table 13.3 Changes in employment and hours in care homes from introduction of the NMW

	Initial proportion paid below NMW	Wage gap
Effect of 10% change in minimum wage measure on:		
Change in employment (%)	–3.8	–2.7
Change in total hours (%)	–3.9	–2.5

Notes: (1) See Machin, Manning and Rahman (2002) for full specification. (2) Regression on 575 care homes. Other control variables are proportion female, proportion with nursing qualification, average age, change in occupancy rate, proportion of Local Authority residents, county and month dummies.

Their results show that those firms most affected by the NMW are more likely to suffer employment falls. This is true if using numbers employed or total hours of work. Depending on the estimated specification a 10 per cent increase in the minimum wage will reduce employment by between 2 and 4 per cent. Machin et al. (2002) also examine whether firms were forced out of business by the introduction of the NMW. They find no evidence that the NMW has affected firm closures in this sector.

So overall the results from this sector suggest that the NMW has had a small negative impact on employment. However, one should exercise caution in generalising these results to other sectors of the UK labour market. This sector has the lowest wages in the UK and is where the impact of the NMW has been largest. Also, it is an unusual sector in that firms are restricted from passing higher costs onto higher prices since prices are largely set by local authorities. Indeed, Machin et al. (2002) find no evidence of increased prices from the NMW. Both of these factors mean that if we are going to find job losses anywhere we would expect them in this sector.

The impact on income inequality and poverty

The NMW was introduced as one of a range of anti-poverty policies designed to make work pay and increase work incentives for low skilled workers. However, many commentators have doubted the effectiveness of the minimum wage as an anti-poverty device. One frequently hears the argument that the low paid are not poor, but those without work and pensioners are the ones to suffer poverty. All that the minimum wage does is to raise the incomes of second earners in middle class households (teenagers and working wives). There appears to be some truth in this argument. But rising wage inequality through the 1980s and 1990s has resulted in a stronger link between low pay and low income and poverty (Dickens, 1999). This has made the minimum wage a more effective tool for tackling poverty.

Table 13.4 presents information on the link between low income and low pay. Presented is the fraction of households in each income decile that are set to gain from the up-rating of the NMW to £4.50 in October 2003.[8] (Income deciles are 10ths of the income distribution arranged in order of the lowest through to highest.) This is reported for all households and then for households of working age, and for working age households with someone in work. When looking at all households we see that the beneficiaries from the NMW are fairly evenly distributed across the income deciles. The largest number of gainers are in deciles 3 through 6, which lends some support to the idea that the NMW mostly helps middle class households. The poorest households have few beneficiaries since they tend to be without work or over retirement age. However, we would never expect the NMW to benefit these groups. When we look at working age households only, we find a stronger link between low income and the NMW, but still many of the benefits going to the middle deciles. Dropping those households with nobody in work strengthens this link much more so. Now we find that about 25 per cent of the bottom two income deciles gain from the increase in the NMW.[9]

Table 13.4   Percentage of households gaining from an increase in the NMW to £4.50 (22+) and £3.85 (18–21) by household income decile (at April 2003 levels)

	% in decile gaining from increase in NMW		
	All households	Households of working age	Households of working age with at least one working person
Household income decile			
1 (Bottom)	5.6	6.8	24.0
2	6.9	10.8	24.6
3	10.3	17.1	19.2
4	10.9	16.3	16.6
5	10.8	16.2	12.9
6	11.6	12.0	10.7
7	8.5	9.9	9.0
8	8.2	7.6	6.2
9	5.0	5.0	4.2
10 (Top)	3.5	3.7	4.1

Source: Figures supplied by Howard Reed at the Institute for Fiscal Studies.

By its design a minimum wage can only help households with somebody in work. As such it will always have a limited role in reducing poverty and income inequality. What these results do show is that when we focus on working households the NMW does have a greater impact on the poor. As such it will have some modest effects on poverty. One must remember that the NMW was introduced as part of a package of reforms designed to create work incentives and make work pay: the Working Families Tax Credit, income tax and National Insurance changes, extra childcare support, etc.

The gender pay gap

Women are still substantially lower paid than men in Britain. On average the pay difference between men and women is around 23 per cent (see Robinson, Chapter 15). This means that a minimum wage has the potential to raise women's pay by much more than men's. Indeed something like three-quarters of the beneficiaries of the NMW are estimated to be women. As such one would expect the introduction of the NMW to reduce the gender pay gap. However, studies of the impact of the NMW on the gender pay gap have found only small effects (Robinson, 2002 and Dex, Sutherland and Joshi, 2000). But, for reasons outlined above, this may be because they are using data that has a large amount of measurement error. We can use our matching methodology outlined above to estimate the impact of the NMW on gender pay differences.

Our results show that the introduction of the NMW raised the pay of about 11.2 per cent of women workers compared to 3.5 per cent of men, and both sexes received on average a 10 per cent pay rise.[10] Thus three times as many women than men had their pay increased by the NMW. So we may expect a large effect on the gender pay gap. Since the gender pay gap is usually reported in terms of the difference between average pay of men and women, we need to work out the impact on the average wages of both sexes. When we do this we find fairly modest effects on gender pay differences. The introduction of the NMW appears to have reduced the gap between men's and women's pay by just 0.5 per cent points. The effect of the October 2001 increase to £4.10 appears to have had a similar impact. So although the NMW clearly raises the pay of many more women than men, since gender pay gaps are often reported in terms of the average pay difference, the impact is small.

Conclusion

When the NMW was set at £3.60 an hour the LPC estimated that close to 2 million workers would have their pay increased by about 30 per cent on average. This prompted fears of wage inflation as workers already above the minimum wage sought to restore pay differentials with those below them. In the event nothing like this many workers received a pay increase. The current set of official estimates suggest that the true figure is closer to 1.2 million workers and even this may be an over-estimate. Also, there were no signs that workers tried to restore the pay differences with their lower paid counterparts. In the month that the NMW was introduced the inflation rate actually fell.

These mistakes were born out of bad data. The quality of earnings data in the UK is just not good enough to measure accurately the proportion of workers at the NMW. The official bodies have made some progress towards rectifying the situation, but one is still forced to estimate wages for a substantial fraction of the workforce. More work is needed to improve the statistics on pay. Indeed in their latest report the LPC call upon the government to ensure that the ONS devote sufficient attention and resources to this problem.

We find that the NMW had no significant impact on aggregate employment. However, we do see significant job loss in the care home sector. This is the lowest paying sector in the UK labour market and it would be foolish to generalise these results. The NMW has less of a role in reducing poverty, but in combination with other policies it can help to increase work incentives. In a situation where the government subsidises incomes with in-work benefits it may well be sensible to have a minimum wage to stop employers cutting wages. Finally, despite the fact that the majority of beneficiaries are women the impact of the NMW on the gender pay gap at average wages is estimated to be small.

Notes

1. The assumption underlying this approach is that once we control for observed individual characteristics, the chances of someone reporting an hourly rate is not affected by their actual hourly rate of pay. This enables us to make accurate predictions about unobserved hourly rates based on individuals' characteristics.
2. Note that the ONS also use data from the New Earnings Survey (NES) and combine the two estimates. The NES also has severe problems because it under-samples low paid workers.
3. See the LPC's first report for these numbers and also for details of the impact of the NMW in different regions, sectors, occupations, etc. (LPC, 1999).
4. The recommendations for 2004 are subject to confirmation by the Commission. They also recommend that workers aged 21 years be paid at the adult rate.
5. For this matching technique to be reliable one must be confident that the observed characteristics on the individuals that are used to match are sufficient to fully capture whether they are hourly paid or not, irrespective of their rate of pay. We find evidence that this is not the case (since our alternative derived hourly wage measure is also a good predictor of whether someone is hourly paid or not, even once we have controlled for other characteristics). If someone is low paid or not is still a good predictor of whether we observe their hourly rate, and if we ignore this, then we will over-estimate the extent of low pay using this methodology.
6. We assume that the actual hourly rate is useful in predicting whether we observe an hourly rate or not, but that the measurement error in the derived hourly rate is not. This amounts to assuming that the measurement error in derived hourly pay is the same whether we observe an hourly rate or not. Beissel-Durrant and Skinner (2003) provide some evidence that in practice the alternative assumptions make little difference to the estimates of low pay.
7. We could not obtain estimates for youth workers due to the low sample sizes in the survey data.

8. These figures were produced for the LPC by the Institute for Fiscal Studies.
9. The measurement error problems noted above will also affect these figures, through both the error in the wage and also the household income. Dickens and Manning (2002) show that controlling for this is unlikely to make much difference to the conclusions here.
10. These are likely to be over-estimates due to the problems outlined above with the matching technique. Unfortunately we cannot use our alternative approach here.

References

Beissel-Durrant, G. and Skinner, C. (2003), 'Estimation of the Distribution of Hourly Pay From Household Survey Data: the Use of Missing Data Methods to Handle Measurement Error', University of Southampton mimeo.
Card, D. and Krueger, A. (1995), *Myth and Measurement: The New Economics of the Minimum Wage*, Princeton University Press: Princeton.
Dex, S., Sutherland, H. and Joshi, H. (2000), 'Effects of Minimum Wages on the Gender Pay Gap', *National Institute Economic Review*, Issue 173, July.
Dickens, R. (1999), 'Poverty, Low Pay and the National Minimum Wage', in *The National Minimum Wage, Incomes and the Low Paid*, Low Pay Commission Occasional Paper 2.
Dickens, R., Machin, S. and Manning, A. (1999), 'The Effects of the Minimum Wage on Employment: Theory and Evidence from Britain', *Journal of Labor Economics*, 17, pp. 1–22.
Dickens, R. and Manning, A. (2002), 'The Impact of the National Minimum Wage on the Wage Distribution, Poverty and the Gender Pay Gap', Report for the Low Pay Commission.
Low Pay Commission (1999), *First Report of the Low Pay Commission*, The Stationery Office: London.
Low Pay Commission (2003), *Fourth Report of the Low Pay Commission: Building on Success*, The Stationery Office: London.
Machin, S., Manning, A. and Rahman, L. (2002), 'Where the Minimum Wage Bites Hard: the Introduction of the UK National Minimum Wage to a Low Wage Sector', Centre for Economic Performance Discussion Paper No. 544.
Robinson, H. (2002), 'Wrong Side of the Track? The Impact of the Minimum Wage on Gender Pay Gaps in Britain', *Oxford Bulletin of Economics and Statistics*, December 2002, Vol. 64, No. 5, pp. 417–48.
Stewart, M. (2002), 'Estimating the Impact of the Minimum Wage Using Geographical Wage Variation', University of Warwick mimeo.
Stewart, M. (2003), 'The Impact of the Introduction of the UK National Minimum Wage on the Employment Probabilities of Low Wage Workers', University of Warwick mimeo.

14
Public and Private Sector Labour Markets

Peter Dolton and Steven McIntosh

Key findings

- Average pay is higher in the public sector than in the private sector, although the difference has shrunk over the last 25 years.
- The distribution of pay is narrower in the public sector than in the private sector.
- The public–private sector pay differential is higher for women than for men.
- In recent years, private sector pay in professional occupations has overtaken public sector pay in these occupations, particularly for men.
- The public–private sector pay differential is lowest in London and the South-East, and indeed is now negative for men in these regions.
- The public–private sector pay differential is lowest for graduates, and again has recently become negative for male graduates.
- Public sector workers are less likely to report that they have a competitive salary or work for a progressive organisation, although they report more challenging work, more socially useful work, and greater long-term security.

Introduction

In 2001 the public sector employed about 5.2 million workers. Hence public sector workers account for around 18 per cent of the UK workforce (*Economic Trends*, No. 583, June 2002). Women form approximately 63 per cent[1] of the public sector workforce and part time workers account for around 30 per cent of public sector workers. Over 39 per cent of public sector workers are aged over 45 and 28 per cent have university degrees. Only 15 per cent of private sector workers have degrees, so public sector workers are relatively highly qualified and highly skilled. Around 59 per cent of public sector workers are trade union members, whereas only 17 per cent of private sector employees are union members.

Although the public sector is still sizeable, it has shrunk to around 18 per cent of the workforce in 2001, from 28 per cent in 1981 (*Economic Trends*, No. 583, June 2002). Gregory and Borland (1999) report that the UK is similar to the US and Australia in this respect. These countries are in sharp contrast to all the Scandinavian countries, Austria, Belgium, France, Portugal, Germany and many other OECD countries, where the public sector has been growing.

One extremely important issue relating to the functioning of the labour market and remuneration in the public sector is the difficulty of observing individual productivity and effort. This means that public sector adminis-trators find it hard to create labour contracts and remuneration policy that reward individual performance and productivity. This is a standard form of principal agent problem. In the public sector there are often several possible measures of performance. When any agent has multiple goals it is unclear how to direct effort, especially when performance may be imprecisely measured. In addition, individual workers (agents) may be affected by many other groups of people (principals) who are in a position of influence, for example members of the public, managers, or local authorities. The existence of several principals makes the overall incentives for the agent much weaker, since each principal will seek to divert the agent's effort to his most preferred dimension. Hence economic theory suggests that it is difficult for the public sector to adopt performance related pay practices or write contracts that induce the best effort of public sector workers.

The process of pay determination in the public sector varies in different occupations. About 25 per cent of public sector employees (for example teachers and nurses) have their pay set directly by government based on the recommendations of Pay Review Boards, which receive evidence from different parties but do not engage in pay negotiations between them. Many public sector employees in the UK are represented by national unions. In recent years there has been a tendency to move away from centralised wage setting towards individual government departments being responsible for wage setting. This has also led to the attempt to introduce individualised pay settlements based on performance related elements or the movement towards more flexible working arrangements. For example, a form of performance related pay was introduced for teachers in 2000 and there are now negotiations taking place about the use of more classroom assistants to cover elements of work done by teachers. (See Dolton et al., 2003.)

Average public sector earnings in the UK are higher than average private sector earnings. Much of this difference is explained by differences in char-acteristics such as educational attainment. Nevertheless some of the premium may be due to rents paid to public sector employees over their private sector counterparts. The perennial problem in gauging the difference between public and private sector earnings and conditions of work is that it is difficult to compare the two sectors as they are fundamentally different.

Much of the literature on public–private sector differences (see Disney et al., 1998; Bender and Elliott, 1999 and Gregory and Borland, 1999) has focused on the difference in pay in the two sectors. A good proportion of this literature has been devoted to trying to account for the different composition of the two sectors. This involves the use of various techniques to attempt to account for the variation in the mix of occupations and other sources of differences in the two sectors. Recent papers have attempted to model the choice of entering one of these two sectors at the same time as modelling the determination of earnings in these two sectors, since there may be some form of self selection in terms of the kind of person who chooses to enter one sector rather than another. Even after using these techniques there is a wide range of estimates for the public–private wage differential after conditioning for all the differences in the two sectors. Gregory and Borland (1999) present a summary of the estimates for the UK which vary from 9 to 38 per cent for women and 5 to –33 per cent for men depending on the year of the data and manual or non-manual workers.

Over the last 30 years, there has been a slow decline in the earnings of individuals working in the public sector relative to private sector earnings (see Figure 14.1).

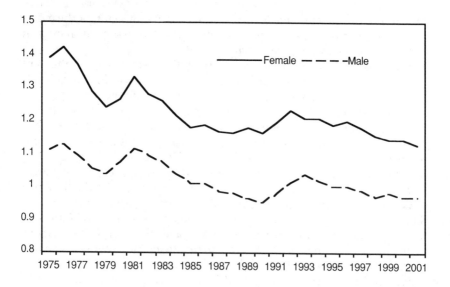

Figure 14.1   Public sector/private sector wage ratio

Source: NES.

In 1976, female earnings in the public sector were 42 per cent higher than those in the private sector. In the same year male earnings were 13 per cent higher in the public sector on average than in the private sector. By 2002, female public sector earnings were only 13 per cent higher than those in the private sector and male public sector earnings were 3 per cent lower than those of their private sector counterparts.

What explains these trends in public and private sector labour markets? The decline in relative public sector pay is partly due to the public expenditure constraints of successive governments over the 1979–2002 period and partly the increasing private sector demand for professional, technological and highly skilled labour which has forced up relative wages in that sector. This declining relative wage has caused real recruitment problems for occupations like teachers and nurses. These problems are most acute in London and the South-East.

Public sector employees also have a more concentrated earnings distribution than private sector workers. The scope for very high salaries in the public sector is limited. Union/non-union, male/female, and ethnic minority/white wage differentials are all lower in the public sector than in the private sector.

Data sources

In what follows we use the New Earnings Survey (NES), the Labour Force Survey (LFS) and several graduate cohort data sets to examine pay and other conditions of work across the public and private sectors. The LFS is particularly useful since 1994 as it contains a direct question about whether the individual works in the public or the private sector. We use the NES to examine basic underlying trends in relative pay, using the variable on sector derived by the data collectors. The graduate data sets provide us with a detailed perspective on the recruitment and retention problems that are commonplace in professional markets.

Pay differences by gender

The public–private sector pay differential is higher for women than for men (see Table 14.1). For men, using LFS data, average real hourly pay, in 2000 prices, in the public sector was £11.25 in 2001,[2] and £10.32 in the private sector (a 9 per cent difference).[3] This differential is down from 20 per cent in 1994. In 2001, average real female hourly pay was £9.03 in the public sector and £7.32 in the private sector, a 23 per cent gap, down from 40 per cent in 1994. Because women are about twice as likely as men to work in the public sector, the earnings growth differential we have reported between the public and private sectors will affect the overall gender earnings gap.

As well as focusing on the average, it is also of interest to examine the distribution of wages in the two sectors. Table 14.1 therefore also shows the wages at the 10th and the 90th percentiles of both the private and the public sector wage distributions.[4] The ratio of these two percentiles is an often-used measure of wage inequality. In 1994, for both men and women we can see that both the 10th and the 90th percentiles of the public sector wage distribution were greater than the equivalent percentiles of the private sector wage distribution, suggesting that the former distribution lay mostly to the right of the latter. It is true, however, that for men the ratio of the two percentiles was lower in the public sector, suggesting less wage inequality there. For women, we observe little difference in wage inequality between the sectors, being actually slightly greater in the public sector. By 2001, however, wages at the top end of the distributions had grown much more quickly in the private sector than in the public sector, particularly for men. The male public sector 90th percentile is now below the equivalent private sector percentile. Overall inequality has fallen in the public sector and risen in the private sector, exacerbating the difference between the two. For women, although the public sector wage distribution still lies much to the right of the private sector distribution at all points, inequality had fallen in the former and risen in the latter by 2001.

Table 14.1   Real gross wages and hours of work in the private and public sectors

| | | Males | | | | | | | |
| | | Private sector | | | | Public sector | | | Public |
	Mean £	10th percentile	90th percentile	90/10	Mean £	10th percentile	90th percentile	90/10	sector premium
1994	8.93	3.72	15.56	4.18	10.71	5.01	17.56	3.50	19.9%
2001	10.32	4.25	18.77	4.42	11.25	5.34	18.25	3.42	9.0%

| | | Females | | | | | | | |
| | | Private sector | | | | Public sector | | | Public |
	Mean £	10th percentile	90th percentile	90/10	Mean £	10th percentile	90th percentile	90/10	sector premium
1994	6.17	3.05	10.22	3.35	8.62	4.13	14.50	3.51	39.7%
2001	7.32	3.61	12.44	3.45	9.03	4.47	14.93	3.34	23.4%

Note: All wages are in constant (year 2000) prices.

Source: LFS.

The structure of occupational pay in public and private sectors

The occupational mix of employees in the public sector is very different from that in the private sector. Public sector employment tends to be concentrated in professional and clerical jobs. Public sector employees are more likely to be union members and their jobs usually require higher levels of education and entail working in large organisations. Hence to compare raw public sector/private sector earnings could be misleading as it may not compare like with like.

Focusing on occupations we know are likely to be wholly or largely made of public sector workers, Figures 14.2 and 14.3, for males and females respectively, display average pay in these occupations as a proportion of average pay in the whole country. The graphs go as far back in time as reliable data will allow.

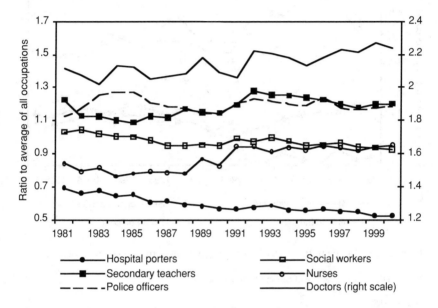

Figure 14.2   Male public sector weekly wages relative to average of all occupations

Notes: Prior to 1984, 'men aged 21 and above'; 1984 onwards, 'men on adult rates'. New occupational classification introduced in 1991.

Source: NES.

Figure 14.2 suggests that for men average pay in these occupations as a proportion of total average pay has been fairly constant over the period considered. This is perhaps surprising, since they are mostly professional occupations and this has been a period of widening wage inequality, when professional wages overall have tended to rise more quickly than average wages. It would therefore appear that, professional male workers in the private sector have pulled away from the median worker in terms of wages, but professional male workers in the public sector have merely kept pace with the average growth of wages in the economy. Lower down the distribution,

Figure 14.2 suggests that the wages of occupations such as hospital porters are falling behind the national average. A similar picture emerges for women in Figure 14.3, revealing, with the exception of nurses, that wages in professional public sector jobs have been increasing at roughly the same rate as the national female average.

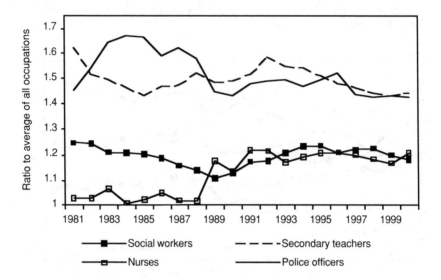

Figure 14.3   Female public sector weekly wages relative to average of all occupations

Note: New occupational classification introduced in 1991.

Source: NES.

Table 14.2 uses LFS data to show average real hourly wages in the two sectors for selected broad (one-digit) occupations, in the years 1994 and 2001.

Public sector pay premia are largest for the lower-ranked occupations captured in the 'other occupations' category. At the top end in 2001, hourly pay is lower in the public sector than in the private sector for each of the three highest-ranked occupations (managers, professional and associate professional) for men, and for professional occupations for women. This contrasts with the situation in 1994, when public sector pay was usually higher in these occupations.

For selected, more detailed occupations (at the three-digit level) that are sufficiently large in both the public and private sectors to make comparisons viable, Figures 14.4 and 14.5, for men and women respectively, show for almost all occupations a declining public sector pay premium.

Table 14.2 Average hourly real gross wages in the private and public sectors, in selected major occupation groups

	Private sector (£)	Male public sector (£)	Public sector premium	Private sector (£)	Female public sector (£)	Public sector premium
Managers						
1994	13.18	13.95	5.8%	9.17	9.83	7.2%
2001	16.26	15.58	–4.4%	12.24	12.47	1.9%
Professional occupations						
1994	12.85	14.21	10.6%	10.80	13.39	24.0%
2001	15.27	14.85	–2.8%	13.77	13.48	–2.2%
Associate professional occupations						
1994	11.59	10.55	–9.9%	8.69	9.69	11.5%
2001	12.11	11.02	–9.9%	9.72	10.26	5.6%
Clerical						
1994	7.25	7.86	8.4%	6.40	6.68	4.4%
2001	8.26	8.66	4.8%	7.48	7.19	–4.0%
Other occupations						
1994	5.31	6.36	20.0%	4.40	4.90	11.4%
2001	5.66	6.50	14.8%	4.71	5.03	6.8%

Note: All wages are in constant (year 2000) prices.

Source: LFS.

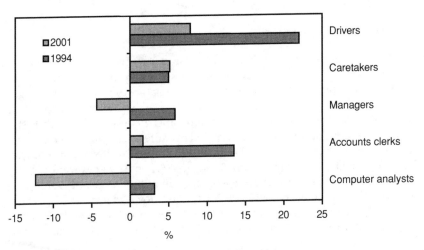

Figure 14.4 Male occupational public sector differentials

Source: LFS.

For males, pay is lower in the public sector than in the private sector for some occupations in 2001, most severely for computer analysts, but also for managers. This compares with a positive public sector pay premium in 1994. For women, secretaries now earn less, on average, in the public sector than in the private sector, while the other occupations graphed show declines in the premia, which nevertheless remain positive.

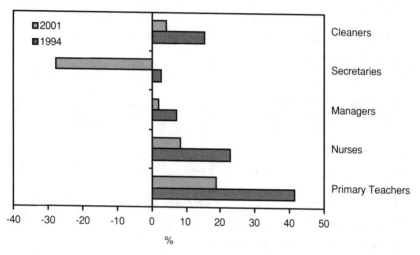

Figure 14.5   Female occupational public sector differentials

Source: LFS.

The regional dimension

Public sector pay premia for the years 1994 and 2001 by region are shown in Figures 14.6 and 14.7 for men and women respectively. In all regions and for both genders, public sector wages have fallen relative to private sector wages over the period. In some regions, however, the fall has not been large. Most dramatic have been the changes in London and the rest of the South-East.

In 1994, London men earned 10 per cent more in the public sector than in the private sector. However, by 2001, they were earning 7 per cent less. Similarly in the rest of the South-East, by 2001 male wages were slightly higher in the private sector. For women, the public sector pay premium remains positive in every region by 2001, but is down to less than 2 per cent in London. Other regions, such as the South-West, the Midlands and the rest of the South-East have also seen large falls in the premium, although in these areas it still remains substantial.

These results show why recruitment has become increasingly difficult in public sector jobs in the South-East, and in London in particular. Real wages

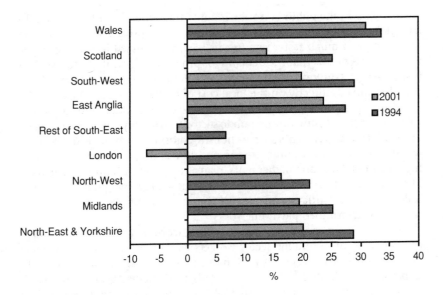

Figure 14.6   Male regional public sector differentials

Source: LFS.

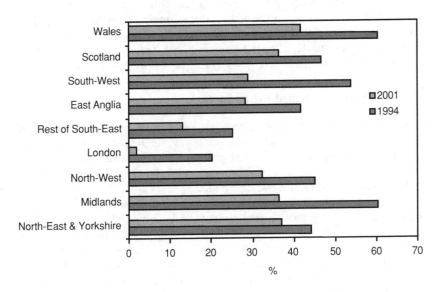

Figure 14.7   Female regional public sector differentials

Source: LFS.

are going up in the public sector by roughly the same amount in the South-East of England as they are in other regions, while private sector wages are increasing at a much faster rate in this region compared to the rest of the country. This means that the demand for professional private sector workers is strongest in London and the South-East. If private sector wages are higher this also impacts directly on the local cost of living and hence the difficulty of recruiting and retaining public sector workers in London and the South-East. This puts pressure on the public sector to pay London allowances and other additional payments such as housing subsidies. It is unclear, however, whether such measures improve the position as they will further induce a higher cost of living and higher rents in an already expensive housing market. The government has, however, recently proposed regional public sector pay indexed to local prices and cost of living, although remaining within nationally determined pay frameworks.

Around 12 per cent of the public sector work in London. There was a considerable shift of public sector workers working for central government departments in the 1980s with the movement of organisations such as the Department of Health headquarters to Leeds, the Benefits Agency to Newcastle and the Employment Service to Sheffield. It is unclear how much scope there is for further redeployment of public servants to the regions since many of the public sector workers who are employed in London are there directly as a result of the support required by Parliament. At present the distribution of public sector workers across the regions is very similar to the distribution of private sector workers across the regions (for example 12 per cent of all public sector workers work in London, while 12.5 per cent of all private sector workers work in London, similarly for the other regions). This balance will probably not be intentionally disturbed.

Quality differences and other issues

Finally, we consider the public sector pay premium for workers of different quality. Figures 14.8 and 14.9 show the public sector pay premia, for men and women respectively, by highest qualification level achieved, using data from the LFS. As usual, at every qualification level and for both genders, the public sector pay premium has declined.

For males, those at the lower end of the qualifications scale earn the highest premia, while those higher up have seen substantial relative wage falls if they work in the public sector. Indeed, male graduates now earn 12 per cent less if they work in the public sector rather than the private sector. For women, the highest premia are earned by those in the middle of the qual-ifications distribution, particularly those whose highest qualification is A-levels. At degree level we observe a large fall in the public sector pay differential for women, although, unlike for men, it has remained positive in 2001 at 4 per cent.

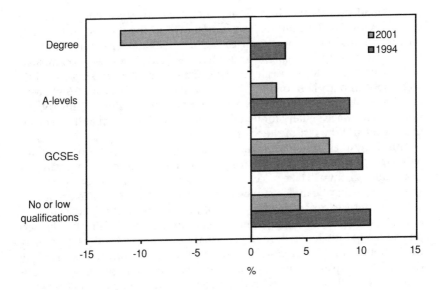

Figure 14.8   Male public sector pay differentials by qualification

Source: LFS.

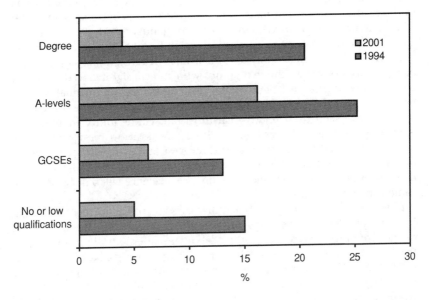

Figure 14.9   Female public sector pay differentials by qualification

Source: LFS.

Thus graduates seem to have been most affected by the decline in relative public sector pay. Further analysis, not shown in the figures, shows that, putting qualifications together with region, graduates in London and the South-East working in the public sector have particularly low wages compared to their private sector equivalents. Thus male graduates working in public sector jobs in both London and the rest of the South-East earn 26 per cent less than male graduates in the private sector in those regions. Similarly, the public sector wage penalty for female graduates is 12 per cent and 4 per cent in London and the rest of the South-East respectively.

This analysis assumes that all people with the same level of qualifications will have the same productivity in a job. This is clearly not the case and part of any adjustment will take place in quality, so that the extent of any particular skill shortage may be underestimated. Nickell and Quintini (2002) argue that a decline in relative earnings should lead to a decline in the average quality of public sector workers, and do find evidence that this is so. Using the datasets on cohorts of individuals born in particular weeks in 1958 and 1970, namely the National Child Development Study (NCDS) and the British Cohort Study (BCS), they compare the average ability in particular public sector occupations amongst the 1970 cohort, to average ability in the same occupations at a similar age among the older, 1958 cohort. Ability is measured by tests of general and mathematical ability taken at the age of 10/11 by the respondents to the two surveys.

The results show that for women, there was a decline between the cohorts in the relative general and mathematical ability scores of nurses and in the relative mathematical abilities of other non-manual workers and teachers, although these falls were not statistically significant. The relative score on the general ability test actually rose for women entering other non-manual occupations. For males, the two groups who show a significant decrease in ability, on both measures, between the two cohorts are non-manual workers excluding police officers and teachers. This is interesting as these two groups of men have seen their relative earnings fall, while ability increased, if anything, for the police grouping whose pay position improved. These results can be viewed as another indicator of labour market pressure. In practice, this kind of evidence is not going to be readily available unless new surveys are undertaken and then any new evidence will only be available some time later.

In the last 30 years, the government has relied on pay adjustments through, for example, Pay Review Bodies to resolve differences in the supply and demand of different types of qualified labour. An alternative to this would be for the government to engage in more active planning based on formal modelling of the underlying labour markets. There was a lot of support for this type of manpower planning approach in the 1960s and 1970s, and some countries, for example the Netherlands, are actively using these tools. There are many difficulties in this approach, which involve the problems of measuring the demand and supply of labour.

How much of the public sector pay premia can we explain?

We next examine how much of the raw difference in wages between the public and private sector can be explained by the factors outlined above. The successive columns of Table 14.3 show, for each year in our LFS sample and for men and women separately, the raw difference in pay between the two sectors, and then the pay premium once we net out differences in the jobs done (occupations) between the two sectors, followed by the premium netting out differences in individual characteristics (age and highest qualification) only, before finally the premium netting out differences in both occupation and individual characteristics between sectors (plus differences in region and workplace size).

Table 14.3 Regression adjusted public sector pay premia (%)

	Male				Female			
	None	Occupation	Individual characteristics	All controls	None	Occupation	Individual characteristics	All controls
1994	26	14	7	5	41	18	18	12
1995	28	15	9	7	39	16	17	11
1996	27	14	7	6	41	17	18	11
1997	25	13	6	5	37	16	16	11
1998	22	10	3	3	35	13	13	8
1999	22	10	2	3	32	12	12	7
2000	19	7	(1)	(1)	31	11	10	7
2001	17	6	(–1)	(1)	28	8	8	6

Notes: The numbers in the table refer to the estimated hourly real (year 2000 prices) gross wage pay premium for working in the public sector relative to the private sector, based on regression equations in which the log of hourly pay was regressed against the control variables indicated at the top of each column. The occupation controls were dummy variables for three-digit occupations. The individual characteristic controls were age and highest qualification. 'All controls' in the final columns for men and women refer to controls for region and workplace size, in addition to the above-mentioned controls for occupation, age and qualification level. An estimated pay pr emium in parentheses denotes that estimate was insignificantly different from zero.

Source: LFS.

The results show that after netting out differences in occupations, the male and female public sector pay premia are reduced by one-half to two-thirds. Netting out the influence of individual characteristics only, the male public sector premium is reduced dramatically, and in 2000 and 2001 is essentially zero. Thus any differences in male wages between the private and the public sector seem to be explained by different types of workers, in terms of age and qualifications, in the two sectors. For women, the impact of individual char-acteristics is similar to netting out the impact of occupation. Netting out all factors (thus controlling for occupation, region, firm size, education and age), public sector and private sector hourly wages are again not significantly different from each other for men. For women, hourly wages remain 6 per cent higher, in 2001, in the public sector, even after we allow for all of these differences in job and worker characteristics across the sectors.

Non-pecuniary differences

There is more to the difference between public and private sector jobs than simply pay, although evidence for such other distinctions is scarce. In Table 14.4 we present some evidence from graduate respondents, which suggests that public and private sector jobs differ in a marked way.

Table 14.4   Percentage of workers saying their job provides: (all that apply)

| | Women | | Men | |
	Private	Public	Private	Public
Competitive salary	37	19*	50	30*
Skill development	65	72*	67	66
Challenging work	67	83*	70	82*
Socially useful	28	58*	21	64*
Long-term security	37	56*	38	57*
Progressive organisation	32	13*	39	17*
People to socialise with	45	41*	43	46

Note: * denotes statistically significant difference at the 5 per cent level.

Source: Authors' calculations from 1990 HEFCE Graduate Survey.

Respondents were asked to rank whether their job had various character-istics on a five-point scale. We test to see if there is a statistically significant difference between responses from those who work in the public sector and those who work in the private sector. Public sector workers are more likely to answer positively that their job is challenging, provides an opportunity for skill development, is socially useful and is expected to offer long-term security. However, public sector jobs have two main drawbacks: one concerns the organisation, the other the financial rewards. A rigid organisation and low financial incentives are traditional criticisms of the public sector, but it is interesting to note that these points are really important to workers. Only 20 per cent to 30 per cent of public sector workers agree that their job provides a competitive salary; the proportion agreeing that the organisation is progressive is even lower. So both pecuniary and non-pecuniary characteris-tics of jobs matter in the difference between public and private sector jobs.

Conclusion

There has been a progressive revolution in the nature of public sector employment in the last 25 years caused by the reforms of successive

Conservative and Labour governments, attracted by the 'market'-led ideas of privatisation, quasi markets, public–private partnerships, contracting out, and performance related pay. The effect of these pressures has been complicated by the introduction of the National Minimum Wage (NMW) and the recognition by the current Blair administration with recent Budgets (in 2001 and 2002) that there will have to be an expansion of the health service and the education system. This is an important potential factor for future pay as all public expenditure is scaled by what is judged to be potentially affordable from taxes. Looking into the future, the advent of large increases in student fees and student debt may have important consequences for the recruitment of graduates into public sector jobs. It is also possible that the important changes on the horizon relating to pension reform will induce changes in the relative attractiveness of the public sector as a career destination.

One important development in the last ten years has been the introduction of public–private partnerships and the contracting out of public sector services to the private sector. This process is often via competitive tendering and the contracts are often won by consortia of the previously employed public sector workers. These changes have resulted in a slow transformation in the composition of the public sector workforce. The proportion of manual employees in the public sector has been falling, as a result of the privatisations and the contracting out process. This contracting out of public services, such as cleaning, catering and various care and personal service functions, has meant that the lowest paid female manual workers have been transferred to the private sector from the public sector. This acts to push up the relative pay in the public sector as many of the occupations involved in the contracting out process are the lowest paid jobs.

Although the introduction of the NMW had much to do with pressure from public sector unions, it is ironic that at the time of its introduction, there were very few public sector workers who were actually affected. Even the lowest paid workers in the public sector working in local government and the health service had won a minimum of a £4 an hour wage by the time the £3.60 an hour NMW was introduced in April 1999. One beneficial consequence of this reform is that it has meant that public sector pay settlements over the last four years have been frequently weighted towards the bottom end of the pay structures and most public sector low paid jobs have managed to secure wages for even the lowest paid which are well above the statutory minimum wage.

The present Labour government has signalled its intention to expand the public sector, emphasising the need to improve provision in education and health. This will inevitably lead to a significant increase in the demand for well-qualified graduates. This has created shortages of public sector employees in key areas, most notably of teachers and health workers. The problem has become more pressing as the relative demand for skilled labour in the UK has increased dramatically during the last 20 years. The government has recognised the implications of this process for the graduate labour market by encouraging the steady increase in the supply of university places with the target of a 50 per cent participation rate in higher education. This will radically change the size of the pool of available qualified people, but the incentives to work in the public sector must still be set at the appropriate level to induce young people to make this career decision.

In recent years there has been a move to introduce performance related pay (PRP) into public sector occupations. Dolton et al. (2003) describe the problems of implementing PRP in teaching and many of their observations would apply to its introduction in other public sector jobs. Of course the main problems in this area are associated with the measurement of performance, productivity or effort in the public sector context. Clearly there is a rationale for PRP-type contracts in the private sector when the output of the individual worker is easily observed and verified. It is not so clear how to implement PRP in a principal–agent type framework in which individual effort is difficult to observe. Often government or consumers want public sector service providers to actually provide more than one outcome. For example, schools are asked to provide, amongst other things, a safe learning environment, a rigorous education in basic skills and an all-round education of a balanced nature for our children. Providing one of these outcomes may divest resources away from the provision of another. It is quite easy to see that the provision of a basic level of education for the average pupil (or the lowest ability pupil) may detract from the provision of a suitable education for the most able pupils.

In the future, the projected increase in university fees and hence the size of personal student loans may have important implications for graduate supply of qualified manpower into the public sector. At current prices the average student graduates with a debt of around £12,000. If this figure was to double then this may have an important impact on recruitment into jobs with relatively low professional pay at the beginning of a career. On the other hand if the public sector has to react to these pressures by introducing fee waivers for certain courses related to public sector jobs, providing subsidised housing in the first years of employment or even paying off student loans and debts at the beginning of the contract, then it is possible that the public sector will be able to compete. However, the question should be addressed as to whether this is an optimal use of public spending funds, especially if the new recruit uses these advantages to an initial public sector job and then moves to a private sector job after a few years.

Notes

1. This and subsequent figures in this paragraph are based upon LFS data.
2. Figure 14.1 does suggest a counter-cyclical pattern in the sector pay differential, with recessions having a larger adverse effect on private sector pay. The decline in

the differential during the 1990s may therefore be purely cyclical, to be reversed as the economy weakens. We cannot be sure of this, however, until the full year's data for 2002 (and then subsequent years) are available.

3. This result contrasts with the NES, which suggests that male pay is now slightly higher in the private sector than in the public sector, as shown in Table 14.1. The difference between the two is likely to be due to the fact that the NES, which bases its sample selection on National Insurance numbers, under-samples the very low paid, who are presumably more likely to work in the private sector. The NES will therefore slightly inflate the estimated wage in the private sector, compared to that in the public sector.

4. The 10th percentile is the wage of the individual ranked 10 per cent from the bottom of the wage distribution, while the 90th percentile is the wage of the individual ranked 10 per cent from the top of the wage distribution.

References

Bender, K. and Elliott, R. (1999), 'Relative Earnings in the UK Public Sector: the Impact of Pay Reform on Pay Structure', in R. Elliott, C. Lucifora and D. Meurs (eds), *Public Sector Pay Determination in the European Union*, Macmillan: London.

Disney, R., Goodman, A., Gosling, A. and Trinder, C. (1998), 'Public Pay in Britain in the 1990s', Commentary No. 72, Institute for Fiscal Studies: London.

Dolton, P., Chevalier, A. and McIntosh, S. (2003), *Performance Related Pay for Teachers*, Institute of Education: London.

Gregory, B. and Borland, G. (1999), 'Recent Developments in Public Sector Labor Markets', in O. Ashenfelter and D. Card (eds), *Handbook of Labor Economics*, Vol. 3, North Holland: Amsterdam.

Nickell, S. and Quintini, G. (2002), 'The Consequences of the Decline in Public Sector Pay in Britain: A Little Bit of Evidence', *Economic Journal*, pp. F107–F118.

15
Gender and Labour Market Performance in the Recovery

Helen Robinson

Key findings

- The average gender employment gap has not changed during the economic recovery.
- The mean gender pay gap has continued to narrow from 26 per cent to 23 per cent from 1994 to 2002. However, the gender pay gap for part-time work is not narrowing.
- The pay gap is partly the result of discontinuous patterns of labour force participation of women. Many mothers are outside the labour market in their 20s and 30s when their male counterparts are experiencing substantial wage growth.
- Women continue to be under-represented in some high-paid occupations and over-represented in other low paid occupations. This situation has not changed notably in recent years.
- The gender job tenure gap has narrowed (partly in response to maternity leave provision and Working Families Tax Credit – WFTC).
- Minimum wage legislation has had some effect on reducing low pay and gender pay inequality. There is also some evidence of an impact of Working Families Tax Credit.

Introduction

Media attention continues to focus on the progress of women in the workplace. More women than ever before hold a full- or part-time job and the traditional pattern of intermittent economic participation over the child-rearing years has virtually disappeared for some groups of women. How much, though, can a typical woman expect to earn at various stages in her working life? How do these earnings compare with the wages of men? Do earnings continue to be affected by the presence of children in the household?

Throughout the post-war period, both the Sex Discrimination and the Equal Pay Acts were put into place, which continue to have some bearing on recent events. The Equal Pay Act of 1970 made the process of offering different wages to men and women illegal. This was later extended in 1983 to cover equal pay for work of equal value. The Sex Discrimination Act implemented in 1975 prohibited gender discrimination in hiring. The subsequent Employment Protection Act, introduced in 1979, established the right to have maternity leave.

Whilst these events of the last 20 years may be heralded as some sort of success story of female labour market improvement, we ask to what extent measurable tallies reveal true progress. In a world where women are still under-represented in the professional occupations, carry out the bulk of household caring/cleaning responsibilities, and are paid less than male colleagues, we document more comprehensive measures of female advancement. This chapter uses cross-section Labour Force Survey data throughout the latest economic recovery to explore the extent of economic gaps that occur between men and women against a backdrop of policy changes that seek to narrow them.

Employment effects

Historically, women in Britain have had lower employment rates than men. Obviously, this is in part because women have tended to withdraw from the labour force in much greater numbers than men. The means-tested component of the unemployment benefit system still offers no incentive for many women to register as unemployed if a partner, if present, is in full-time work. More women than men have traditionally shown up as economically inactive in their child-rearing years. When in work, women are more likely than men to combine a job with time spent with their family by working part-time. This situation, however, continues to change.

Table 15.1 and Figure 15.1 confirm that more women than ever are now in work. The aggregate employment rate for women rose from 69 per cent in 1996 to 72 per cent in 2002. The employment rate for men rose 2 percentage points over the same period, from 80 per cent in 1996 to 82 per cent in 2002. As a result of these different employment trends, by 2002 the absolute difference in employment rates between men and women had fallen to the lowest ever observed level, at around 10 percentage points. This narrowing has been the result of males failing to make recent employment gains, though the gap has changed little over recovery.

Table 15.1   Employment rates by age

	Age 16–24	Age 25–34	Age 35–49	Age 50+	Total
Female					
1996	68	68	74	61	69
1998	70	69	74	62	70
2000	69	72	75	64	71
2002	71	71	76	65	72
Male					
1996	76	86	87	66	80
1998	78	88	87	68	81
2000	79	89	89	69	82
2002	79	88	88	70	82
Gap					
1996	−8	−18	−13	−5	−11
1998	−8	−19	−13	−6	−11
2000	−10	−17	−14	−5	−11
2002	−8	−17	−12	−5	−10

Note: Including schemes and excluding students.

Source: LFS. Weighted using the LFS sample weights.

At what age does the employment gap emerge?

Although inequality between the employment rates remains, it is much less than in the 1970s. Figure 15.1 illustrates employment rates for both men and women over the life cycle. The upper panel shows that in 1979 there was quite a clear double-peaked female employment effect with rates as low as 50 per cent for women in their mid-20s and mid-30s. This pattern has for the most part disappeared in recent years. Despite high staying-on rates in education, more young men currently enter employment in their teenage years than women, and the employment rate gap is negative. The employment gap widens to 18 per cent for the 25–34 age group in 1996, before eventually beginning to narrow.

The obvious explanation for the emergence of the employment gap is that women still carry the bulk of childcare responsibilities and continue to find the dual roles (and associated costs) of paid work and motherhood incompatible. Table 15.2 reports female employment rates broken down by the age of the youngest child present in the household. Employment rates for women with children younger than eight years are always much lower than those for women with no dependent children. One explanation of the constraining force of the presence of young children on female labour supply is that children have high costs in terms of time and thereby raise the reservation wage of being in work (Becker, 1964). As the age of the youngest child rises, the decision to participate in formal work is affected less and less.

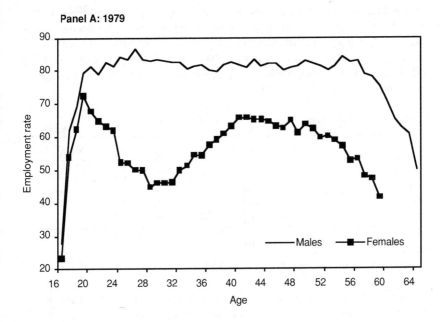

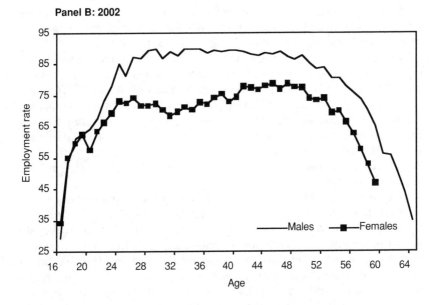

Figure 15.1   Employment rates over the life-cycle by gender, 1979 and 2002

Source: LFS.

This is what we observe from the data. Female employment rates rise with the age of the youngest child. The absence of children in the household is associated with a pattern of female employment rates that most closely mimics the aggregate employment rate of men. Note that, although not shown in the table, there is no association between employment rates and the age of youngest dependent child for men.

Table 15.2   Female employment rates by age of youngest child

	0–1	2–3	4–5	6–7	8–16	16+	No children
1996	44	52	60	64	73	74	74
1998	48	53	60	67	73	76	76
2000	51	54	63	68	74	76	76
2002	50	54	63	70	74	77	77

Note: Including schemes and excluding students.

Source: LFS. Weighted using the LFS sample weights.

The employment rate for women with children under one year old has traditionally been low and stable, but there is some recent evidence for this particular group of a recent increase in this rate (from 44 per cent in 1996 to 50 per cent in 2002). It is increasingly likely to now find women with very young children in employment, and the difference in employment rates for these and other groups of women is narrowing quite quickly.

In the autumn of 1999, the British government introduced more finely tapered in-work benefits for which the major recipients were women. Subject to working at least 16 hours each week, a parent may qualify for WFTC in the form of a monetary benefit and help with childcare costs, administered through the Inland Revenue. Such a policy is geared at facilitating the participation of women, even in very low paid jobs, whilst their children are young. Hitherto, some of these women would have withdrawn from the labour market and the policy is directly aimed at reducing their intermittent economic participation.

In April 2003, the rules governing WFTC change again and the benefit will be split into two tax credits: the Working Tax Credit (WTC) and the Child Tax Credit (CTC). The WTC represents a payment top-up that helps to make paid work financially worthwhile for individuals on low incomes and it also includes some help with the costs of recognised childcare. The CTC brings together all income-related financial support for children into one single payment paid directly into the bank account of the primary carer (usually the mother). It is likely that the WTC will further promote the trends in female employment observed above.

Lengthening female job tenure

The changing nature of job tenure has been well documented elsewhere (see amongst others, Burgess and Rees, 1996 and Gregg and Wadsworth, 2002). Table 15.3 shows the increase in proportion of jobs for men of short to medium length since 1990. Male tenure in jobs of over five years continued to decline steadily, while female tenure continued to rise, such that the gender tenure gap has recently narrowed.

Table 15.3 Male and female job tenure by year and age of youngest child

Length of tenure	Men (%)	Women (%)	Difference	Women		
				With child aged 0–5	With child aged 5–16	No children or child over 16
1990						
0–12 months	14.7	20.3	–5.6	30.1	21.5	16.2
12 months–5 years	29.8	39.9	–10.1	40.1	47.5	33.1
5 years plus	55.4	39.8	15.6	29.7	31.0	50.7
1997						
0–12 months	19.6	21.5	–1.9	26.6	24.0	19.2
12 months–5 years	28.4	33.9	–5.5	34.3	38.4	30.6
5 years plus	52.0	44.6	7.4	39.2	37.7	50.1
2002						
0–12 months	17.8	20.8	–3.0	22.9	22.7	18.7
12 months–5 years	32.2	36.7	–4.4	37.7	39.7	33.7
5 years plus	50.0	42.5	7.5	39.4	37.7	47.5

Source: LFS.

Higher female employment rates now occur alongside lengthier female job tenure. The retention of good jobs over the life-cycle is sometimes associated with improved firm-specific human capital and an increase in the marginal productivity of labour. Maternity leave legislation, introduced in Britain in 1978 and then amended in 1993, has allowed increasing numbers of women to retain a job match over their child-rearing years. Whilst the length of job tenure for men in Britain has been falling, job tenure for women, even for those with young children, has generally been rising.

Indeed, Table 15.3 confirms how average job tenure for women with young children has continued to increase more than for other groups of women. The percentage of mothers with young children and job tenure of more than five years rose from around 30 per cent in 1990 to 39 per cent in 2002. However, the percentage of women with no children (or with offspring older than 16 years) with tenure of more than five years fell slightly. What we may be observing is the effect for mothers of young children of the take-up of maternity leave for high-wage women, alongside the impact of the WFTC (encouraging low-wage women to retain a foothold in the labour market). Maternity leave legislation would be further enhanced by the formal right to return to part-time work enabling additional women to keep the link with an existing employer. Such an improvement does not yet seem likely to occur in Britain. It might of course be argued that part-time jobs allow women to manage both home and work and serve to commit women to the traditional, yet constraining, role of homemaker.

Breaking through the ceiling: occupational categorisation of gender

If women remain in occupations and industries with low rates of pay and poor working conditions, then do relative improvements in employment rates and average job tenure truly reveal progress? Table 15.4 reports the

Table 15.4   Gender segregation by occupation in 2002

Main job	Share in female (male) employment (%)	Within occupation gender share: % female	Hourly wage (£)
Manager & senior	10 (18)	31	
Corporate manager		19	25.80
Functional manager		29	20.70
Protective services		7	17.40
Professional	10 (12)	43	
Health		48	21.10
Business & statistics		32	20.30
Legal professional		41	19.60
Associate professional	13 (13)	47	
Legal associate		47	17.50
Transport		5	16.70
Business & finance		38	14.90
Administrative	24 (5)	81	
Secretary		98	9.40
Skilled trade	2 (20)	9	
Printer		28	9.70
Personal service	13 (2)	86	
Leisure		61	8.90
Sales	12 (4)	72	
Salesperson		75	6.70
Processing, plant	3 (13)	17	
Construction		2	9.40
Elementary	12 (12)	47	
Cleaning		73	6.60

Source: LFS, 2002.

occupations in which men and women are employed in 2002. Skilled manual occupations, such as work as a printer, dominate the areas where women have made little in the way of inroads, whilst secretaries are nearly always women. However, it is now possible to observe an almost equal gender split in some occupations. For example, 48 per cent of health professionals and 47 per cent of legal associate professionals are female.

The hourly wage of some occupations selected from the nine major occupational categories are reported in the final column. The amounts are roughly hierarchical, such that managers (at the top of the table) earn more than cleaners (at the bottom). What is interesting is that whilst there are many female managers, further investigation reveals that these women are not located in the particularly high-paying managerial subgroups. Around 31 per cent of managers are female compared with 69 per cent male. But amongst these managers, the highest hourly wages occur for corporate managers. In 2002, only 19 per cent of corporate managers are female compared with 81 per cent male.

Pay

We report, above, the occupational split by gender at average hourly wages for certain occupations. Can it be said, however, that the economic recovery and the introduction of the National Minimum Wage (NMW) reduced gender disparities in earnings in all occupations? Figure 15.2 shows the pay distributions for both men and women for the years 1997 and 2002. Despite the use of the recent, improved LFS hourly pay information for 2002, we still expect some measurement error and employer non-compliance, and we continue to observe observations below the level of the minimum wage (Dickens and Manning discuss this at length in Chapter 13). The left-hand tail of the male pay distribution is not as concentrated as that of the female. So relatively more women earn less than men and this has neither changed over time, nor in the advent of minimum wage legislation. Indeed, Robinson (2002) notes that the minimum wage would have had to be £6.00 an hour in 1999 in order to reduce the average gender pay gap to around 20 per cent.

Table 15.5 shows that, in 1994, a typical woman could expect to be paid an average of £7.00 an hour. However, a man could expect to earn £9.50 an hour (in January 2002 prices). As recently as 2002, a woman could be paid an average of £8.20 an hour whilst a man could earn £10.70. So in 2002, women earned, on average, some 77 per cent of the typical male wage. The usual way to represent this is by looking at the simple difference in pay; or by calculating the female wage as a proportion of the male wage (the wage ratio); or by normalising this by subtracting the ratio from unity (the wage gap). The wage gap would then range from zero (complete equality in pay) to one (complete inequality). Table 15.5 shows that there has been a modest

Panel A: 1997

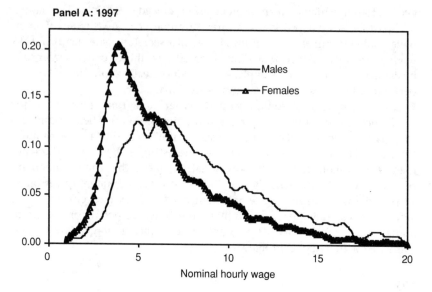

Nominal hourly wage

Panel B: 2002

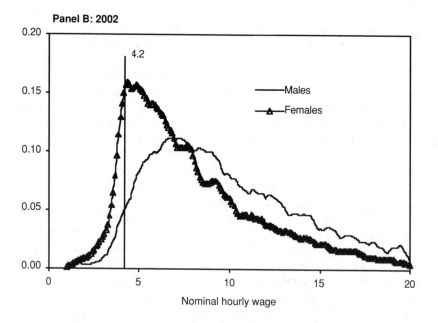

Nominal hourly wage

Figure 15.2   Nominal hourly wage distribution in 1997 and 2002

Source: LFS.

Table 15.5 Real hourly wage rates by gender

Year	Male total	Female total	Difference	Mean gap (%)	Gap at 10th percentile (%)	Gap at median (%)	Gap at 90th percentile (%)	FT male gap (%)	PT male gap (%)
1994	9.50	7.00	2.50	26	16	26	25	18	35
1996	9.60	7.10	2.50	26	15	27	26	18	36
1998	9.70	7.20	2.50	26	16	26	25	16	37
2000	10.30	7.70	2.60	25	14	25	25	17	36
2002	10.70	8.20	2.50	23	12	24	25	15	36

Source: LFS.

narrowing of the average (mean) gender pay gap (from 26 per cent to 23 per cent) during the periods of New Labour administration.

Given that the pay distributions of men and women are so very different, we may ask what is the extent of narrowing of the pay gap at various points in the wage distribution? Column 5 shows that there is some evidence of a fall in the size of the pay gap at the 10th percentile. At the 90th percentile of the distribution, there is virtually no change. What we are probably observing here is the impact of the NMW at the bottom end of the wage distribution.

Since the majority of part-time workers are women, any part-time pay penalty will influence the gender pay gap. So it may be more meaningful to split the gender pay gap by part- or full-time work status, as in the last two columns. Now we see that any narrowing of the gap is reserved solely to women working full-time. There has not been a narrowing of the pay gap for women working part-time, despite minimum wage legislation.

The gender pay gap. At what age does the gap emerge?

So far, we have something like the following: employment rates of women have continued to converge to those of men, but occupational and pay differences between the genders remain. It is insightful to ask at what point in the life-cycle these differentials begin to emerge. Differences in educational attainment or on-the-job training may mean that pay for older women may lag behind, if younger cohorts are more educated or receive more training. When we disaggregate by age, Table 15.6 reveals that the gender pay gap for workers aged between 16 and 24 has widened recently. These women earned less than their male counterparts since 1996, but the relative female position worsened in 2002. The difference in pay for teenagers is still only relatively small. The differential is more pronounced when young workers reach their mid-20s and it really begins to widen for the 35–49 age range. (This is perhaps more clearly seen in Figure 15.3.) Once again, the linking factor may be the constraining effect of young children (see Joshi, Paci and Waldfogel, 1999). Their presence may preclude women from taking, or continuing in, high-paying jobs, or from generally maintaining a foothold in the labour market over their child-rearing years. Recently, the gender pay gap has narrowed most among 25–34 year olds: it does not appear to be closing significantly elsewhere. That it is indeed narrowing for those women in their mid-20s is in part due to the fact that the labour market participation of this group has been increasing over time: greater attachment and less intermittent work behaviour is generally associated with higher wages. The lower panel of Table 15.6 gives the gender pay gap for workers split by educational level attained. It shows that there is not much variation in the gap for groups of women by highest educational qualification. So the explanation for the pay gap must partly lie elsewhere.

Table 15.6 Gender wage gaps by age and education

	Gap (%)			
	Age 16–24	Age 25–34	Age 35–49	Age 50+
1996	–6	–20	–32	–28
1998	–6	–19	–31	–30
2000	–6	–17	–29	–30
2002	–8	–15	–29	–26
	Graduate	A-level	GCSE	No qualifications
1996	–20	–20	–18	–24
1998	–22	–21	–20	–22
2000	–23	–21	–20	–22
2002	–20	–18	–23	–20

Source: LFS.

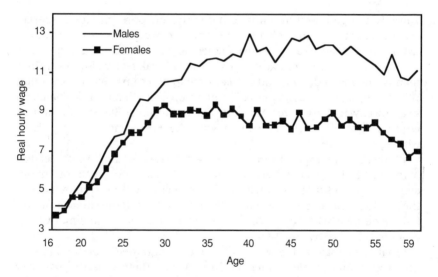

Figure 15.3 Age–earnings profile by gender, 2002

Source: LFS.

Table 15.7 reveals that those women who do actually manage to combine working life and motherhood (especially those who can do so when their children are very young) earn more than those with older children. So, for example, a mother with a baby less than one year old who remains in employment could expect to earn around £9.10 in 2002, whilst a working mother of a child aged between 6 and 15 years could earn around £7.50.

Increasing numbers of women are remaining in employment whilst their children are young. With the passage of more recent cohorts of mothers through time, we would expect them to have accumulated relatively more work experience than earlier cohorts.

Table 15.7   Wage rates by age of youngest child

	Female Total	Child 0–1	Child 2–5	Child 6–15	No children
1996	7.10	7.80	7.30	6.60	7.20
1998	7.20	8.10	7.20	6.60	7.40
2000	7.70	8.90	7.90	7.10	7.90
2002	8.20	9.10	8.50	7.50	8.40

Source: LFS.

Entrants

There is a large literature on whether better measures of labour market experience can help in explaining the gender pay gap. The estimates of the returns to experience can be biased if potential, rather than actual, experience measures are used. Women who have a career break receive lower earnings than women who do not, and it takes time to make up these lost earnings. When returning to the labour market after a break, both men and women do so at lower wages. However, Manning and Robinson (1998) show that men return at higher wages than women, with the entry gender pay gap rising with age.

We divide our sample of workers observed in a single annual cross-section of the British Household Panel Survey into two groups: those with continuous employment and those who have had some period of non-employment in the previous year, but who are currently in work. We call the latter 'entrants', but we define this group to have come from the pool of unemployed or economically inactive workers.

What can be said of the wages of the female entrants? Table 15.8 reports the proportion of male and female entrants and their respective pay over recent years. The proportion of female entrants is routinely higher than the male figure, and the wages that accrue to these women is consistently lower than for the men. Manning and Robinson (1998) decompose the gender wage gap by breaking down wages as follows. The observed current average wage comprises a weighted average of the average wage of new entrants and the average wage of continuing workers. Entrant wages are lower. Women are far more likely to be entrants, and this, combined with the fact that women are more likely to have repeated breaks in paid employment, and the timing of these breaks, is the explanation for why the pay of women increasingly falls behind the pay of men. Further, women working part-time are paid less than full-time women because they are much more likely to be entrants and because they have slightly lower wage growth when in paid employment.

Table 15.8   Proportion of entrants and entrant wages

	Male entrants (%)	Female Entrants (%)	Difference	Male entrant wage	Female entrant wage	Difference
1992	11	14	–3	7.00	5.60	–1.40
1993	11	14	–3	6.80	5.60	–1.20
1997	12	13	–1	6.80	5.60	–1.20
2000	11	14	–3	6.80	6.00	–0.80

Source: BHPS.

Low pay

In April 1999, the British government introduced the NMW at an adult rate of £3.60 an hour across all occupations. Figure 15.2 illustrates that women are disproportionately represented amongst the low paid, so it was anticipated that the NMW would overly affect poorly paid women, and so reduce the overall gender pay gap. Table 15.9 suggests that there is evidence of some compression in both male and female wage distributions from the bottom end. This is reflected in the compression in the within-gender pay ratios. Both the

Table 15.9   Summary statistics of nominal hourly wage distribution before and after NMW (adults 22 years and over)

	Females				Males			
	10th p'tile	50th	90th p'tile	Mean	10th p'tile	50th	90th p'tile	Mean
1998	3.40	5.90	12.20	**7.00**	4.5	8.4	16.5	**9.70**
1999	3.70	6.20	12.70	**7.40**	4.8	8.6	17.1	**10.10**
2000	3.80	6.60	13.80	**8.00**	4.9	8.9	18.4	**10.50**
2002	4.10	7.10	14.60	**8.50**	5.3	9.6	19.5	**11.30**

	Gender pay ratios				
	$10_F^{th}/10_M^{th}$	$50_F^{th}/50_M^{th}$	$90_F^{th}/90_M^{th}$	$10_F th/90_M^{th}$	$10_F^{th}/50_M^{th}$
1998	0.75	0.70	0.74	0.21	0.40
1999	0.77	0.72	0.74	0.22	0.43
2000	0.78	0.74	0.75	0.21	0.42
2002	0.77	0.74	0.75	0.21	0.43

Note: Pay estimates rounded to nearest tenth of a pound.

Source: LFS.

90/10 and the 50/10 ratios fall further than the 90/50 following the immediate introduction of the NMW. This is to be expected if there is a process introduced that compresses the wage distribution from below.

Consistent again with the effect of the NMW benefiting women more than men, we observe that the percentage change in the nominal mean of female hourly earnings rises by more than that of men in the year 1998/99. In the year 1999/2000, the distribution for women appears to widen again (see also Machin, Chapter 12), which suggests that most of the action on the gender wage gap in this year was coming not from the lower end of the distribution but from the top. The lower panel of Table 15.9 shows that the cross-gender pay ratios are little changed at the top, though they may have narrowed at the bottom between 1998 and 1999. And so whilst we observe an overall narrowing of the (average) gender pay gap over time, there seems little move to close the gap at the upper end of the occupational ladder.

Conclusion

The gender employment gap does not appear to have changed substantially during the New Labour administration. However, the average gender pay gap continues to narrow, but this process has disguised the widening divide between women who work full-time and those who work part-time. The gender pay gap for part-time work has not narrowed.

Much of the pay gap is the result of the discontinuous labour force participation of women. However, intermittent participation has continued to become less prevalent over the years. Those women who are outside the labour market in their 20s and 30s miss out on crucial amounts of wage growth experienced by their counterparts. They are also precluded from attaining higher occupational levels. For as long as this continues, we will observe the existence of the average gender pay gap.

The increasing length of female job tenure for women with young children proxies to a certain extent how well maternity leave is encouraging women to remain in work. Where maternity leave is operating effectively we would expect to see women remain with their pre-break employer, and ever-increasing lengths of job tenure. The average gender tenure gap has indeed been narrowing: this may also be the result of WFTC.

The advent of the NMW seems to have had some effect on removing gender pay inequality at the bottom of the wage distribution. But the WFTC is also aiding this process by encouraging women to remain in the labour market. The timing, and repetition, of exit and re-entry of women into jobs over their child-rearing years would seem to be a huge part of the explanation of the gender pay gap and WFTC attempts to counteract this. However, although many processes have been acting in the interests of women, the occupational segregation of women remains and women are noticeably absent from the high-paid occupational subgroups.

References

Becker, G. S. (1964), *Human Capital*, Columbia University Press: New York.

Burgess, S. and Rees, H. (1996), 'Job Tenure in Britain 1975–1992', *Economic Journal*, 106(435), pp. 334–44.

Dickens, R. and Manning, A. (2002), 'Has the National Minimum Wage Reduced UK Wage Inequality?', Centre for Economic Performance Discussion Paper No. 533, London School of Economics.

Gregg, P. and Wadsworth, J. (2002), 'Job Tenure in Britain 1975–2000. Is a Job for Life or Just for Christmas?', *Oxford Bulletin of Economics and Statistics*, 64(1), pp. 111–34.

Manning, A. and Robinson, H. (1998), 'Something in the Way She Moves: A Fresh Look at an Old Gap', Centre for Economic Performance Discussion Paper No. 389, London School of Economics.

Joshi, H., Paci, P. and Waldfogel, J. (1999), 'The Wages of Motherhood: Better or Worse?', *Cambridge Journal of Economics*, 23, pp. 543–78.

Robinson, H. (2002), 'Wrong Side of the Track: The Impact of the Minimum Wage on Gender Pay Gaps in Britain', *Oxford Bulletin of Economics and Statistics*, 64(5) December.

16
Skills in the UK

Steven McIntosh

Key findings

- The UK has more adults with poor basic skills of literacy and numeracy than many countries in Europe.
- Younger cohorts of adults in the UK perform no better (literacy) or even worse (numeracy) than older cohorts, which suggests that the UK labour force is not replenishing itself with more skilled workers, contrary to the situation in many European countries.
- Those who do have good literacy and numeracy skills in the UK enjoy a substantial wage premium over those who do not, showing the value of these skills to individuals and employers.
- There has been a small recent increase in the proportion of adults holding at least intermediate (Level 3) vocational qualifications, although the growth of academic qualifications remains faster.
- With the exception of professional qualifications, the returns to other vocational qualifications are not large, suggesting a relatively low worth in the labour market.
- For individuals with no school qualifications at all, vocational qualifications at Level 3 do seem to provide real benefit, although qualifications below Level 3 continue to have little value.

Introduction

In terms of higher education, the UK compares reasonably favourably with competitor countries. It is at the lower end of the skills distribution that the UK seems to be falling behind. There has been a growth in the demand for skilled labour, which many commentators seem to attribute to skill-biased technological change. These changes have led to a large fall in the demand for unskilled labour, and a rise in the demand for professional and managerial non-manual workers at the top of the skills distribution, and for skilled manual/intermediate non-manual workers in the middle of the skills distribution. It could perhaps be argued that the UK education system is satisfying the former demand through the expansion of higher education, but the latter demand for skilled manual and intermediate non-manual workers does not seem to be being met.

Thus, the British skills distribution is becoming bi-polar, with large numbers obtaining high levels of qualifications and skills equivalent to graduate level, but also a long tail of low achievers continue to exist with no or only low level qualifications to their name. Other countries have been more successful in reducing the size of this latter group in line with their falling demand, essentially by ensuring that more individuals reach an intermediate (Level 3[1]) level of attainment. The 1996 Skills Audit shows precisely this when comparing the UK with France and Germany (DfEE, 1996). It is not just in terms of formal qualifications that the UK is falling behind, however. The Moser Report (DfEE, 1999) shows that the UK has higher proportions of adults with poor basic skills in literacy and numeracy, compared to many European countries.

The recent emphasis on education in UK public policy has attempted to alleviate the problems identified above. It has been recognised that if larger numbers of low achievers are to reach an intermediate level (Level 3) then they are more likely to do this through vocational qualifications, rather than A-levels for which they are ill-equipped to study. A problem in the provision of vocational qualifications was identified in that, although many vocational qualifications are on offer in the UK, they fall under the control of various awarding bodies, principal amongst which are the City and Guilds, the Business and Technician Education Council (BTEC) and the Royal Society of Arts Examinations Board (RSA). Thus there was no unified system of vocational education, with little structure and hence recognised pathways of progression, and little understanding, by individuals or employers, of the relative worth of the various qualifications. Therefore, although the older vocational qualifications still remain available, a system of National Vocational Qualifications (NVQs) and General National Vocational Qualifications (GNVQs) was introduced in the early 1990s, which was intended to provide clarity and structure to vocational education.[2] In addition, towards the end of the 1990s, apprenticeships re-appeared on the agenda in the UK, with the idea that Advanced Modern Apprenticeships should lead to the critical Level 3 qualification.

As for basic skills, programmes have been put in place to improve literacy and numeracy amongst both children and adults. For the former, a 'Literacy Hour' was introduced in 1998 covering all primary school children. The literacy hour takes place every day, and concentrates on developing literacy skills in a prescribed way. In 1999 a corresponding 'Numeracy Hour' was introduced every day. For adults, the 'Skills for Life' programme was established in 2001. This programme targets those individuals who are likely to have low literacy and numeracy skills, such as the unemployed, prisoners and low-skilled people in employment, and offers them an entitlement to free basic skills training, in a format, time and location acceptable and appropriate to such individuals.

This chapter discusses and evaluates some of these issues. We begin by focusing on basic skills. Unfortunately, no nationally representative tests of such skills have recently been undertaken. We therefore use a data set from 1995 to document the UK's position on basic skills relative to other countries, and to evaluate the impact of basic skills on labour market outcomes. We then consider more formal vocational qualifications, for which time series data are available, allowing us to chart changes in their acquisition, before we again move on to a consideration of their value.

Basic skill levels in Britain compared to other countries

To obtain comparative information on the basic skills of literacy and numeracy across countries, we make use of the International Adult Literacy Survey (IALS). This survey was conducted in 1994–95 in 12 countries, using an identical questionnaire in each country. The respondents were all adults of working age. The most useful aspect of the survey for the purpose of this chapter is that it included direct measures of the respondents' literacy and numeracy skills, in the form of tests given as part of the survey. Since the same questions were asked in each country, this has allowed users of the data to make comparisons of skill levels across countries. Based on their answers to the test questions, respondents were given a score of between 0 and 500 for both literacy and numeracy.[3] These scores are then translated into five levels for each skill, based on certain cut-off points. The cut-off points are the same in each country, so that the levels are again comparable across countries.

The designers of IALS suggest that Level 3 skills in their survey are the minimum required to function successfully in modern economies, so we examine the proportions of the various national populations who fail to reach this Level 3 standard. Table 16.1 reveals that Britain does not fare too well in terms of the basic skills relative to the other countries in IALS.

Britain has more of the working age population scoring at the lowest two levels than all other countries in the survey except Ireland and Poland. For example, considering literacy, over one-fifth (22 per cent) of Britons fall into the lowest category, measuring a very limited level of skills, while over half fall into the lowest two categories. These figures compare, for example, to 14 per cent and 49 per cent respectively in Germany and just 7 per cent and 28 per cent respectively in Sweden. For numeracy, the gap between Britain and her European colleagues seems even wider. Some 23 per cent of Britons are at the lowest skill level for numeracy and again over half, 51 per cent, can be found in the lowest two categories. Using Germany and Sweden (the best-performing country) for comparison purposes again, only 7 per cent of adults in each country score at the lowest level for numeracy, with 25 per cent in Sweden and 33 per cent in Germany falling into the lowest two categories.

Table 16.1   The percentage of working age adults scoring at Level 1 or Level 2 and below for literacy and numeracy

	Literacy		Numeracy	
	% at Level 1	% at Levels 1 and 2	% at Level 1	% at Levels 1 and 2
Sweden	7	28	7	25
Germany	14	49	7	33
Netherlands	11	41	10	36
Canada (English)	15	40	16	39
Belgium (Flanders)	18	47	17	40
Switzerland (German)	19	55	14	40
US	21	46	21	46
New Zealand	18	46	20	49
Britain	**22**	**52**	**23**	**51**
Ireland	23	52	25	53
Poland	43	77	39	69

Source: IALS.

Table 16.2 looks at low basic skills by age group. If a country is to improve its stock of skills, then the most likely route is through cohorts of youngsters entering the labour market with better basic skills than the older cohorts leaving it. If this process is occurring, then we should observe a smaller proportion of the younger age groups being classified at IALS Levels 1 and 2 than the older age groups.

Table 16.2   Percentages at Level 2 or below for literacy and numeracy, by age group

	Literacy % at Levels 1 and 2			Numeracy % at Levels 1 and 2		
	16–25	26–35	36–45	16–25	26–35	36–45
Sweden	21	19	27	23	18	24
Germany	38	43	46	31	28	29
Netherlands	30	27	39	29	27	35
Canada (English)	39	37	30	39	33	28
Belgium (Flanders)	31	35	47	28	31	39
Switzerland (German)	43	43	59	29	34	45
US	54	43	41	57	41	41
New Zealand	44	46	40	50	46	45
Britain	**47**	**47**	**46**	**51**	**47**	**43**
Ireland	44	47	51	48	50	51
Poland	65	74	80	62	66	68

Source: IALS.

This is indeed what we observe in all of the mainland European countries. For literacy, the proportion of 36–45 year olds scoring at IALS Level 2 or below is significantly higher than the proportions of 16–25 year olds or 26–35 year olds scoring at the same level in Sweden, Germany, the Netherlands, Belgium, Switzerland, Ireland and Poland. In Britain, however, we do not see this pattern. Amongst 36–45 year olds, 46 per cent are in the lowest two categories for literacy, with this proportion being 47 per cent in each of the two younger cohorts. Britain does not seem to making any progress in terms of replenishing its workforce with better literacy skills. With respect to numeracy, although it is true that the improvements in the central European countries are not as large as with literacy, in Britain the situation again compares poorly, with the younger cohorts actually performing *worse* on the numeracy test than their older counterparts. Amongst 16–25 year olds, over half (51 per cent) have numeracy skills that score in the bottom two IALS categories, compared to 47 per cent amongst 26–35 year olds and 43 per cent amongst 36–45 year olds. It is interesting to note that the other English-speaking countries in the sample, with the exception of Ireland, namely the US, Canada and New Zealand, also experience poorer skills amongst the younger age groups, for both literacy and numeracy.

The returns to basic skills

How important are basic skills for success in the labour market? By examining the differences in wages between those at a higher level and a lower level of skills, we can get an idea of the value that is placed on these skills. Table 16.3 reports the results of such an analysis, for five countries in the IALS data set. In particular, the table shows how much more those at IALS Level 3 and at IALS Level 4 or 5[4] earn, compared to those at IALS Level 2 or below. We focus on these levels because, as stated earlier, the collectors of the IALS data view IALS Level 3 as the minimum level that individuals should be aiming for to function successfully in modern society. The results net out other factors that influence wages, such as gender,[5] age and father's education. For each country, column '2' also controls for highest qualification achieved.

Whether we want to control for qualifications or not depends on what question we want to answer. When qualifications are excluded from the analysis, then the observed returns to basic skills will be the full effect of basic skills on wages, incorporating the fact that more able individuals in terms of literacy and numeracy are more likely to obtain higher qualifications, and so earn more for this reason. If we net out the effect of qualifications attained, then the observed returns to basic skills will be the increase in wages due to higher skills, over and above any rise in qualification attainment attributable to those higher skills. Thus, if we want to know the benefit of raising literacy and numeracy amongst school children, then we may be interested in the full effect, including any knock-on effects from higher qualification attainment. If we are focusing on raising the skills of adults, then we may wish to know the effect of an increase in literacy and numeracy skills for a given level of qualifications already attained, in which case we would focus on the partial effect, netting out qualifications. Table 16.3 considers both scenarios, for each country in turn.

Table 16.3 The wage returns to higher level literacy and numeracy

	Britain		US		Netherlands		Sweden		Germany	
	1	2	1	2	1	2	1	2	1	2
Literacy										
IALS Level 3	+2	0	+14	+8	+8	+1	+5	0	0	0
IALS Level 4/5	+12	+4	+17	+8	+14	+3	+6	0	+2	0
Numeracy										
IALS Level 3	+23	+20	+26	+21	+9	+5	+2	+2	+8	+8
IALS Level 4/5	+39	+29	+44	+32	+20	+15	+6	+6	+6	+7

Notes: The equations control for gender, age, father's education and, in the column '2's only, for highest qualification achieved.

Source: IALS.

In Britain, there are big differences in wages between those at IALS Level 3 or above, and those below this level, particularly for numeracy. Thus, individuals whose numeracy skills are ranked at Level 3 earn, on average, 23 per cent more than those with numeracy skills below this standard. If we move to the highest IALS categories for numeracy (Levels 4/5), there is a 39 per cent difference between the wages of this group and those with low level (below Level 3) skills. Clearly good numeracy skills earn a substantial premium in the British labour market, and are highly valued. Column '2' reveals that these findings are not simply a result of more numerate individuals obtaining better qualifications. Even when we control for highest qualification acquired, there are still substantial returns to numeracy skills, of 20 per cent and 29 per cent for those at IALS Levels 3 and 4/5 respectively, compared to those below Level 3.

The value attached to literacy skills in Britain is lower than for numeracy skills, although it should be noted that the scores on the tests are very strongly related, and our analysis might not be too successful in identifying the separate effects of literacy and numeracy on wages. Nevertheless, as far as the results stand, they indicate only a small, 2 per cent difference between the wages of those with Level 3 literacy skills and those with Level 2 or below literacy skills. At the higher level, we do observe a substantially higher return of 12 per cent to Level 4/5 literacy skills. Column '2' shows that the impact of good literacy skills works to a large extent through the achievement of good qualifications, since, once we control for the fact that those with better literacy skills acquire better qualifications, we do not observe any difference in wages between those at Level 3 and those below this level, while those whose literacy skills score at Level 4/5 earn only 4 per cent more than those below Level 3, on average. There is an even larger difference in wages between those with good and bad basic skills in the US than in Britain, with numeracy again dominating. Thus individuals with numeracy skills at IALS Level 3 earn 26 per cent more than those whose numeracy skills fall below this level in the US, with the premium at Level 4/5 for numeracy skills being 44 per cent. Although differences in wages by literacy score are smaller than these numeracy differences, they are still substantial, being 14 per cent at Level 3 and 17 per cent at Level 4/5, both compared to Level 2 or below. Moreover, column '2' shows that each of these wage impacts act in part independently of any effects on better qualification attainment, with the wage differences even after controlling for qualifications being 21 per cent at Level 3 and 32 per cent at Level 4/5 for numeracy, and 8 per cent at both Levels 3 and 4/5 for literacy.

The remainder of the table shows that the returns attached to skill levels are much lower in mainland European countries than in the UK and the US. In the Netherlands, the wage premia attached to numeracy skills are less than half those observed in the UK (although the literacy differentials are similar). In Sweden and Germany, wage differentials by skill level are even smaller, being less than 10 per cent in all cases at all levels, even when we do not control for qualifications and observe the full impact of skills on wages.[6]

What can account for these differences in the impact of basic skills on wages across countries? Two possible explanations spring to mind, given that the countries where the returns are higher, the UK and the US, have more workers with low level skills, and also higher wage inequality than the countries with the smaller returns, the Netherlands, Sweden and Germany. The relative shortage of individuals with a good standard of basic skills in the US and the UK could lead to a higher premium being paid to those who do possess these skills. In addition, just as high wage inequality in the Anglo-Saxon countries is well known to be associated with higher returns to formal qualifications than in central European countries, we may be observing a similar effect on the returns to basic skills here. It would appear that the high wage inequality that we observe in the UK and US may be due in part to a wider distribution of skills, with a longer tail at the bottom end in those countries, but also in particular due to higher returns to particular skill levels in the UK and the US with fewer institutional props to low wages for the low-skilled.

Vocational qualifications

We turn now to a consideration of more formal qualifications, focusing in particular on vocational qualifications, which are more likely to be acquired by those at the lower end of the skill range. Although formal qualifications are included in the IALS data set, far more information is available in the Labour Force Survey (LFS), which being yearly also allows us to consider changes over time. We use data for the years 1993 to 2001, 1993 being the first full year in which wage data were collected in the LFS. In each year we merge the data from the four quarterly surveys to produce annual data sets. The usefulness of the LFS for this analysis is the detailed information that it contains on qualifications held. Beginning in 1996, individuals have been asked to list *all* qualifications that they hold. Prior to 1996, the LFS only asked respondents for their three highest qualifications, and so there is an inconsistency in the data at this point in time. This is clearly likely to lead to an under-reporting of lower level qualifications in these years.

Table 16.4 reveals the percentage of the UK adult working-age population that holds each of the main qualifications on offer in this country, in 1993,

Table 16.4   The proportions holding each of the qualifications – all of working age

Qualification	1993	1997[a]	2001
Academic			
Higher degree	2.0	1.9	2.6
First degree	8.8	9.9	12.2
Other HE	1.7	2.4	2.7
A-levels	17.3	21.3	23.7
Academic qualification at Level 3 or above	*20.8*	*23.5*	*26.9*
GCSEs A*–C	41.5	53.0	56.4
GCSEs D–F	7.0	4.8	4.3
Vocational			
Professional qualification	4.2	1.5	1.8
Teaching qualification	2.6	2.9	2.8
Nursing qualification	2.4	2.6	2.5
HND/HNC	4.0	4.5	4.8
RSA higher	0.6	0.4	0.3
ONC/OND	4.0	4.0	4.1
City & Guilds Advanced Craft	2.4	3.2	4.1
NVQ/GNVQ 3–5	0.3	1.7	3.8
Vocational qualification at Level 3 or above[b]	*14.5*	*16.6*	*19.2*
City & Guilds Craft	5.1	5.6	4.9
BTEC diploma	1.0	1.2	0.8
NVQ/GNVQ 2	0.5	2.6	4.2
City & Guilds other	4.6	8.3	7.1
NVQ/GNVQ 1	0.2	1.0	1.4
RSA lower	6.3	7.5	7.0
Other	22.3	38.7	36.9
Apprenticeship/no other qualification	2.0	1.0	1.1
No qualification	24.7	19.1	17.3

Notes: [a] In 1996, the LFS changes from asking about the highest three qualifications held, to asking about all qualifications held. [b] Total does not include professional qualifications, as their level is unknown.

Source: LFS.

1997 and 2001. The first thing to note is that the percentage holding no qualifications at all has fallen from 25 per cent in 1993 to 19 per cent in 1997 and 17 per cent in 2001. In deciding where the growth in qualifications has been strongest we focus on qualifications at Level 3 or above, firstly because this is the level that the government wants young people to reach, and secondly because such qualifications should fall within individuals' top three qualifications, and so should have been picked up when only the top three were recorded prior to 1996, thus making a reasonably consistent series over the period. Table 16.4 shows that in 1993, a larger percentage of the adult population held Level 3+ academic qualifications than Level 3+ vocational qualifications, and that the difference has widened since. Thus the percentage holding academic qualifications at Level 3 or above has increased by 6.1 percentage points, from 20.8 per cent to 26.9 per cent between 1993 and 2001, while the percentage holding vocational qualifications at Level 3 or above has increased by 4.7 percentage points, from 14.5 per cent to 19.2 per cent. Thus while there has been some growth in the acquisition of intermediate vocational qualifications, in particular the new NVQ qualifications, this is dominated by the growth in academic intermediate qualifications, in particular A-levels.

The returns to vocational qualifications

We turn now to an evaluation of one factor that may influence the take-up of vocational qualifications, namely their return, or value, in the labour market. Table 16.5 shows estimates of the wage returns attached to the principal vocational qualifications on offer in the UK, calculated by netting out other factors that can influence wages, namely academic qualifications held, age, ethnicity, region, workplace size and sector worked in (public or private). The estimated returns should be viewed as cumulative. For example, if a man holds both a City and Guilds Craft and a City and Guilds Advanced Craft qualification, he can expect to earn on average 11.3 per cent (4.5 per cent + 6.8 per cent) more than a man with neither of these qualifications in 2001, holding constant demographic characteristics and any other qualifications held.

Returns have been fairly stable over the period from 1997 to 2001. Although we do observe a growth in the returns to professional qualifications, consistent with the well-known increasing wage inequality at the top end of the distribution, the returns to the other vocational qualifications are remarkably similar in the two years. The small increase in the supply of these qualifications, noted in Table 16.4, does not therefore seem to have depressed their returns, suggesting that the demand for these qualifications is also rising in line with supply.

The largest returns are received, as expected, by graduate level professional qualifications (such as in law or accountancy), which raise wages by 43 per cent for men and by 49 per cent for women in 2001. Below this, however, the returns to vocational qualifications are not as high, and in particular are not as high as the academic qualifications at the notionally same NVQ level.[7] At NVQ Level 4, teaching qualifications receive a return of about 8 per cent, nursing qualifications 9 per cent and HNC/HNDs 14 per cent for men in 2001. However for women, although the female returns to an HNC/HND are lower, at 9 per cent, than the equivalent returns for men, women with teaching or nursing qualifications do much better than other women, compared to the male gains from these qualifications. A woman with a teaching qualification earns 29 per cent more than a woman who does not, while a nursing qualification carries an 18 per cent wage advantage. It would appear that although gender segregation in occupations is slowly breaking down, these two professional qualifications still remain amongst the most advantageous to women.

At Level 3 there is again a gender difference in returns to ONC/OND qualifications, being 10 per cent for men and 5 per cent for women in 2001. The

Table 16.5 Estimated percentage wage returns to vocational qualifications

	Males		Females	
	1997	2001	1997	2001
Professional qualification	33.4	42.7	36.1	48.6
Teaching qualification	6.0	7.9	28.0	29.4
Nursing qualification	7.2	9.2	15.6	17.6
HND/HNC	12.1	13.5	7.6	9.1
RSA higher			5.2	0.1
ONC/OND	10.7	9.7	6.3	5.4
City & Guilds Advanced Craft	6.8	4.5		
NVQ/GNVQ 3–5	1.0	2.8	3.3	4.2
City & Guilds Craft	3.5	6.8		4.5
BTEC diploma	4.8	3.4	3.6	1.5
NVQ/GNVQ 2				
City & Guilds other				
NVQ/GNVQ 1				
RSA lower			1.0	
Other	5.1	6.1	6.2	6.5
Apprenticeship/no other qualification	1.6	2.1		

Notes: The equations control for academic qualifications held, age, ethnicity, region, workplace size and public or private sector. Where a cell is left empty indicates a negative return to the qualification was estimated. This is likely to be due to unobserved ability bias, whereby the type of individual acquiring the qualifications involved, which are typically low level qualifications, are likely to be individuals with low earning power for unobserved reasons such as ability, ambition or commitment. We would therefore not suggest that acquiring these qualifications actually reduces the wages of such people, preferring instead to say that there is no evidence of any positive impact of the qualifications, hence shown by the blank cells in the table.

Source: LFS.

results also show differences between the genders with respect to craft vocational qualifications, in particular City and Guilds qualifications, which have a positive impact on wages for men, but have little benefit for women.[8] Again, therefore, we observe men and women earning returns in their traditional stereotyped occupations.

Finally, the NVQ/GNVQ qualifications introduced in the 1990s appear to have little value in the labour market. Such qualifications at Level 3 or above raise male wages by just 3 per cent and female wages by 4 per cent, while NVQ/GNVQ qualifications at Levels 1 and 2 appear to give no benefit at all.

The returns to vocational qualifications for those with no school qualifications

These estimated returns to vocational qualifications are, however, an average, calculated across all individuals who hold them. It could well be that the returns are actually very different for individuals at different points in the skills distribution. This section considers such a possibility, and continues the focus of the chapter on the lower end of the skills distribution, by calculating the returns to the various vocational qualifications for those individuals who did not obtain any qualifications at school. We merge data for the years from 1996 to 2001, because in a disaggregated analysis such as this some of the results using a single year's data would be based on only a limited number of respondents. Merging seems reasonable, given that the returns to most qualifications have remained stable over this time period, as reported above.

Table 16.6 shows the returns to the various vocational qualifications for the group of unqualified school-leavers. We will not focus on the returns to high level qualifications such as professional qualifications, to which the returns are naturally very large for the (very limited number) of unqualified school-leavers who acquire them. Focusing lower down the scale some of these vocational qualifications are clearly beneficial for the group who have left school without a certificate to their name, more so than in the average returns across all individuals calculated in Table 16.5 above. For example, for male unqualified school-leavers, those who acquire an NVQ/GNVQ qualification at Levels 3–5 (in practice, almost all at Level 3) earn 9 per cent more than the similarly unqualified without the NVQ. This is clearly a substantial return, showing the worth of acquiring such a qualification for individuals who have not done well at school, and the worth of investing in such qualifications for society. It is perhaps surprising that there is no estimated return to NVQ/GNVQ qualifications at Levels 1 or 2 amongst this group of low-achievers at school. It seems that these qualifications really do have little value in the labour market, and it is at Level 3 that the benefits kick in. Table 16.6 also shows the benefits of undertaking an apprenticeship for male unqualified school-leavers (even when that apprenticeship does not lead to a qualification[9]) namely a 6 per cent increase in wages. Other trade qualifications, such as City and Guilds qualifications, do not seem to be more beneficial to unqualified school-leavers, however, the returns to this group being very similar to the average returns calculated across all individuals above. Finally, amongst the Level 3 vocational qualifications, an ONC/OND qualification raises the wages of male unqualified school-leavers by 16 per cent, more than the average return across all men of 10 per cent.

For women, the value of NVQ/GNVQ qualifications at Levels 3 or above (though again not below this level) to unqualified school-leavers, raises wages by 7 per cent (as compared to an average figure of 4 per cent for all women). Apprenticeship training, however, does not have the same benefits for unqualified women as for unqualified men. On the other hand, we observe real value attached to RSA qualifications (typically secretarial qualifications) for women who have left school with little to show, RSA higher and lower qualifications raising their wages by 13 per cent and 11 per cent respectively. As with men, ONC/OND qualifications are of significantly more value to female unqualified school-leavers (a return of 11 per cent), than to women on average (5 per cent).

Table 16.6 Estimated percentage wage returns to vocational qualifications for those with no school qualifications, 1996–2001

	Males	Females
Professional qualifications	70.7	79.0
Teaching qualification	10.3	38.7
Nursing qualification	24.7	31.4
HND/HNC	31.7	21.8
RSA higher	0.5	12.9
ONC/OND	16.2	10.7
City & Guilds Advanced Craft	5.7	8.1
NVQ/GNVQ 3–5	8.5	6.6
City & Guilds Craft	6.5	0.4
BTEC diploma	2.7	6.0
NVQ/GNVQ 2		
City & Guilds other	1.9	
NVQ/GNVQ 1		
RSA lower	0.4	11.0
Other	8.1	9.6
Apprenticeship/no other qualification	5.7	

Notes: The equations control for academic qualifications held, age, ethnicity, region, workplace size and public or private sector. Empty cells indicate a negative return was estimated (see notes to Table 16.5).

Source: LFS.

Conclusion

More adults in the UK have poor literacy and numeracy skills, compared to most of our European neighbours. The UK also gets fewer lower achievers up to at least Level 3 in formal qualifications, in contrast to many mainland European countries, which use mainly vocational qualifications to achieve this aim. Policies have been put in place in an attempt to rectify both of these problems. For basic skills, programmes have been set up to improve the literacy and numeracy skills of both school children and adults. Unfortunately no new nationally representative data on the basic skills of the adult population have become available in the UK since the mid-1990s, and so we have been unable to evaluate how successful these policies have been in terms of improving basic skills. What we have shown is the value of any success that these programmes might have. The large wage gaps between those with higher and those with lower level literacy and numeracy skills in the UK reveal the benefit of acquiring these skills to individuals, as well as the value put on them by employers, and hence by society in general. It is hoped that basic skills have improved, and that these benefits have been reaped.

An attempt has been made to provide structure and clarity to the vocational education programme through the provision of NVQs. The new qualifications have helped to raise the number of adults with Level 3 or higher vocational qualifications, although the number with Level 3 or higher academic qualifications is still rising more quickly. A potential reason for this is that the wage returns to such vocational qualifications are lower than the wage returns to academic qualifications at the same notional level. Vocational qualifications below Level 3 do not seem to lead to higher wages, on average. For those with no school-level qualifications, then there are real benefits to be had by this group from acquiring Level 3 vocational qualifications. However, vocational qualifications below Level 3 still provide no real benefit, even for this group of low achievers.

This would suggest that such low level qualifications need to re-designed so that they are of some worth, or even scrapped altogether. Given that the government's aim is to get as many people to Level 3 as possible, it may be better to stop awarding certificates below this level, with their message that individuals have succeeded in reaching a goal which has little worth. Without the 'escape route' at lower levels, more individuals may continue to Level 3, thus helping the UK to close the skills gap.

Notes

1. Level 3 qualifications include academic qualifications obtained at upper secondary level, for example A-levels in England and Wales (Highers in Scotland), or advanced vocational qualifications, such as an NVQ/GNVQ Level 3 qualification, an ONC/OND or an Advanced Craft City and Guilds qualification.

2. NVQs were originally intended to certify the possession of relevant skills in a workplace setting, while GNVQs were less occupation-specific and more likely to be taught outside work. The distinction has blurred somewhat with the provision of full-time NVQ courses in FE colleges.
3. There are three separate tests in the IALS survey, namely 'prose literacy', 'document literacy' and 'quantitative literacy'. The 'prose literacy' test seems to have been used more in the literature as a measure of literacy, which we follow here, while the 'quantitative literacy' test is used as our measure of numeracy.
4. There are insufficient numbers scoring at IALS Level 5 to meaningfully analyse this category on its own.
5. Because of the small sample sizes of IALS in some countries, it was decided to pool the data, rather than present separate results for men and women.
6. There are potentially some problems with the data in these two countries. The Swedish test scores seem to be much better than in other countries, as revealed in Table 16.1, while in Germany there are some problems with the coding of the qualifications variable, and there are many missing responses to the income question. Nevertheless, these problems are very unlikely to have created the general pattern of results, and it seems safe to assume that the returns to basic skills are lower in these countries.
7. Though consideration should be given to the amount of time required to obtain these qualifications, as was done in Dearden et al. (2002), to derive a truer *rate of* return to the various qualifications. When this is done, the gap between the rates of return to academic and vocational qualifications closes.
8. The 4.7 per cent effect of City and Guilds Craft-level qualifications for women in 2001 is actually statistically insignificant, as a result of a high standard error caused by few women in the sample having this qualification.
9. Had a qualification been achieved, the apprenticeship training would have been classified under that qualification, rather than 'apprenticeship'.

References

Dearden, L., McIntosh, S., Myck, M. and Vignoles, A. (2002), 'The Returns to Academic and Vocational Qualifications in Britain', *Bulletin of Economic Research*, 54, pp. 249–74.
Department for Education and Employment (DfEE) (1996), 'The Skills Audit: A Report from an Interdepartmental Group', Department for Education and Employment, London.
Department for Education and Employment (DfEE) (1999), *Improving Literacy and Numeracy: A Fresh Start*, Great Britain Working Group on Post-School Basic Skills chaired by Sir Claus Moser, Department for Education and Employment: London.

Further reading

Dearden, L. (1999), 'Qualifications and Earnings in Britain: How Reliable are Conventional OLS Estimates of the Returns to Education?', Institute for Fiscal Studies, Working Paper No. W99/7.

Part IV:

Incomes, Education and Opportunity

17
Access to Education

Alissa Goodman and Leslie McGranahan

Key findings

- Educational inequalities start early in life, and are magnified throughout childhood. Children aged three and four from poorer backgrounds spend less time in education than those from higher income families, though research evidence indicates that these children stand to gain the most from high quality pre-school learning.
- During compulsory schooling, educational inequalities become more pronounced. Schools with the highest concentration of poor children (measured by the proportion eligible for free school meals) see worse results at Key Stages 1, 2 and 3 than schools with fewer poor children. Poorer children obtain considerably lower GCSE grades than those from richer backgrounds.
- Some of these educational gaps arise because of differences in ability and motivation between children, or are simply the product of varying educational choices. But financial barriers also play a role. House prices are higher in the catchment areas of the highest performing schools, whilst the cost of private schooling and tuition can also be prohibitive.
- Educational choices after 16 have been the subject of an ongoing policy experiment over the last four years. The Education Maintenance Allowance (EMA) pilots aimed to increase after-16 education participation amongst children from low income families by offering £30 or £40 a week to encourage children from poorer backgrounds to stay in school. Evaluation results show that more young people have been induced both to stay on, and to remain, at school or college. These increases in participation, though substantial, will not be sufficient to remove the socio-economic gap in participation entirely.

- The financial returns to obtaining qualifications are substantial: this means that the economic effects of educational choices made early persist throughout the child's entire life and are perpetuated across generations.

Introduction

Securing equal access to education has become a central focus of recent government policy, from the early years' learning intervention programmes introduced over the last five years, to new policies to encourage young people from low income backgrounds to stay on in school beyond 16, to the newly created role of the 'access regulator' governing university admissions. Much of the recent concern about access to education is driven by the now well-established role of education in the transmission of both deprivation and privilege across generations (Blanden et al., 2003). Children of parents with low incomes and low levels of educational attainment tend to attend worse performing schools and to leave school with fewer qualifications. Lower achievement on average translates into worse labour market performance and lower earnings, perpetuating economic divisions. Relative to other developed nations, Britain has a highly polarised educational system. Sixty-eight per cent of individuals aged 25–34 in 2001 achieved a level of education at least equivalent to five or more GCSEs at grades A to C. This is lower than the OECD average of 74 per cent and places Britain 22nd among 30 OECD countries. By contrast, 30 per cent of British 25–34 year olds had obtained a degree. This was higher than the OECD average of 28 per cent, and put Britain 13th (OECD, 2002). In this chapter we examine educational differences between children of different family backgrounds in Britain, and where possible we try to assess how these have been changing over time.

The term 'access' to education is now frequently used in the public policy domain, though finding a precise definition, particularly one against which progress can be measured is far from straightforward. Ideally we would present evidence showing the extent to which there are systematic differences according to a child's family background in the availability of educational opportunities. Such differential opportunities could arise because of differences in the quality of state education available to people of different backgrounds, combined with differences in parents' and pupils' access to finance to pay for the quantity or quality of education they desire (for example due to credit constraints). It could also arise because of lack of information on the part of parents to make the best educational choices on behalf of their children. Measuring the existence of differential opportunities is extremely difficult. Parents and young people from different backgrounds systematically make different choices about their education because they have different abilities, preferences regarding education, and different expectations about the future returns. Because of this, the finding that educational outcomes differ by family income does not necessarily imply that access is lacking.

We do not attempt to separate out differences in educational preferences and choices from the opportunities available to children of different backgrounds. Instead we consider differences in participation rates and educational attainment by family income or other measures of socio-economic status. We also highlight a number of policy reforms that have taken place in recent years that have attempted to equalise educational availability.

Changes in access and participation

Social and economic divisions in educational choices start early in life and continue into school and adulthood. Such divisions have long-lasting effects on individuals and, in turn, on the lives of their own children. Here we examine differences in participation, and in some cases attainment, at each stage of the education system prior to higher education. Even before schooling becomes compulsory, there are important differences in both the amount, and the quality of education received by children from different backgrounds. By contrast, for students in compulsory formal schooling the issue is mostly one of quality, since a free place at school is available to everyone. For over 16s, the issue of access is again closely linked to the issue of participation.

Early years learning

Before-school education assists a child's transition to formal schooling by helping them become accustomed to an academic setting, teaching basic skills and generally assuring that children do not start off already behind. Such catch-up is likely to be especially relevant for the children of poorer parents who are less likely to be read to and otherwise prepared for schooling within the home environment. Links between the quality of a young child's home learning environment and parental socio-economic status have been well-established. Melhuish et al. (2001) document strong correlations between factors such as reading, library visits, educational play and parents' socio-economic status for children as young as three. The children of professional fathers are three times as likely as children of unskilled fathers to be read to every day.[1]

As a result, we would expect that disadvantaged children have the most to gain from early entry into formal schooling. However, recent UK survey data, presented in Table 17.1, find that although overall participation rates in nursery school are high (since some children aged three and all aged four are entitled to free nursery education for up to 2.5 hours a day during term time, regardless of income), children of higher income parents are more likely to attend nursery school, to attend more sessions each week, and to also attend over the summer holidays. In part this is a reflection of a greater need for childcare among higher income families – since both parents are more likely to be in work. But, wealthier parents are also more likely to believe that their children are receiving a high quality pre-school education. Interestingly, repeated surveys show that the gap in attendance between low and high income families has been narrowing over time (Fitzgerald et al., 2002).

Table 17.1   Participation in nursery education last week, by parental income, 2000–01

	Parental income			
	< £10,000	£10,000–£19,999	£20,000–£29,999	£30,000+
Participation rate	93%	96%	96%	98%
Mean number of sessions a week	3.1	4.2	4.4	4.8
Summer holiday participation in nursery or childcare	22%	31%	42%	52%

Source: Fitzgerald et al., 2002.

Academic research indicates that low income children have the most to gain from pre-school attendance. The best-known research on the benefits of early education for disadvantaged children is based on evaluations of need-based pre-school programmes in the US. This research generally finds that intensive early intervention improves the academic outcomes of disadvantaged children. Evaluations of Head Start, the large, long-standing, national targeted pre-school programme in the US, also point to increased social and academic school readiness among participant children. However, because of the lack of experimental design, these studies are less persuasive than those looking at smaller programmes (Currie, 2000).

By contrast, research into the benefits of early education for the overall population tends to be more inconclusive. While some studies show early gains in achievement, these benefits tend to dissipate over time. Similarly, cross country studies have not found systematic links between long-term achievement and the age of starting compulsory schooling (Sharp, 2002). This all indicates that disadvantaged children benefit from early schooling even if their more advantaged peers may not gain as much. This is echoed in recent UK research looking at the effects of pre-school education for three and four year olds (the EPPE project). This research has found that disadvantaged children in particular can benefit significantly from good quality experiences before school, especially if they attend centres that cater for a mixture of children from different social backgrounds (Sammons et al., 2002).

Compulsory schooling years

Between ages five and 16 the issue is one of access to quality schooling and in particular, access to schooling that facilitates continuing education beyond compulsory level. Against a backdrop of increasing resources directed towards schools over the last five years (Figure 17.1 shows average spending on each

---

Box 17.1 **Government policies aimed at pre-school education**

The launch of the National Childcare Strategy in May 1998, and the introduction of the Sure Start programme (also in 1998) marked the start of a set of government policies aimed at narrowing educational gaps for children below school age. The first set of Sure Start early learning interventions focused largely on children growing up in disadvantaged areas – providing significant funds to pay for early education, childcare, health and family support services. Sure Start aims to provide free part-time early education for *all* three and four year olds by April 2004.

Significant increases in childcare subsidies to low income families paid since the introduction of the Working Families Tax Credit in 1999 (paid through the childcare tax credit), could also redress early educational imbalances, though this depends crucially on the quality of the childcare which is subsidised, and is generally seen more as a tool to encourage labour supply rather than early education.

---

pupil), and falling class sizes especially at primary school level (Figure 17.2), differences in educational attainment according to parental background remain large, even at the earliest stage in a child's schooling. This can be seen from Figure 17.3, which shows the proportion of pupils achieving benchmark standards in reading and English tests at Key Stages 1, 2 and 3. In order to differentiate between children from different backgrounds, results are presented separately for schools divided according to the proportion of children in them known to be eligible for free school meals.

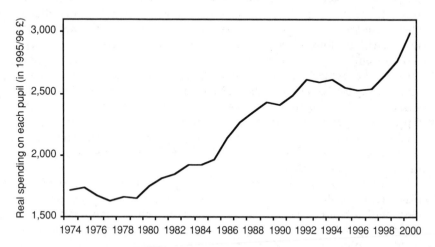

Figure 17.1 Average spending on schoolchildren

Source: (1) Number of pupils: DFES (2002a) 'Class Sizes and Pupil:Teacher Ratios in Schools in England', http://www.dfes.gov.uk/statistics/DB/SBU/b0329/index.html. (2) Expenditure: authors' calculations.

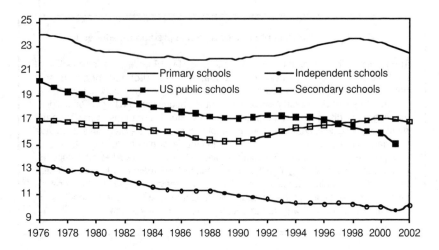

Figure 17.2   Pupil to teacher ratios, 1976–2002

Sources: DfES (2002a); and National Center for Education Statistics, *Digest of Education Statistics, 2001* (Washington, DC: US Department of Education, 2002), http://nces.ed.gov/pubs2002/ digest2001/

Figure 17.3 shows that, starting at Key Stage 1 (when children are seven), more children attain specified minimum levels in the 'richest' schools, where there are fewest children known to be eligible for free school meals. By contrast, pupils in 'poorer' schools, i.e. those with higher concentrations of children eligible for free school meals, do progressively worse in terms of Key Stage 1 results, with the lowest levels of achievement in schools where 40 per cent or more of children are known to be eligible for free school meals. These differences in achievement are then magnified across each of the Key Stages, with the gap between the results the widest at Key Stage 3 when children are 14. For example, as many as 84 per cent of children in schools where less than 5 per cent of pupils were eligible for free meals attained Level 5 or above in English in 2001, compared to just 39 per cent of those in schools where more than 40 per cent were known to be eligible.[2] The gaps are of similar magnitude in mathematics and science.

There is some evidence, however, that these gaps may have been narrowing over time, especially among younger children. Table 17.2 shows the percentage of students attaining the minimum standard in Reading/English, Maths and Sciences in 1998 and 2001 by educational stage, separately for students in 'rich' and 'poor' schools. While the proportion of students attaining each level shown has improved in the schools with the lowest concentration of poor pupils, the scores of schools having the most poor pupils improved even more. Though this is partly due to the fact that students in 'rich' schools were doing so well to begin with that there was less room for improvement,

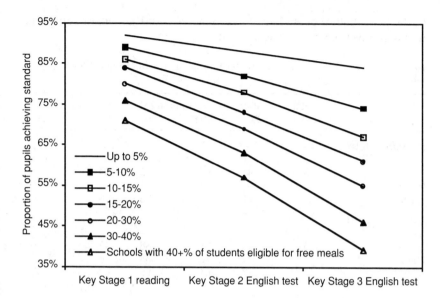

Figure 17.3   Proportion of pupils achieving expected level or above, by eligibility for free school meals, 2001

Note: Only results of pupils in maintained schools are included.

Source: DfES (2002b), 'Statistics of Education – National Curriculum Assessments of 7, 11 and 14 Year Olds in England: 2001', Statistical Bulletin, http://www.dfes.gov.uk/DB/SBU/b0333

this convergence has been more dramatic for tests administered at ages seven and 11 than at age 14. Although the improvements made by students in poorer schools are impressive, the performance of poor schools remains extremely bad especially at age 14 Key Stage 3 (Glennerster, 2001). Moreover, there is little evidence of any 'value added' as children age among poorer schools. The cohort of children who were 11 in 1998 and who were 14 in 2001 in poor schools are doing less well at 14 in English, Maths and Science in terms of attainment than they were at age 11. No such decline can be observed among children in richer schools. Data not shown also suggest that girls are doing better than boys.[3]

Two issues should be kept in mind when interpreting these test scores. First, as Glennerster and others have pointed out, high stakes testing gives schools incentives to teach to the test at the expense of other subjects and skills. As a result, while the indications from test scores are encouraging they may not indicate true increases in skills. Second, while pupils at poorer schools are doing better, they are still not doing well especially at higher levels of education. Nonetheless, the test score data point to two encouraging trends: an increase in school quality since 1995 and a particularly impressive increase in the performance of students in the schools with the highest concentration of pupils from poorer backgrounds.

Table 17.2   Percentage achieving key stages by share in school eligible for free school meals

	Total population		<5% children FSM		40+% children FSM	
	1998	2001	1998	2001	1998	2001
Key Stage 1, Level 2, Age 7						
Reading	80	84	90	92	64	71
Writing	81	86	91	93	66	73
Maths	84	91	92	95	73	82
Key Stage 2, Level 4, Age 11						
English	65	75	81	88	45	57
Maths	59	71	76	83	38	54
Science	69	87	84	95	49	75
Key Stage 3, Level 5, Age 14						
English	65	65	83	84	39	39
Maths	59	66	81	86	30	38
Science	56	66	80	86	26	35

Notes: FSM = free school meal. Sources: DfES 'National Curriculum Assessments of 7, 11 and 14 Year olds in England – 1998' Statistical Bulletin: Issue No 6/99, April (1999) and 'Statistics of Education – National Curriculum Assessments of 7, 11 and 14 Year olds in England: 2001', Statistical Bulletin (2002). http://www.dfes.gov.uk//DB/SBU/b0333

A further indication of the persistent gap in attainment between richer and poorer students is the large disparity in GCSE performance. In 2000, 65 per cent of children of parents of non-manual occupations had passed five or more GCSEs at grades A* to C, while only 42 per cent of children of parents whose occupations were manual had attained the same qualifications. The gap in performance has been fairly consistent since the introduction of the GCSE exam, though attainment has been increasing over time across all parental occupation groups. (Figure 17.4 shows GCSE attainment by more disaggregated parental occupational groups.) To what extent are these disparities the result of differences in access to quality education between families with different incomes, and how much to do with other factors? Some of these differences are no doubt driven by differences in ability and motivation between different pupils, and the amount of time and knowledge parents are able (or choose) to devote to their children's learning, and choice of school. But parents' financial circumstances also have a direct impact on the quality of schooling available to a child.

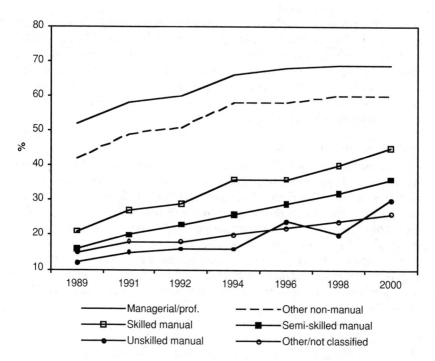

Figure 17.4 Attainment of five or more GCSE grades A*–C in Year 11, by parental occupation, 1989–2000

Source: DfES (2001), 'Youth Cohort Study: The Activities and Experiences of 16 Year Olds: England and Wales 2000', National Statistics First Release, SFR 02/2001, 23 January.

One example of this is the ability of higher income families to pay for extra tuition or private education for their children. A relatively small number of children attend private schools in Britain – around 7 per cent in 2002 – and this number has remained fairly stable since the mid-1990s. Private school quality is generally higher. For example, in 2002, state schools spent £3,735 on each primary school student compared to £5,602 in the independent sector and £4,855 on each secondary school student compared to £6,364 at independent schools (Pollard, 2002). Figure 17.2 showed that pupil to teacher ratios in state schools have been roughly twice those in independent schools since the mid-1970s. Though some lower income children do receive need-based bursaries to attend independent schools, fee relief available from schools is quite limited,[4] whilst the phased abolition of the Assisted Places Scheme is now all but complete.

Perhaps a more widespread way in which financial circumstances influence the ability of poorer students to attend high quality schools is the indirect effect of differential school quality on house prices. Recent research finds that parents pay significant house price premiums to live within the catchment areas of popular or better performing schools. Gibbons and Machin (2003) find that parents are willing to pay a 5.2 per cent to 8.4 per cent premium to live in a postcode where 10 per cent more students pass the minimum standards at age 11. Though education can be seen as an investment which can generate a return over time, poorer parents are less likely to be able to borrow to finance such investment.

Education after 16

Once a student reaches 16, the issue of further education hinges on the student's decision to continue to participate. In part this decision depends on GCSE results and GCSE results differ quite substantially according to parental background. But at this point other time-use options for young people, including training and employment, also become important. This means that the decision to stay on at school depends not just on differing educational opportunities, but also on differing labour market opportunities for young people from different backgrounds, and the extent to which individuals are willing to defer entry into the labour market in return for potential – but uncertain – future returns.

Participation in full-time education amongst 16, 17 and 18 year olds increased dramatically over the five-year period following the introduction of GCSEs (see Figure 17.5). Less than half of all 16 year olds remained in full-time education in 1988 – the year before the GCSE replaced the O-Level and CSE – rising to about 70 per cent by 1992. Recent research has shown that in the period *prior* to the introduction of GCSEs, the expansion in education after 16 disproportionately benefited children from higher income backgrounds – increasing educational inequalities considerably. Blanden et al. (2003) show that over the first half of the 1980s (a period of rapidly increasing income inequality in Britain), the gap between the participation rate in education after 16 between children from low and high income backgrounds (measured by parental income at age 16) rose substantially.

Since then, the evidence points in the opposite direction. Staying-on rates in full-time schooling have remained roughly stable at around 70 per cent of 16 year olds since the mid-1990s, but the gap in educational participation after 16 between young people of different socio-economic backgrounds appears to have narrowed, returning to 1970s levels (Blanden et al., 2003). Not surprisingly however – in the light of the evidence we have shown about the differences which pervade throughout the education system prior to age 16 – educational differences after 16 remain significant. For example, this same research shows that in 1998–2000 children of parents in the highest fifth of incomes were 26 percentage points more likely to stay in school at 16 than those in the lowest income quintile (compared to a gap of 40 percentage points in 1986–88).

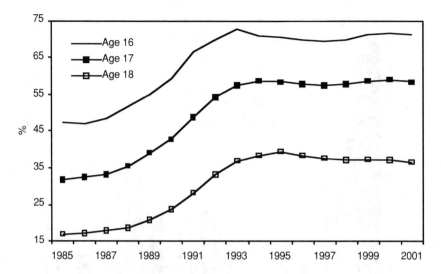

Figure 17.5   Participation in full-time education by age, 1985–2001

Note: Figures for 2001 are provisional.

Source: DfES (2002c), 'Participation in Education, Training and Employment by 16–18 Year Olds in England: 2000 and 2001', http://www.dfes.gov.uk/statistics/DB/SFR/s0341/index.html

These results are paralleled in evidence on the social class composition of those who stay on in school in post-compulsory education. Figure 17.6 shows participation rates by parental social class for 18 year olds based on data from the Youth Cohort Study (YCS). It shows that educational participation is highest for children whose parents' social class is highest. Higher social class children are also less likely to be in neither education, employment nor training, whilst young people with parents of lower social classes are also for the most part more likely to be in employment, both with and without training. The patterns are similar for 16 and 17 year olds.

Data for earlier cohorts of the YCS show that the gap in staying on by social class has narrowed quite substantially since 1989. In 1989, children of managerial/professional parents were 41 percentage points more likely to stay in school. By 2000, they were only 23 percentage points more likely to stay on. The data from the YCS also show the important role of previous attainment as an influence on the decision to stay in school, though of course poor GCSE results may also reflect a prior decision not to stay on. For example, 75 per cent of 17 year olds who had achieved Level 2 or above (five or more GCSE grades A*–C) were participating in full-time education as compared to only 29 per cent of those having attained below Level 2 (DfES, 2000).

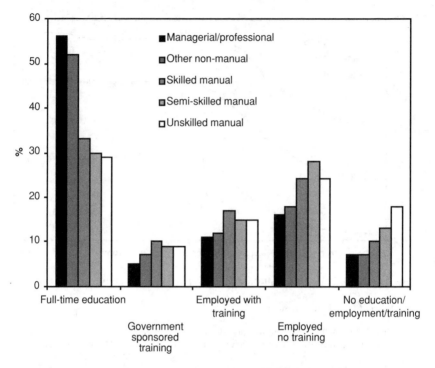

Figure 17.6   Participation in further education by 18 year olds in 1998, by parental occupation

Source: DfES 2000.

A recent government policy initiative aiming to increase the proportion of young people from low income backgrounds staying on in post-compulsory education is the Education Maintenance Allowance (EMA) (see Box 17.2). The EMA provides financial incentives to young people to remain in education. By comparing average outcomes amongst 16 and 17 year olds in areas where the EMA was offered to the average outcomes amongst a matched group of individuals in control areas where the EMA was not made available, the effect of the policy can be estimated.

The first two years of the evaluation showed that the EMA pilots, which offered £30 or £40 a week to young people from low income families, together with retention and achievement bonuses (if they remained in full-time education and signed a learning agreement), raised participation in post-16 education by 5.9 percentage points – from an average staying-on rate of 65.5 per cent in the matched control sample, to 71.3 per cent amongst matched young people in pilot areas. This increase in participation appears to have drawn young people from both employment, and inactivity. Increases in participation were found to be particularly strong amongst those eligible for the full award (this was amongst young people whose parents were on a joint annual income of less than £13,000).

By looking at differences in outcomes amongst 17 year olds as well as 16 year olds, the evaluation found that EMA has also appeared to have a positive effect on retention rates in post-compulsory education, particularly in the areas with the largest retention bonuses. The proportion of students dropping out after Year 12 was lower in the areas where the EMA was offered to young people than in the control areas where the EMA was not offered.

To what extent is this policy likely to close the gap in participation between young people in low income and higher income families? The evaluation results indicate that although the financial incentives offered will go some way towards reducing inequalities in participation, it will not close the gap entirely. Children from higher income families are still significantly more likely to stay on in education in the pilot areas where the EMA is offered. For example, in the first year of the EMA pilots, around 71 per cent of students with parental income below £30,000 a year stayed on in school at age 16, compared to 83 per cent of those with parental incomes above this (making them ineligible for EMA). Another important issue currently under evaluation is how the EMA will affect the achievement of those students from lower income families who are induced to stay in education. This will be particularly important for

---

Box 17.2   The Education Maintenance Allowance (EMA)

Educational choices after 16 have been the subject of an ongoing policy experiment over the last four years: the Education Maintenance Allowance (EMA) pilots aimed to increase participation in education after age 16 amongst children from low income families by offering £30 or £40 a week to encourage children from poorer backgrounds to stay in school.

Four different variants of the EMA were piloted from September 1999 in selected Local Education Authorities in England. The variants were designed to test the effectiveness of making the payments to the parent or to the child, the impact of different retention and achievement bonuses, and the level of the maximum weekly award.

In the light of the results from an ongoing national evaluation of the EMA pilots – which measured the effects of the new incentives offered on pupils' participation, retention, and achievement in post-compulsory education (and a range of other outcomes) – the government has announced plans to roll the EMA out nationwide.

From September 2004, the EMA will be made available to 16–19 year olds throughout England. It will be will be a means-tested allowance of up to £30 a week during term time, which will be paid directly to young people who remain in full-time education. Additional bonuses will also be paid at periodic intervals to reward pupils for retention and achievement.

This new benefit will be means-tested against parental income: children from families on the lowest incomes (at a level yet to be determined) will be entitled to the full EMA award (£30); for those on slightly higher incomes entitlement will then be tapered away.

determining the knock-on effects of the policy on the number of children from low income backgrounds who go on to higher education. This is because amongst those who stay on at school until 18, A-level grades play an extremely important role in determining continuation into higher education.

Conclusion

The role of parental income and social class in determining the quality and quantity of education obtained by children is very strong. At every point in the educational system, parental income and social class are strongly related to educational participation and achievement. Poorer children are less likely to attend pre-school, are educated in worse performing primary and secondary schools, have less choice over their schooling and are less likely to stay in school once compulsory schooling ends. Recent reforms including the introduction of Sure Start, the increase in standards at the primary and secondary level, and the EMA appear to have gone (or promise to go) some way towards reducing the gap in educational access between rich and poor. Nonetheless, significant gaps remain.

These educational gaps are the product of differences in choices amongst parents and young people from different backgrounds, and differences in opportunities – both informational and financial. The extent to which these gaps can (or indeed should) be narrowed by government, and the best means of achieving their reduction, depends on the balance between these different contributory factors. At the same time as these gaps persist, the education received by children continues to have a powerful influence on their later life earnings. The combination of continuing educational inequalities, and significant financial returns to qualifications serves to perpetuate economic divisions across generations.

Notes

1. Source: authors' calculations based on British Cohort Study.
2. Sixteen per cent of schools at Key Stage 3 contained less than 5 per cent of pupils eligible for free school meals, with roughly the same number containing more than 40 per cent of pupils eligible.
3. For more evidence on this see Machin and McNally (2003).
4. While schools affiliated with the Independent Schools Council (the ISC) receive nearly £3 billion in fees, total academic and need-based fee relief is approximately £190 million – just over 6 per cent.

References

Blanden, J., Goodman, A., Gregg, P. and Machin, S. (2003), 'Changes in Intergenerational Mobility in Britain', in M. Corak (ed.), *Generational Income Mobility*, Cambridge University Press: Cambridge.

Currie, J. (2000), 'Early Childhood Intervention Programs: What Do We Know?', Working Paper 169, Joint Centre for Policy Research.

DfES (2000), 'Youth Cohort Study: Education, Training and Employment of 16–18 Year Olds in England and the Factors Associated with Non-Participation', http://www.dfes.gov.uk/statistics/DB/SBU/b0162/index.html

Fitzgerald, R., Finch, S., Blake, M., Perry, J. and Bell, A. (2002), 'Fifth Survey of Parents of Three and Four Year Old Children and Their Use of Early Years Services (Summer 2000 to Spring 2001)', Research Report RR351, National Centre for Social Research.

Gibbons, S. and Machin, S. (2003), 'Valuing Primary Schools', *Journal of Urban Economics*, forthcoming.

Glennerster, H. (2001), 'United Kingdom Education 1997–2001', Centre for the Analysis of Social Exclusion Paper 50, November.

Machin, S. and McNally, S. (2003), 'Gender and Educational Attainment in Schools', presented at a conference on 'The Economics of Gender Issues: Widening the Debate', ZEW Mannheim and University of Mannheim, 28–29 March.

Melhuish, E., Sylva, K., Sammons, P., Siraj-Blatchford, I. and Taggart, B. (2001), 'Social/Behavioural and Cognitive Development at 3–4 Years in Relation to Family Background', *The Effective Provision of Pre-School Education (EPPE) Project, Technical Paper 7*, Institute of Education, University of London.

OECD (Organisation for Economic Cooperation and Development), *Education at a Glance 2002* (2002). http://www.oecd.org/EN/links_abstract/0,,EN–links_abstract–604–20–no–no–1239–604,00.html

Pollard, S. (2000), 'Brown Must Stop Throwing Money at State Monopolies', *Guardian*, 16 July.

Sammons, P., Sylva, K., Melhuish, E., Siraj-Blatchford, I., Taggart, B. and Eliot, K. (2002), 'Measuring the Impact of Pre-School on Children's Cognitive Progress Over the Pre-School Period', *The Effective Provision of Pre-School Education (EPPE) Project, Technical Paper 8a*, Institute of Education, University of London.

Sharp, C. (2002), 'School Starting Age: European Policy and Recent Research', Paper presented at the LGA Seminar 'When Should Our Children Start School?', LGA Conference.

18

Higher Education, Family Income and Changes in Intergenerational Mobility

Stephen Machin

Key findings

- Links between higher education and parental income have strengthened over time in the UK, portraying a significant rise in educational inequality.
- This means the rapid expansion of the higher education system seen in recent years disproportionately benefited children from richer families.
- Intergenerational mobility of economic status has also declined over time, as the labour market success or failure of individuals has become more closely connected to parental income than it was in the past.
- A key transmission mechanism underpinning falling intergenerational mobility is the strengthened link between individuals' education participation and attainment and parental income.

Introduction

Education has long been seen as a powerful force with the potential to increase opportunity and promote social mobility. Equality of access to education is seen by some as key to advancing children from less well-off backgrounds to break generational cycles of deprivation and encourage economic growth. Indeed, people from across the political spectrum advocate equality of opportunity as a vital part of building a fair society. At the same time, education is an important mechanism underpinning the extent of intergenerational mobility in society, namely the extent to which the economic and social success or failure of people is correlated with that of their parents.

In this chapter I consider connections between education, income and the extent of intergenerational mobility in economic status, with particular reference to how they have changed through time. The findings make grim reading for proponents of equality of opportunity because: 1) the link between education and parental income has strengthened over time, as the rapid expansion of the higher education system disproportionately benefited children from richer families; 2) at the same time, intergenerational mobility of economic status declined, as the labour market success or failure of individuals has become more closely connected to parental income than it was in the past.

Higher education and family income

Whether family income is a key factor determining educational attainment, and if this has shifted over time, is a critical policy question. It matters for questions to do with equality of opportunity, for questions of child welfare and for broader questions of fairness in society. Recent decades have seen sharp increases in educational attainment and participation in the UK. It therefore seems important to consider whether these increases have been evenly distributed amongst children and young people from different social backgrounds. This section considers this question in some detail showing that educational inequality – measured by the sensitivity of education to parental income – has increased over time.

Trends in higher education participation and income

Figure 18.1 shows the rapid expansion of higher education participation seen in Britain in recent years. The figure shows the Department for Education and Skills (DfES) higher education age participation index. Participation was at low levels at the start of the 1960s, with around 6 per cent of the 18–19 year old age cohort participating in higher education. This rose to around 14 per cent by the mid-1970s, before dropping back a little in the late 1970s. Most of the 1980s saw small increases in higher education participation but the expansion from the late 1980s thereafter was very rapid indeed. By the year 2000 participation reached around one in three.

At the same time income inequality rose sharply. Figure 18.2 shows a very sharp increase in income inequality for families with children in the UK. The figure shows the evolution over time of the 10th, 50th and 90th percentiles of the income distribution (measured in real terms) where each percentile is indexed to 1 in 1968. It shows real income growth at each of the percentiles. After not much change in the 1970s, the figure shows the by now familiar pattern of no real income growth at the 10th percentile for most of the post-1979 period. Only in the last few years does the 10th percentile income start to grow in real terms. On the other hand there is significant growth at the

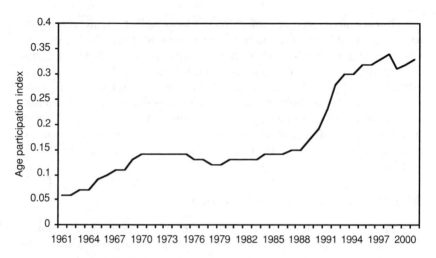

Figure 18.1   Higher education participation

Note: Higher education age participation index is the number of young (under 21) home initial entrants expressed as a proportion of the averaged 18–19 year old population.

Source: DfES.

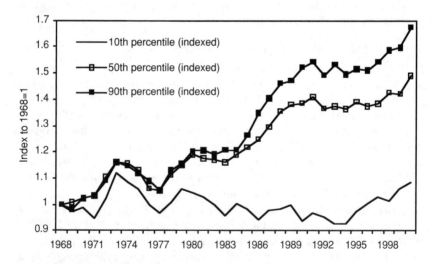

Figure 18.2   Changes over time in the distribution of real income for families with children

Note: Sample is all non-pensioner families with children.

Source: Own calculations from FES, 1968 through 2000.

median (of over 40 per cent) and very substantial growth (of over 60 per cent) at the 90th percentile. The conceptual difficulty in connecting these two phenomena (rising education participation and rising income inequality) is the dearth of data that one can use to match up university age individuals with their parents' incomes. The critical problem is that one cannot do this with the usual large scale household surveys as most students have left the family home and so one cannot match them up with their parents. However, one can do this with longitudinal data that follows people through time, and then allows one to track back and match with parents' income at an earlier age. I therefore draw on British cohort data that permits one to carry out this matching procedure.

British cohort data

The National Child Development Study (NCDS) is a very rich data source that has been used in previous work looking at the effects of family background on child outcomes in the UK (e.g. Gregg and Machin, 1999). It consists of the birth population of a week in March 1958 with follow-up samples at cohort member ages 7, 11, 16, 23, 33 and 42.[1] The British Cohort Study (BCS) is very similar in style, covering a full birth population in a week of April 1970 with data collected at ages 5, 10, 16, 26 and 30. As well as being similarly structured the questions asked in the two cohorts are frequently identical, although there remain some difficulties inherent in using them in a comparative study over time. The use of cohort data allows one to follow the sequence of post-16 education decisions for the cohort members in a way that is very difficult from even rich cross-sectional sources.

The cohorts are certainly the largest source of detailed information on family background and educational transmissions. Unfortunately they are also a little dated. But one can create a third pseudo cohort from the British Household Panel Survey (BHPS). The BHPS began in 1991 with a sample of 5,500 households. All individuals over 15 years old were asked to provide extensive information including details of income and education. Individuals were then contacted in subsequent years and followed through the panel (adding new respondents from the household as they reached 16). The sample size is thus increased by taking people of eligible ages as the panel progresses through time.

Changes in the relation between education and income over time

Table 18.1 shows higher education participation (at age 19) by parental income group from the cohort data at three points in time: the late 1970s, the late 1980s and the late 1990s. The table shows that children of higher income parents improved their higher education participation substantially in the 1980s. There was then less change across the income spectrum through the 1990s. In fact, children from the middle 60 per cent seemed to improve their position by a little more than the top quintile during the 1990s and the top quintile itself did better than the bottom.

Table 18.1   Higher education participation at age 19 (%) by parental income

	Parental income group		
	Lowest 20%	Middle 60%	Highest 20%
NCDS 1977	8	12	28
BCS 1989	10	17	38
BHPS 1997 (Ave)	15	28	46
Change 1977 to 1989	2	5	10
Change 1989 to 1997	5	11	8
Change 1977 to 1997	7	16	18

Sources: Own calculations from National Child Development Study (NCDS), British Cohort Study (BCS) and British Household Panel Survey (BHPS) data on people aged 19, studied in Blanden, Gregg and Machin (2003).

Table 18.2 repeats the same exercise for degree acquisition by age 23. The rise in educational inequality is clear to see as the percentage of children from upper quintile families rose rapidly over time (from 20 per cent in 1981 to 48 per cent by 1999). At the same time the percentage from the lower quintile group rose from a very low level (6 per cent) by only 5 percentage points to 11 per cent by 1999.[2]

Table 18.2   Percentage with a degree by age 23 by parental income

	Parental income group		
	Lowest 20%	Middle 60%	Highest 20%
NCDS 1981	6	8	20
BCS 1993	7	15	37
BHPS 1999	11	23	48
Change 1981 to 1993	1	7	17
Change 1993 to 1999	4	8	11
Change 1981 to 1999	5	15	28

Sources: Own calculations from National Child Development Study (NCDS), British Cohort Study (BCS) and British Household Panel Survey (BHPS) data on people aged 23, studied in Blanden, Gregg and Machin (2003).

It therefore appears that educational inequality – defined here as the link between higher education participation and family income – has tended to rise in recent years. These patterns are confirmed in the more detailed statistical analysis in Blanden, Gregg and Machin (2003) that controls for factors that are correlated with both parental income and education participation, and looks for different income impacts at different stages of the education process. The statistical models show university participation and degree acquisition to have become more strongly connected to parental income. Even the sharp expansion of higher education participation of the 1990s did not benefit poorer children. If anything, it strengthened the position of the middle classes.

The same story is borne out if one considers recent trends in higher education participation by social class. Table 18.3 reproduces some of Glennerster's (2001) analysis of Social Trends data to show no differential improvement for the lower social classes in the link between higher education participation and parental social class. There has been an actual worsening in absolute percentage points, despite the rapid increase in enrolment in higher education seen in the 1990s.

Table 18.3   Higher education participation (%) and social class in the 1990s

	1991–92	1998–99	Change 1991–92 to 1998–99
Professional	55	72	17
Intermediate	36	45	9
Skilled non-manual	22	29	7
Skilled manual	11	18	7
Partly skilled	12	17	5
Unskilled	6	13	7
All social classes	23	31	8

Source: Glennerster 2001, Table 11.

Changes in intergenerational mobility over time

The education–income patterns reported above have clear ramifications for future inequality, both within and across generations. We know that graduates subsequently get paid more in the labour market. It therefore appears that if more children from relatively rich backgrounds get degrees, this will generate increased links between people's income and that of their parents, and this can therefore reduce intergenerational mobility. This section shows that this was the case, at least for a comparison across the NCDS and BCS cohorts.[3]

Measuring the extent of intergenerational mobility

A simple (and commonly used) approach to estimate the extent of inter-generational mobility uses statistical regression techniques to relate children's economic status to that of their parents. The typical formulation relates the economic status (usually labour market earnings) of children and parents in matched-up families and summarises the extent of intergenerational mobility by a coefficient β which reflects how strongly children's status is associated with parental economic stature. The literature usually proceeds to say β of zero (where child and parental Y are uncorrelated) corresponds to complete intergenerational mobility and β of unity (child Y is fully determined by parental Y) corresponds to complete immobility.

Due to data issues this exact framework cannot be implemented with the NCDS versus BCS comparison. Ideally one would like to have measures of the same permanent economic status (be it wages or income) for both generations from both cohort studies. Unfortunately, due to different survey design, this is not possible for the majority of the current analysis. The NCDS parental income data comes from separate measures of father's earnings, mother's earnings and other income (all defined after taxes). Because of this breakdown earlier work on the NCDS was able to compare sons' and fathers' earnings (Dearden, Machin and Reed, 1997) but a cross-time comparison cannot as the BCS only has data on parents' combined income. One is therefore forced to base estimates on the relationship between the cohort member's earnings or income and parental income. This can produce different point in time β estimates if there is a different relation between earnings and the components of family income, but these are easily reconciled with the earlier work (see Blanden et al., 2002). Anyway the changes over time are consistent and of most interest here.

Estimates

Table 18.4 reports a set of estimates of intergenerational mobility from both cohorts, for male and female cohort members separately. Three sets of results are reported for each. The first, in the top panel of the table, considers the relationship between cohort members' earnings and parental income. The second adds a large set of pre-labour market entry control variables (detailed in the notes to the table) to the first specification. These variables are a set of child-specific and family factors. The inclusion of these variables is an attempt to identify the effect of changes in family income for otherwise identical individuals.[4] The final set of results (bottom panel) looks at intergenerational correlations in family income.

The main interest concerns changes in the extent of mobility over time. The results in Table 18.4 paint a strong and very consistent pattern. In all cases the BCS parental income coefficient is higher than the comparable NCDS coefficient.[5] This remains the case when an inequality adjustment is implemented so as to allow for the fact that the income distribution for the later cohort is characterised by greater inequality.

The changes over time, showing falls in intergenerational mobility, are sizeable with the inequality-adjusted estimates rising by 0.95 to .260 for men and by .059 to .227 for women. Similarly strong rises in the link with parental income are seen in the augmented and family income regressions. All of the increases for sons are strongly significant, showing a steep rise across cohorts that resulted in substantial falls in the extent of intergenerational mobility.

Links between child and parent economic status appear to have strengthened considerably in this cross-cohort comparison. This, of course, has occurred at the same time as the strengthened link between education and income described in the previous section of this chapter.

Table 18.4   Estimates of changes in the extent of intergenerational mobility

	Earnings regressions		
	β Adjusted for changes in inequality		Change in adjusted β
	NCDS	BCS	
Sons	.166*	.260*	.095*
Daughters	.168*	.227*	.059*

	Conditional earnings regressions		
	β Adjusted for changes in inequality		Change in adjusted β
	NCDS	BCS	
Sons	.103*	.194*	.091*
Daughters	.099*	.154*	.054*

	Family income regressions		
	β Adjusted for changes in inequality		Change in adjusted β
	NCDS	BCS	
Sons	.123*	.261*	.139*
Daughters	.137*	.221*	.085*

Notes: All regressions control for parents' age and age-squared. Augmented regressions include controls for ethnicity, parental education, family structure, whether father was unemployed during childhood and maths and reading test score quintiles at age 10/11. In the family income regressions the dependent variable is the sum of cohort member's earnings plus those of any partner. * denotes statistically significant at conventional levels (5 per cent significance level).

Transition matrices

The other commonly used research tool for estimating the extent of inter-generational mobility is the use of transition matrices which show where child–parent pairs are moving across the distribution of economic status. Tables 18.5a and 18.5b report a set of transition matrices for NCDS and BCS sons and daughters.

The tables show the percentage in each parental income quartile that move into each quartile of the sons' or daughters' earnings distribution. The extent of immobility can be summarised by an immobility index that computes the sum of the leading diagonal and its adjacent cells. These are reported at the top of the tables. These numbers can be interpreted relative to the immobility index in the case of perfect mobility. If all individuals had an equal chance

Table 18.5a   Quartile transition matrices for sons

Immobility index: NCDS 278 BCS 295

NCDS Parental income quartile	Sons' earnings quartile			
	Bottom	2nd	3rd	Top
Bottom	31	29	23	17
2nd	30	24	23	23
3rd	23	26	26	26
Top	17	20	29	34
BCS Parental income quartile	Sons' earnings quartile			
	Bottom	2nd	3rd	Top
Bottom	39	25	22	14
2nd	28	29	24	19
3rd	20	28	27	25
Top	13	17	28	42

Note: Immobility index defined as the sum of the leading diagonal and its adjacent cells.

Table 18.5b   Quartile transition matrices for daughters

Immobility index: NCDS 269 BCS 286

NCDS Parental income quartile	Daughters' earnings quartile			
	Bottom	2nd	3rd	Top
Bottom	27	31	25	17
2nd	30	24	22	24
3rd	25	24	26	24
Top	19	20	27	34
BCS Parental income quartile	Daughters' earnings quartile			
	Bottom	2nd	3rd	Top
Bottom	33	31	23	13
2nd	28	28	25	19
3rd	24	22	28	26
Top	16	19	26	39

Note: Immobility index defined as the sum of the leading diagonal and its adjacent cells

of experiencing an adult income in each quartile all cells would contain 25 and the immobility index would be 250. As we might expect, given what we learned from the regression analysis, all the immobility indexes we observe in the tables are above this number.

It is clear that transition analysis confirms the regression finding that mobility has fallen between the cohorts. In almost every case a higher percentage remain in the same quartile as their parents in the later cohort and there are less extreme movements between generations. In the NCDS 17 per cent of sons and daughters with parents in the bottom quartile rise to the top; in the BCS this falls to 14 per cent for sons and 13 per cent for daughters. Moving in the other direction the growth in immobility is more marked with almost one-fifth (17 per cent for sons and 19 per cent for daughters) of those who start life in the top quartile falling to the bottom in the NCDS while in the BCS the corresponding percentages are 13 for sons and 16 for daughters. The overall pattern of reduced mobility is very much confirmed by the pattern of results in the transition matrices.

Conclusions

This chapter considers changes in inequality across generations. It first considers how links between higher education and parental income have strengthened through time in Britain and second how the extent of inter-generational mobility has altered across two British birth cohorts considered (the first born in March 1958 and the second born in April 1970).

It is very clear that, even though these cohorts are only 12 years different in age, the education and economic status of the 1970 cohort are much more strongly connected to parental economic status than they were in the 1958 cohort. One can use the estimates to calculate the difference in the earnings of young people born into the top and bottom quintiles of the family income distribution in the two different years. In the NCDS, families in the top income quintile had an average income 2.78 times that of families from the bottom quintile. The estimates of intergenerational mobility therefore suggest that the sons of the richest parents earned 120 per cent more than those of the poorest. The same calculation for the BCS, where the parental income distribution is wider, shows that sons from the richest quintile earned 140 per cent more than sons from the poorest family income quintile.[6]

This fall in intergenerational mobility can partly be accounted for by the fact that a greater share of the rapid educational upgrading of the British population has been focused on people with richer parents. The unequal increase in educational attainment is thus one factor that has acted to reinforce more strongly the link between earnings and income of children and their parents. This seems to be an unintended consequence of the expansion of the university system that occurred in the late 1980s and early 1990s and an issue that needs to be borne in mind when considering future educational reforms.

Notes

1. The NCDS data have also been used to look at the transmission mechanisms that may underpin intergenerational mobility: see Gregg and Machin (1999).
2. One might query some of the differences between higher education participation at age 19 and degree acquisition at age 23. The reason they may differ is that it is

participation in any higher education at 19, then getting a degree by 23 and some may obtain vocational qualifications from attending a higher education institution.

3. Sample sizes are prohibitively small to consider intergenerational mobility patterns in the BHPS cohort.

4. One way of thinking about the inclusion of these characteristics is that they in some sense 'level the playing field' between cohort members by controlling for detailed observables and as such proxy child/family fixed effects. Or at least that they show how the coefficients would alter if one moved more towards a fixed effects specification that would wash out child and family characteristics not previously controlled for.

5. There are some potentially serious pitfalls associated with estimating β from data on children and their parents. Indeed estimates will be biased downwards if parental income is measured with error so that one is not measuring permanent, or lifetime, income (Solon, 1999). In this application the focus on changes over time means that this may not present such a problem. Simulations in Blanden et al. (2002) do in fact show this to be the case for the results reported in Table 18.2 as the rise in the intergenerational correlation does not seem attributable to differential bias across the two cohorts considered.

6. In the BCS the top quintile of parents had an average income 4.36 times that of the bottom quintile.

References

Blanden, J., Goodman, A., Gregg, P. and Machin, S. (2002), 'Changes in Intergenerational Mobility in Britain', Centre for the Economics of Education Discussion Paper No. 26, London School of Economics, forthcoming in M. Corak (ed.), *Generational Income Mobility in North America and Europe*, Cambridge University Press.

Blanden, J., Gregg, P. and Machin, S. (2003), 'Changes in Educational Inequality', Centre for the Economics of Education mimeo.

Dearden, L., Machin, S. and Reed, H. (1997), 'Intergenerational Mobility in Britain', *Economic Journal*, 107, pp. 47–64.

Glennerster, H. (2001), 'United Kingdom Education 1997–2001', Centre for the Analysis of Social Exclusion CASE Paper 50.

Gregg, P. and Machin, S. (1999), 'Childhood Disadvantage and Success or Failure in the Labour Market', in D. Blanchflower and R. Freeman (eds), *Youth Employment and Joblessness in Advanced Countries*, National Bureau of Economic Research, Cambridge, MA.

Solon, G. (1999), 'Intergenerational Mobility in the Labor Market', in O. Ashenfelter and D. Card (eds), *Handbook of Labor Economics*, Volume 3A, North Holland: Amsterdam.

19
Child Poverty in Britain

Richard Dickens and David T. Ellwood

Key findings

- Relative child poverty rose sharply over the period 1979–97/98 and has since fallen by about half a million (4 percentage points). Absolute poverty changed little between 1979 and 1997/98 but has fallen sharply since then. Absolute poverty fell by 1.7 million between 1997/98 and 2001/02, with a half million fall in the last year alone.

- Changes in work patterns, wages and demographics all contributed to rising relative child poverty between 1979 and 1997/98. Demographics and work changes were responsible for the rise in absolute poverty. Benefit changes offset some of these increases. The absence of work was particularly severe on children in lone parent families.

- The Blair government's welfare reforms raised work incentives and resulted in more work among low income families with children. These increases in work had modest effects in reducing child poverty and much of the reduction is attributable to benefit changes – work itself is not enough to pull many families over the poverty line.

- The Clinton administration introduced a range of welfare to work reforms in the US, increasing aid to those in work but cutting it to those out of work. Child poverty there has fallen but not as sharply. Increased work and demographic change have been the driving forces in poverty reductions.

- Median incomes, and hence the poverty line have increased rapidly and in conjunction further small increases in wage inequality and demographic shifts have meant that the government is making slower progress in reducing relative poverty than anticipated.

- While much progress has been made, current and planned policy reforms may not raise the incomes of the poor enough relative to median income to achieve the sort of poverty reductions needed to meet the stated poverty targets.

Introduction

The proportion of children living in poverty increased threefold in the two decades up to 1997 such that over a third of children were living in poverty. At the same time the number of children living in households with nobody in work had risen to one-fifth (see Chapter 2 on workless households). The newly elected Labour government responded to the growing hardship among children with a range of welfare reforms designed to reduce child poverty. So central was this issue to the new government that the Chancellor of the Exchequer pledged to halve child poverty in one decade and to abolish it in two.[1]

At the heart of these welfare reforms was a desire to 'make work pay' for low income families. Research suggested that a possible reason for the large numbers of workless households was that low paid jobs were just not worth taking for those in receipt of benefits. A number of policies were introduced to increase work incentives and hopefully raise work among those on low incomes. But alongside these reforms benefits for families with children who were not in work were raised substantially.

The government claimed that this package of tax and benefit reforms would reduce child poverty by 1.2 million over the first parliament (over what would otherwise have been in the absence of policy change). But estimates from Brewer, Clark and Goodman (2003) and Piachaud and Sutherland (2002) show that child poverty only fell by half a million over this period. Although poverty would probably have risen in the absence of the policy change these significant reductions in child poverty are clearly not as much as had been hoped.

In this chapter we investigate the forces that have had an impact on child poverty in Britain since the late 1970s. We are interested in the period under the Conservative government, 1979–1997, when child poverty rose and then under the new Labour government since 1997, when poverty fell. We examine changes in both *relative* and *absolute* poverty and decompose these into changes in demographics factors, wage changes, changes in work patterns and changes in the benefits structure. We then assess why the government has failed to achieve its stated targets so far and the likely success of the policy reforms announced.

Changes in child poverty since the late 1970s

Measuring poverty

Poverty is usually defined as a situation where the income of the household that a person lives in falls below some threshold. So for children we take the income of their household and examine the proportion whose income falls short of the poverty threshold. The choice of this poverty threshold can vary (both across countries and from year to year). In Britain we have no official poverty line but the commonly used definition favoured by the government and researchers is based on 60 per cent of median household income in each year with an adjustment for household size. Because the poverty line is related to median income the poverty line will rise and fall as the median household's income rises or falls. Using this poverty definition means that one is comparing the position of a low-income child relative to children in middle class households. If incomes of the disadvantaged children rise but those of the median child rise even more then poverty will increase under this measure. For this reason it is known as a relative poverty measure.

An alternative is to utilise a fixed poverty threshold that doesn't change over time (except to adjust for changes in inflation). Indeed, the US has an official poverty measure that is based upon an absolute threshold that has been fixed in real terms for 35 years. This poverty threshold assumes that what is important is the absolute household income of children, and is useful for measuring the ability to purchase a fixed bundle of essential goods.

The relative poverty standard is essentially a measure of inequality. It depends on the distance between a disadvantaged child and the median child. The absolute standard measures the extent of low income irrespective of what is happening to incomes in the rest of society. The government's poverty targets for children in Britain are phrased in terms of a relative standard. However, from a policy perspective both are of interest. Are the poor gaining on the middle class, or are the incomes of the poor rising? Let us now turn to examine the evidence.

Changes in poverty

Figure 19.1 presents relative child poverty in Britain for the period 1979–2000/01, based on the proportion of children whose household income falls below 60 per cent of median income. Household income here includes total income from employment, government benefits, investments, pensions, etc., minus taxes to obtain a measure of disposable income. Often when defining poverty, researchers examine incomes both before and after housing costs have been taken out. This removes some of the differences due to regional variation in housing costs.[2] Figure 19.1 therefore presents relative poverty based on net income both before and after housing costs. Note that after housing cost poverty rates are higher since the poor spend a greater proportion of their income on housing.

A couple of points stand out. First, relative poverty rose sharply over much of the 1980s and early 1990s. In 1979, some 15 per cent of children were living in poor households (using the after housing cost measure). By 1996/97 this had increased to an astonishing 33 per cent. A similar rise is observed using income before housing costs. This sharp rise in child poverty followed a period of fairly stable poverty rates for children. Gregg, Harkness and Machin (1999) show that child poverty rates rose by just a few percentage points between 1968 and 1979. Since 1997, child poverty has fallen quite rapidly. The proportion of children in relative poverty fell by over 4 percentage points in

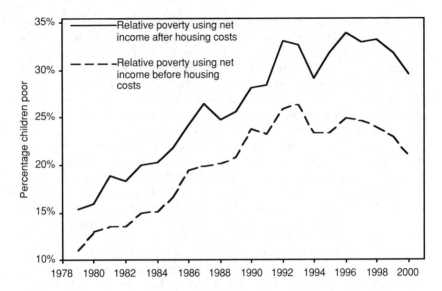

Figure 19.1   Percentage of children below relative poverty line in Britain, 1979–2000/01

Sources: Authors' tabulations of annual FES (1979–1995/96) and FRS (1996/97–2000/01).

just five years, with much of that fall occurring since 1998/99 when many of the new anti-poverty policies were introduced.

Figure 19.2 presents measures of child poverty based on an absolute poverty standard of 60 per cent median household income in 1997 (adjusted for inflation). The pattern of absolute child poverty over this period is very different from relative poverty. Absolute poverty fluctuates over the economic cycle; increasing in the recessions of the early 1980s and 1990s but falling in the late 1980s and 1990s recoveries. As such, child poverty changed little between 1979 and 1996/97, but has since fallen very sharply. In fact child poverty (after housing) fell from 34 per cent in 1996/97 to under just 23 per cent by 2000–01. Again, much of this fall occurred after 1998/99. Indeed the latest government figures show absolute child poverty fell by half a million in 2001–02 alone (Department for Work and Pensions, 2003).

Comparing the two figures throws some light on the differences obtained from the two types of poverty measures. If income grows and inequality increases, then absolute poverty can fall while relative poverty increases. This was the situation in Britain through much of the 1980s, when incomes of both the disadvantaged and the middle classes were rising but the middle classes were experiencing much faster increases in incomes. In the latter part of the 1990s both relative and absolute poverty rates have fallen, as incomes have risen faster for the disadvantaged than for the middle class.

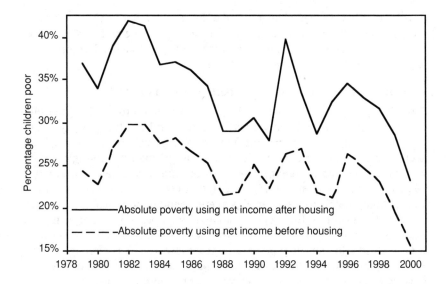

Figure 19.2   Percentage of children below absolute poverty line in Britain, 1979–2000/01

Source: Authors' tabulations of annual FES/FRS.

What has caused poverty to change?

Poverty changes as incomes rise and fall. A child is defined to be poor if their household's income falls below a certain poverty threshold. This income is composed of earnings from work for each household member, government benefits received by the household and any other household income. Earnings can further be split into the number of hours worked by each household member and their wage rate per hour. We want to know how much of the change in poverty is due to changes in wage rates, hours of work and government benefits. Poverty rates can also change if people live in different types of households. If children are now more likely to live in single parent households poverty may rise since these tend to be poorer than households with two adults.

The problem we face in trying to explain the change in poverty is that all of these factors change at the same time. Wage rates have changed, as have patterns of work, government benefits and the type of households children live in. In trying to explain the change in poverty say between 1979 and 1997 a natural question to ask is what would have happened to poverty if the structure of households, work and benefits had remained constant and only wages had changed. This then gives us the component of the poverty change that is attributable to wages. We can then ask what would have happened to poverty if only work had changed, and so on for the other factors. In Dickens and Ellwood (2003a) we developed a methodology that enables us to answer questions such as these. We next examine the results of such a decomposition for the period 1979–1997/98 when poverty rose.

Why did child poverty rise in the period 1979–1997/98?

Table 19.1 presents the results of this decomposition for the period in Britain when child poverty rose. Reported is the relative and absolute poverty rate in 1979 and in 1997/98 and the contribution to changing poverty arising from each of the factors; demographic change, wage changes, changing work patterns and changing benefits.[3] In 1979 the child poverty rate based on this relative standard was just over 15 per cent. By 1997/98 this had risen by almost 15 percentage points to just over 30 per cent. Demographic change accounted for some 9 per cent of this rise, wage changes for 4 per cent, changes in work patterns 5 per cent and benefit changes offset these increases by 3.4 per cent.

Over this period absolute poverty increased by some 3 percentage points. Here demographics and work changes in particular had an upwards effect on poverty but some of this was offset by benefit changes.

Table 19.1 Decomposition of changes in relative and absolute poverty between 1979 and 1997/98

	Relative poverty (based on 60% of median income)	Absolute poverty (based on 60% of median income in 1997)
All children		
Poverty in 1979	15.2	26.9
+ Demographics	+9.2	+2.3
+ Wage changes	+3.9	+0.3
+ Work patterns	+5.1	+5.0
+ Government benefits	–3.4	–4.5
= Poverty in 1997	30.1%	30.1%

Sources: Authors' calculations using FES/FRS data.

Demographics – Household composition changed considerably over this time period. The number of single parent households increased substantially; with the proportion of children living in single adult households more than doubling from 10 per cent in the late 1970s. Since single parent households are poorer this is expected to raise both relative and absolute poverty, which it did. Furthermore, the educational structure of the population also changed, with increases in the average level of educational qualifications achieved. This will serve to change the poverty rate through changes in incomes at the bottom and will increase the relative poverty standard as median incomes rise.

Wages – The wage structure underwent large changes over this period. Average wages rose in Britain for both men and women but the distribution of pay increased at an unprecedented rate through much of the 1980s, so that the difference in pay between the low and high paid was larger than it had been at any other time over the last century (see Chapter 12 on wage inequality). Despite these huge increases in pay differentials, real wages did rise over this period for the low paid, but average wages and wages for the high paid increased by substantially more. Since the early 1990s, increases in wage differentials slowed with some signs of falling inequality since the introduction of the minimum wage in 1999. We would expect these changes in pay to have differing effects on relative and absolute poverty. If wages rose at the same rate at all pay levels then we may expect modest increases in relative poverty since the incomes of the non-working often do not keep pace. But absolute poverty would fall as more working individuals are taken over the fixed threshold. However, increases in wage inequality will work to raise both relative and absolute poverty. This is precisely what we observe; relative poverty is increased by wage changes but the two impacts on absolute poverty offset one another so the overall effect is zero.

Work – Unemployment rose sharply in the early 1980s and 1990s recessions but recovered in the 1990s boom so that overall employment rates are now as high as they were in the mid-1970s. However, while employment of women has risen over this period, employment among men has fallen (see Chapter 1). Also, while average employment rates among women have increased substantially, this is wholly due to an increase among women with working partners. Employment rates among single women and those with a non-working partner have not risen. This has led to a massive change in the distribution of work across households, particularly among those with children. The proportion of children living in households with no working adult increased from 8 per cent in 1979 to over 21 per cent in 1996 (Gregg and Wadsworth, Chapter 2). These changing work patterns pushed up relative and absolute child poverty by about 5 percentage points.

Benefits – The above factors all pushed up child poverty over this period. However, changes to benefits offset some of this increase. Benefit rates were linked to prices over much of this period; which one would expect to raise relative poverty. But a number of changes in the benefit system cushioned this impact. More individuals were shifted from unemployment benefit onto sickness benefits, which were more generous. Income Support rates were raised quite substantially for single parents in the late 1980s and Housing Benefit increased substantially as rents rose.

Table 19.2 shows the poverty decompositions separately by family type. The results suggest that much of the overall rise in poverty was due to rising poverty among single parents where relative poverty rose from 44 per cent to 59 per cent. The biggest factor in this rise was work, which contributed to 13 percentage points of this rise. Worklessness increased sharply among single parents in Britain over this period with a corresponding increase of children living in single parent households with no work (although lone parents' employment did start to increase again in 1993, see Chapter 7). But demographic change also played a large part.[4] Benefit increases had the effect of heavily offsetting what would have been an even larger rise in poverty. But it may also have been the case that increases in benefits actually contributed to falls in work, as incentives to working fell.

Table 19.2   Decomposition of changes in poverty between 1979 and 1997/98 by family type

	Relative poverty (based on 60% of median income)	Absolute poverty (based on 60% of median income in 1997)
Children living in couple households		
Poverty in 1979	12.3	23.3
+ Demographics	+3.1	−3.9
+ Wage changes	+4.0	+1.0
+ Work patterns	+2.6	+2.5
+ Government benefits	−1.0	−1.9
= Poverty in 1997	21.0%	21.0%
Children living in single adult households		
Poverty in 1979	44.1	61.6
+ Demographics	+9.5	−0.8
+ Wage changes	+3.6	−1.9
+ Work patterns	+13.0	+13.0
+ Government Benefits	−11.1	−12.7
= Poverty in 1997	59.2%	59.2%

Sources: Authors' calculations using FES/FRS data.

The causes of this rise in child poverty leaves policy makers intent on reversing this trend with a difficult task. Household composition is hard for governments to influence, and often it is not an area policy makers are willing to tackle. Also, the growth in wage differences between the rich and poor are hard to tackle in a decentralised market such as the British labour market, although a minimum wage may have some role here. Probably, work and benefits have the potential for most influence. Benefit reform can be used to change work incentives and to raise the incomes of those out of work. But there is a balancing act to be performed here if one is to make work more attractive without increasing hardship for those not working.

Policy change under the Blair government

When the Labour government came to power in 1997 they announced a major set of welfare reforms with an emphasis on getting people back into work. The aim was to increase work among the disadvantaged and reverse the huge increase in the number of workless households. Many of these reforms were aimed at families with children in an attempt to achieve the reductions in child poverty required to meet the explicit targets that had been set. The reforms centred on increasing work incentives among those who previously faced little gain from entering work. The centrepiece of the new policy agenda was the Working Families Tax Credit (WFTC), which substantially raised in-work benefits for those with children. The hope is that boosting incomes in work for the low paid will encourage more families to enter employment. Lack of affordable childcare is clearly a significant constraint for many low income families who want to return to work. The Childcare Tax Credit provided generous increases in childcare support for low income families in work. In addition, the starting rate of income tax was reduced from 20 per cent to 10 per cent. National Insurance reforms reduced payments for those on low pay and a National Minimum Wage was introduced at £3.60 an hour for workers over the age of 22 (see Chapter 13). The aim was to 'make work pay' through a range of increases in financial incentives.

In addition the government sought to increase work with a range of non-financial incentives. Various New Deal policies for improvements in childcare provision were introduced (see Chapter 1). Again, none of these schemes aimed at families with children had any compulsion to enter work built into them. Out-of-work lone parents now have to attend a case management interview but face no compulsion to find work. The National Childcare Strategy was introduced to create a wider supply of childcare opportunities. Although work was at the centre of the anti-poverty strategy, this was not the only means used by the government to raise low income and tackle child poverty. Benefit rates for out of work families with children were also increased. Child Benefit rates, which are non-means tested and paid to every household with children, were increased substantially. Income Support rates for low income families with children were boosted, while those for families without children stagnated in real terms.

Clearly there is a balancing act here. Increasing in-work benefits will raise the financial incentives to working. But increasing out of work benefits will reduce work incentives through two mechanisms. Firstly, the return to working will fall as the gap between incomes in and out of work is reduced (this is known as a *substitution effect*). Secondly, the extra income benefits provided to those out of work will also reduce work incentives (this is known as an *income effect*). That is why if the government is to raise benefits for non-working families, they also need to provide generous increases in in-work benefits to induce families back into work (see also Chapter 7 for more details on welfare reform).

The impact of the reforms

Employment increases

There has been considerable debate in Britain about whether the changes in incentives would induce people into work. Prior to the WFTC's introduction, Blundell et al. (2000) estimated that it would raise work among parents in aggregate by only about 35,000. This is largely because the generous gains in WFTC are largely offset by reductions in housing benefits. However, this aggregate figure hides some important changes in the distribution of work across households. Employment increases among couple and single adult families with nobody working but falls among couple households with both adults working due to the changed incentives discussed above. The result is a fairly large reduction in the number of workless households with children, in the order of 60,000 (or 100,000 children). The government's own estimates of employment change from the whole package of reform is somewhat higher with an aggregate increase of 80,000.

The early evidence suggests that employment has risen due to the introduction of the WFTC. Employment growth had been strong in late-1990s Britain due to the strong economy. Employment of lone parents had been rising strongly and the number of children in workless households falling. However, the evidence suggests that since the introduction of WFTC in 1999 this employment growth has accelerated. Chapter 7 by Gregg and Harkness estimates that within a year of its introduction the WFTC had reduced the number of workless households with children by about 40,000. But it is not clear that raising work will reduce poverty. If one forces individuals into low wage jobs they may not be much better off in terms of overall household income.

Poverty change under the Blair government

We saw above that child poverty rates have fallen since 1997/98 in Britain, but it is not clear whether the policy change is responsible. To try and understand why child poverty fell over this period, Table 19.3 presents the results of a poverty decomposition for the period 1997/98 to 2000/01 for relative and absolute poverty change. Relative poverty fell by just over 3 percentage points while the fall in absolute poverty was much larger at nearly 8 percentage points. Demographics and wage changes tended to push up relative poverty somewhat, but reduced absolute poverty. This is presumably because these factors pushed up median incomes, and so raised the relative poverty standard by more than the incomes of the disadvantaged. The impact of the substantial increases in work discussed above was to reduce relative and absolute poverty by just 1.1 percentage points and 1.2 percentage points respectively. Apparently many of the jobs the parents are taking do not pay enough to push them out of poverty. Much of the reduction in poverty can be traced to higher benefits, which has resulted in a fall in relative and absolute poverty of 3.1 percentage points and 4.5 percentage points respectively.

Table 19.3   Decomposition of changes in poverty between 1997/98 and 2000/01

	Relative poverty (based on 60% of median income)	Absolute poverty (based on 60% of median income in 1997)
All children		
Poverty in 1997	30.1	30.1
+ Demographics	+0.5	–0.9
+ Wage changes	+0.6	–1.3
+ Work patterns	–1.1	–1.2
+ Government benefits	–3.1	–4.5
= Poverty in 2000	**27.0%**	**22.3%**

Sources: Authors' calculations using FES/FRS data.

Table 19.4   Decomposition of changes in poverty between 1997/98 and 2000/01 by family type

	Relative poverty (based on 60% of median income)	Absolute poverty (based on 60% of median income in 1997)
Children living in couple households		
Poverty in 1997	21.0	21.0
+ Demographics	–0.5	–1.6
+ Wage changes	–0.0	–1.2
+ Work patterns	–1.1	–0.6
+ Government benefits	–1.8	–2.4
= Poverty in 2000	**18.1%**	**15.2%**
Children living in single adult households		
Poverty in 1997	59.2	59.2
+ Demographics	+0.4	–1.7
+ Wage changes	+2.3	–1.4
+ Work patterns	–2.8	–2.6
+ Government benefits	–6.8	–10.6
= Poverty in 2000	**52.4%**	**42.9%**

Source: Authors' calculations using FES/FRS data.

This impact can be seen even more starkly in Table 19.4 which gives the decomposition of poverty change for couples and lone parents separately. The impacts of demographic and wage changes are similar to the aggregate figures above, raising relative poverty but reducing absolute poverty for both couples and lone parents. For couples, the impact of work is modest and reduces relative poverty by 1.1 percentage points and absolute poverty by just 0.6 points. Again much of the work is done by benefits. Among lone parents the poverty falls are much larger. Relative poverty fell by 7 percentage points and absolute by more than 16 points. Work changes had a significant impact contributing almost 3 percentage points towards these falls but the lions share was done by increased benefits. This reduced relative poverty by almost 7 percentage points and absolute by a huge 10.6 points.

The United States

In the United States, child poverty had also been rising before the advent of the Clinton government, albeit not as fast as in Britain. Clinton came to power also with a promise to make work pay and to 'end welfare as we know it'. But the Clinton strategy was very different from that of the Blair government. Out of work benefits were cut substantially and time limits were introduced. At the same time welfare payments to those in low wage work were raised substantially through increases in the Earned Income Tax Credit. The changes in welfare were dramatic so that after the reforms, welfare payments to those out of work were substantially lower than to those in work. The effect was a huge increase in work incentives largely brought about by forcing people into work. This is in sharp contrast to the Blair approach, which was more reliant on *carrots* than *sticks*.

Child poverty rates fell by a similar amount in the US since Clinton came to power as they did in Britain since the advent of the Blair government.[5] The differing forces driving the reductions in poverty in Britain and the US do appear to reflect the differing policy approaches. The stated aim of US policy was to increase work and reduce welfare roles. It was never an explicit goal to reduce poverty. These changed incentives really did increase work in the US which in turn helped to reduce child poverty.

In Britain a gentler approach was taken. The stated goal was a reduction in child poverty and an increase in work was one of the mechanisms used to achieve this. Work incentives have changed and as a result work has risen among families with children. But the impact on poverty is fairly modest from these work changes alone, as low wage jobs themselves are not enough to push many families over the poverty threshold. The other mechanism used was to simply increase benefit payments to the working and non-working alike. This resulted in a large amount of the observed drop in child poverty.

Conclusion

The government has made substantial gains in reducing child poverty over the first term of the parliament. However, despite substantial policy reform the numbers of children living in poverty are still high and much more needs to be done to achieve the targets of reducing child poverty by 1.1 million by 2005, halving it by 2010 and abolishing it a decade later. A number of factors suggest these are going to be difficult to meet.

Firstly, we saw above that the predictions made by the government (and other researchers) suggested that child poverty using a relative standard would be reduced by 1.2 million as a result of the welfare reforms introduced over the first parliament relative to a base of no change in policy. If benefits had only risen in line with prices (the no policy change situation), then poverty rates would have risen against this relative income threshold. Even so the half a million fall in the number of children below this relative threshold is certainly less than hoped for. But, if the government had set themselves an absolute poverty standard (based on 60 per cent median 1997 income) they would have indeed met their goal. The problem here is that the predictions about falling poverty failed to account for the rapid increases in median incomes, especially after housing costs due to the very low mortgage rates. With a relative poverty standard such as this, one is always going to be chasing a target moving at an uncertain speed in a growing economy. The government can only reduce poverty if they generate faster income growth for the poor than the middle classes. Over the first term of the Labour government this was achieved but not as much as expected. The paradox here is that the stronger the economy the faster the incomes of the poor have to be raised. The sensitivity of median incomes after housing costs to mortgage interest rates introduces another paradox – lower interest rates increase relative poverty. This is likely to be a problem over the next two decades in trying to reach the stated child poverty targets.

Another factor that may make it difficult to reduce poverty further is that the policies that have been introduced so far may have targeted the poor who are easier to help. This means that the remaining poor may well have incomes further below the poverty line and be harder to place in work. Evidence from Brewer, Clark and Goodman (2003) shows that the average incomes of the remaining poor are now further below the poverty line than they were in 1996/97. They report that the gap between median income and the relative poverty line, for those below the poverty line, in 1996/97 was £39 a week. By 2000/01 this had risen to £44 a week. Their results suggest that although a substantial number of children have had their incomes raised above the poverty line over this period, the incomes of those left behind are now somewhat further away from that line. Remember that this poverty line has increased over this period, it is just that the incomes of those still below (on average) have not risen as fast. This suggests that the group 'left behind' by the current crop of policy reforms may be harder to help with future policy. However, one needs some caution in making this interpretation. Many households with low incomes below the poverty line contain self-employed workers or at least one employee. The reported income data of the self-employed is notoriously prone to errors. It may well be that many of those with incomes at the bottom of the distribution are misreporting their household income and we are falsely classifying them as poor. Indeed, Brewer, Clark and Goodman (2003) find sharply falling incomes for those at the very bottom of the distribution. If this is the case then no policy intervention will raise this group out of poverty.

These factors may well make it more difficult to achieve the stated poverty objectives. But the government is pressing ahead with further policy reforms. Child Benefit rates have effectively been frozen but in 2000/01 the Children's Tax Credit was introduced. This provides means tested support for households with children regardless of work status; so there is a general shift in support towards low income families with children. The WFTC is being replaced with the Working Tax Credit, which extends entitlement to many low income households without children. The minimum wage is being up-rated so that in October 2003 it will be £4.50 an hour.

Piachaud and Sutherland (2002) simulate the impact of these future policy reforms to estimate the impact on child poverty between 2000/01 and 2003/04. They find that the new policies (introduced after 2000/01) will reduce the number of children below 60 per cent 2000/01 median income by over half a million or 4 percentage points. However, over these two years median incomes are likely to grow. They estimate that with current projections about median income growth, relative child poverty will fall by about half these estimated numbers as a result of the policy interventions introduced since 2000/01. While a welcome move in the right direction this still leaves the government with a significant amount of work to do.

Notes

1. This includes a commitment to reduce child poverty by 1.1 million by 2005.
2. It also accounts for the fact that those who own their own houses outright have a hidden income compared to those paying rents.
3. Note that the poverty definition here is based upon gross income before housing, which is different from the net income standards presented in Figures 19.1 and 19.2.
4. Note that this is the impact of demographic change in the whole population on child poverty in lone parent households. So demographics could be pushing up the relative poverty threshold and children in lone parent households are not keeping up.
5. This is using a consistent relative poverty standard of 60 per cent median incomes. See Dickens and Ellwood (2003b) for a comparison of the different experiences of Britain and the US.

References

Blundell, R., Duncan, A., McCrae, J. and Meghir, C. (2000), 'The Labour Market Impact of the Working Families Tax Credit', *Fiscal Studies*, Vol. 21.

Brewer, M., Clark, T. and Goodman, A. (2003), 'What Really Happened to Child Poverty in the UK under Labour's First Term?', *Economic Journal*, Vol. 113, No. 488.

Department for Work and Pensions (2003), *Households Below Average Income 1994–95 – 2001–02*, The Stationery Office: London.

Dickens, R. and Ellwood, D. T. (2003a), 'Whither Poverty in Great Britain and the United States? The Determinants of Changing Poverty and Whether Work Will Work', in R. Blundell, D. Card and R. Freeman (eds), *Seeking a Premier League Economy*, University of Chicago Press: Chicago.

Dickens, R. and Ellwood, D. T. (2003b), 'Child Poverty in Britain and the US', *Economic Journal*, Vol. 113, No. 488.

Gregg, P., Harkness, S. and Machin, S. (1999), 'Poor Kids: Child Poverty in Britain, 1966–96', *Fiscal Studies*, 20, pp. 163–87.

Piachaud, D. and Sutherland, H. (2002), 'Changing Poverty Post 1997', CASE Paper 63, Centre for the Analysis of Social Exclusion, London School of Economics, November.

Index

Compiled by Sue Carlton